DIGITAL BANKING

SECOND EDITION

SECOND EDITION

DIGITAL BANKING

Guide on Digital Banking and Payments for Industry Professionals

ALBERT MUTONGA MATONGELA

REACH PUBLISHERS

Second edition 2025

Published by Albert Mutonga Matongela using Reach Publishers' services,
P O Box 1384, Wandsbeck, South Africa, 3631

Edited by Karen Hoy for Reach Publishers
Cover designed by Reach Publishers
Website: www.reachpublishers.org
E-mail: reach@reachpublishers.org

REACH PUBLISHERS

ALBERT MUTONGA MATONGELA
mutonga.matongela@gmail.com

Disclaimer

This guide or book on digital banking helps individuals and other stakeholders to have a general understanding of the inner core of digital banking and payments. The information contained herein is based on the author's opinion and should not be interpreted as providing personal financial advice. Please consult qualified personal financial advisors or relevant service providers should you wish to seek appropriate financial advice or guidance. The author prepared the content herein to the best of his ability and as a result assumes no responsibility for errors and omissions that may be found, as well any liability for any damage arising from using the information as provided in this publication.

Table of Contents

Preface

Are you an employer in the financial services industry, that includes banking institutions and non-bank financial institutions, whose drive is to provide financial and payment services to a wide range of customers and stakeholders? Are you a student at a university or any other institution of higher learning who would like to pursue banking or payment systems as a career in future? Are you an employee working for a financial services provider who needs to upgrade knowledge and skills around payment systems and digital banking? Are you a researcher whose interest is to understand what is happening in the field of payment systems? Are you a policy maker interested in payment systems going forward? Are you an entrepreneur who is interested in selling books related to the financial services industry to the general public? Or are you a training provider with special interest in the financial services industry? This guide is for you if you have answered "Yes" to at least one of the above questions.

Banking has long been known to include components such as savings, investments and lending. These three components relate to moving money from surplus units or those with surplus cash, to deficit units or those with a shortage of cash. Recent and available knowledge is that banking is more than these elements that you have known for a long time. Banking now includes the provision of payment services to as many stakeholders as possible. This implies that next time you hear of someone referring to banking they will be talking about savings, investments, lending and also payment services.

This book will help you to understand the inner workings of payment systems, sometimes called "payment, clearing and settlement systems", "payments" or "the national payment system". It is a branch of banking that is evolving and the time to understand this field is now, in order for you as a reader to have appropriate knowledge and skills in this very important area.

The scope of this guide has been carefully selected to make sure that the inner core of payment systems is well understood. Presentation is at a fairly basic level with every attempt having been made to avoid some technical words or jargon, and to explain it where required. Core and special topics are covered so that you as a reader can have total understanding of payment, clearing and settlement systems not only in Namibia but also around the world. These topics include those related to payment streams, regulation, domestic payments, regional payments, international payments and related topics.

The undersigned here-below has every trust that you will enjoy reading this book on digital banking and payments, and that the information that you will accumulate will be useful in your sphere of life and future endeavours.

Albert Mutonga Matongela
Windhoek, Namibia
January 2025

CHAPTER 1

Introduction

Payment systems are not easily understood in our society. What are they? Is it wrong to just say "payment system"? What then is the national payment system? Is there a difference between payment, clearing and settlement systems? The list of questions is endless, but useful and important if one is to understand the differences or similarities between these concepts that are sometimes used interchangeably.

Three distinct illustrations can be used to provide more clarity on what payment systems are all about. The first illustration that can be used is a *canal*. This is a man-made waterway that can be used for transportation, recreation and for provision of water for human, industrial, agricultural and animal use. It is believed that the longest and oldest canal in the world is the Beijing-Hangzhou Grand Canal, which measures 1782 kilometres and connects several provinces and rivers in China. What a long canal! This distance is almost like from Aroab to Kongola in Namibia. Canals are common in Namibia as well. The common canal in Namibia is the 150-kilometre-long Calueque-Oshakati canal, which runs from Omahenene near to Onesi in the Omusati region all the way to Oshakati in the Oshana region. In this illustration, the canal itself can be referred to as a payment system with what moves on it referred to as funds or transactions.

A river can be seen as another illustration. This can be extended to a lake or ocean, as the three belong to the same collection system. While a lake fills up when there are good rains, the other two, a river and an ocean, are perennial. The Zambezi River in the Zambezi region in Namibia always has water in it. This is not the same with respect to Lake Liambezi in the same region, which dries up every few years before it fills up again. Some lakes such as Lake Victoria, Lake Tanganyika and Lake Malawi are massive and contribute positively to economic activities in Uganda, Tanzania and Malawi respectively. The two longest rivers in the world are said to be the Nile River and the Amazon River measuring over 6500 kilometres each. A river can be thought of as a payment system, while what is moved on or through a specific river can be thought of as funds or transactions.

A garden is the last illustration that can be considered. Gardening can traditionally be thought of as an agricultural activity that can be done at school or at home. Those who have done agricultural science can recall that this activity was a must as part of school curriculum. This was because most families did back yard gardening, which refers to growing plants at the back of the house within the yard for household consumption.

Think about a situation where plants are grown on distinct raised beds, areas or plots as opposed to in-ground gardening. They might be within a yard as part of a school project or purely as a way of substituting things we often buy from the supermarkets. Raised garden beds of say 1,2 meters wide and a minimum of 0,15 meters high is good in terms of retention of moisture and improves the structure of the soil as well. Gardening with raised beds relates well to a payment system environment where closed loop systems are common as opposed to open loop systems. A closed loop payment system is an environment where payment systems of different providers don't communicate with each other, with an open loop payment system allowing communication.

The above illustrations – canal, river and garden – provide a solid basis for understanding what payment systems are all about. Which one of the abovementioned illustrations have you enjoyed or is appealing to you? Whichever one it is, the goal was to enable you as a reader grasp the concept of payment system.

The terms "payment systems" and "the national payment system" are normally used interchangeably. The national payment system is a collective term that includes such things as payment systems, clearing systems, settlement systems, legal and regulatory framework, participants and institutions. You might be wondering about an automated teller machine (ATM) or the payment card in your pocket. They all form part of payment systems and the national payment system. An ATM is a delivery channel normally used for dispensing cash, depositing cash and other services, while a card is used for purchases at point-of-sale and online as well as making cash withdrawals at a payment channel such as an ATM.

The above provides a glimpse of what is to come as you continue to enjoy reading this book. Reading until the end will make you feel empowered in terms of the knowledge you are going to accumulate for the future. This is like doing an investment now with the goal of reaping the benefits at some point later on. The effort and time spent in reading this book is your investment, while the benefits include knowledge gained as well as the opportunity to apply what has been learned.

Several stakeholders are expected to benefit from the content of this useful guide. These stakeholders include students, banking professionals, finance professionals, researchers, regulators and the general public. They are highly likely to benefit in a number of ways. The question is, "How?" This depends on the stakeholder in question.

Students are some of the stakeholders that this guide is targeting. Some students are pursuing banking related courses while others are in the science, technology, engineering and mathematics (STEM) field. This guide covers all student types including those studying banking related courses and others who might be interested in learning about this particular field of banking: payment systems. The bottom line is: don't pass-by this book while seeing it on the shelf or online simply because it might seem to be written for banking and finance professionals. Life is such that there is a need to break away from familiar territory to an area that might seem to be unfamiliar to us. In this way we get to learn both horizontally and vertically in order to embrace a complete approach to learning.

This book will be useful to banking professionals as well. The banking profession covers different areas such as project management, lending, investment, operational support with respect to payment queries and other payments related matters, legal, compliance, information technology, relationship management and several other areas. Knowledge of payment systems can therefore empower a banking professional to be aware of the universe of payment systems. It is good at this juncture to say that awareness or knowledge accumulation is not enough. Applying what has been learned is key and is a differentiator. Besides, it is like faith. Faith implies not only to believe, but also to do something. Believing that one can pass an exam without opening a book to study is not enough. Using the knowledge gained in this book in everyday discussions and possibly implementing something is a way to go.

Finance professionals need to learn about payment systems. There are differences and similarities between mainstream banking and finance. Banking is a subset of finance and not the other way around. Other sub-sectors that can be found in finance include insurance, retail, investment, development banking and agricultural banking. One finds system operators and a host of service providers in this sub-sector as well. System operators and service providers are traditionally called non-bank financial institutions (NBFIs). Some NBFIs traditionally provide payment services and lending while others provide services, including insurance and other products.

It is therefore imperative for NBFIs to have a good grasp of payment systems as well. Knowledge of payment systems enables these entities to: know the payment solutions their bankers are implementing, be familiar with payment solutions to offer to their customers, assess if direct participation in the payments environment is an option, and understand key developments in payments that relate to policies and standard that apply.

Researchers will also find this book useful. These can be individuals associated with academic institutions, commercial entities, banking institutions, professional associations, other organisations or even individuals who are doing research on their own. There are different reasons why research is crucial in every-day life. Research is done to create and extend knowledge, aid in decision making, create general awareness on market trends, and serve as basis for product development. Research is a basis for any development endeavour. One cannot think of anything that was created without a research component as input, be it a small or big research activity that was involved. Research should be viewed as a necessity and not as something that is optional.

What about regulators? This material will be beneficial to them too. Regulators come in a number of forms. These include principal regulators, self-regulators, banking regulators, non-bank regulators, telecommunication regulators, competition regulators, and other regulators that have a stake in payment systems. Essentially, regulators put in place legal and regulatory frameworks that they use to oversee environments they are responsible for, with the view to protect the general public from unfair practices and also achieve certain public policy objectives. It is easy to conclude that regulation leads to an increase in cost. The other side of the coin can also be true: to say that lack of regulation also leads to an increase in cost. Does it matter which side one looks at? Certainly not. Regulation is important in our daily lives to make sure that the interests of all stakeholders are protected. This aspect of regulation will be expanded upon ahead.

The general public is not left out as far as this book is concerned. In this regard, the general public includes all stakeholders not included above. Stakeholders included above are students, banking professionals, finance professionals, regulators and researchers. The general public should therefore include businesses, other organisations, and individuals with a vested interest in payment systems. Armed with payments knowledge, these stakeholders are able to understand both domestic and international trends as well as using the information to make important decisions that affect their operations and daily lives.

Consequently, this book dovetails different aspects in the inner core of payment, clearing and settlement systems in a clear and concise manner. It provides answers to common questions in digital banking and payment systems while at the same time covering diverse topics including but not limited to payment instruments, payment streams, regulation and supervision, special topics and other matters you need to know in your everyday interactions around payments. All stakeholders will find the book useful.

CHAPTER 2

Importance of Payment Systems

We all value certain things or items at times or even most of the time. The question is: why put a value on something we think is important to us? And how do we show that we value these things? A car can be used as an example. Many of us value a car because it helps us to move from one place to another – say, taking kids to and from school or going to work and back. In addition, a car is used for carrying grocery shopping and other items. We show that we value a car if it is kept clean, taken for an annual service, repaired if damaged, or even handled well so that it remains durable into the future. The concept of value applies to payment systems as well.

Learning Objectives

By the end of this chapter, you should be able to

- understand the usefulness of payment systems in several markets;
- appreciate the need for reforming payment systems; and
- know the relationship between payment systems and gross domestic product.

Payment Systems and Markets

Studies confirm that payment systems are important for our daily living. Carstens (2020) points out that payment systems are vital for the functioning of the economy because they enable the purchase and sale of goods, services and financial instruments. This aligns with Lawack-Davids (2012) who indicates that payment systems are critical to the effective functioning of financial systems in a country and globally and that, if insufficiently protected against risks such as credit, liquidity and settlement risks, disruption within the systems could trigger or transmit further disruptions among its participants, or generate systemic disruption in the financial markets or more widely across the economy.

There is a difference between a good, a service and a financial instrument. First of all, they are all called products. Some products can be seen and touched while others have a feeling associated with them as a result of consuming them. For example, bread is a good, hairdressing is a service, and a bond is a financial instrument. Payment systems therefore facilitate the exchange of ownership and money between those that are selling products and those that are buying them. The end result is that the seller receives money and the buyer receives a product arising from the transaction in question.

An illustration can be used. Tom learns that there is a big Black Friday sale that is coming the following month at one of his favourite clothing shops. He decides to save now by spending less from his salary in order to buy shoes. The following month seems far away but he convinces himself that he will have to wait for that moment to realise his goal of buying new shoes that he cannot afford at the normal price. Tom is not the only one looking forward to Black Friday; there are others too. The young man is so anxious to the extent that he wants to be number one in the queue when the shop opens on Black Friday.

The day finally arrives. Tom heads to his favourite shop as early as possible to secure his number one spot in the queue. He whisks himself to the men's department where he finds the shoes. The price tag catches his eye: "Buy 2 pair of shoes and get one for free". "Well, what a discount!"

he says. The normal price for a pair of his preferred shoes is NAD400 and for three pairs this becomes NAD1200. He saves a whopping NAD400 as the price tag says take two and get one pair of shoes for free and in total it follows that he is supposed to pay NAD800 only.

Tom puts his shoes in a shopping cart and heads to checkout counter. He does not have physical cash on hand but rather a plastic payment card. This card is handed to the cashier to process the payment. The young man keys in his personal identity number (PIN) and then signs off the till slip and off he goes with a smile on his face.

What is the lesson above? Tom benefited from payment systems. He used a payment card to buy shoes from the shop owner as that was the most convenient way to pay for the shoes. The shop owner did not receive physical cash but was very sure to receive funds via electronic means from their bank.

Payment systems are applicable in all markets. These markets are depicted below and consist of labour, product, capital and money markets.

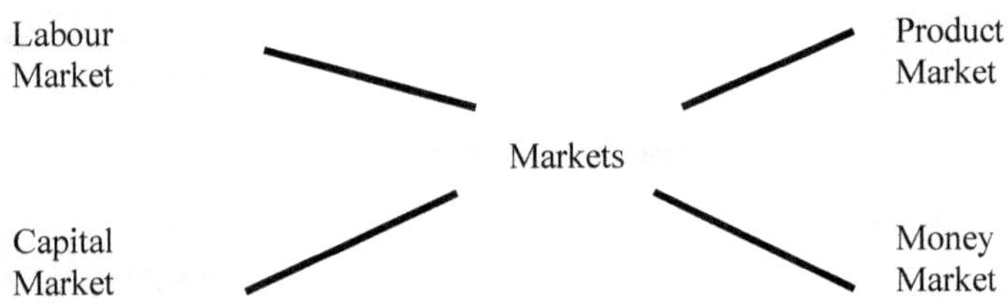

Figure 2.1. Types of Markets

The labour market is a place where supply of and demand for labour takes place, while the product market is a market for goods and services. The money market is for short-term securities such as treasury bills and other short-term investments, while the capital market is a market for long-term securities such as buying and selling shares via a stock exchange. Payment systems therefore facilitate the initiation, processing, clearing and settlement of funds for all these markets.

Reforming Payment Systems

Payment systems need to be taken care of, given their importance in several markets. This can imply ensuring that there are controls on how risks are managed in the national payment systems. Outlining controls on a piece of paper is one thing; using those controls to make sure that players in the market undertake their business operations in accordance with the regulatory framework is another.

Modernising or reforming payment systems is another way to show that these systems are important. Reforming payment systems means making changes to, enhancing or improving these systems so that they respond to the changing needs of the society or communities these systems need to support. This implies that payment system reforms are done to respond to the changing needs in a given society. HPS (2024) outlines strategies for platform modernisation that include big bang migration (switching from old to new in a single move), parallel running (two systems running for a period allowing for gradual transition), incremental modernisation (updating components rather than overhauling at once), phased migration by product (launching specific products at a time), and selective migration by customer segment (introducing to a specific segment before rolling out to the broader customer base). All these strategies are important for implementing systems and products as well as for customer onboarding.

Let us assume there is a complaint from members of a certain locality regarding the long distance they must travel to access automated teller machines. Most people in that locality are not well off and are dependent on subsistence farming to earn a living. There is therefore a general state of poverty as farming is susceptible to changing climatic conditions. The locality prospers when the rains are good and does not during drought times.

There are several interventions that can be put in place to address the situation mentioned above. Service providers such as banking institutions and other financial institutions can deploy access points that include automated teller machines, speed points or other cash-in and cash-out points to serve the locality. This can only be done if it is profitable and safe to do so. Regulatory intervention cannot be ruled out to make sure that there is access to financial services as limited access to such services can dampen economic activities.

Payment systems reforms are not only driven by changes in customer tastes, preferences or attitudes as indicated above. Other sources of reform are technological changes, regulatory changes, and other macroeconomic or environmental changes. There is a need to continuously monitor these sources of possible payment system reforms to inform the kind of enhancements that are required for the benefit of the general public or the national payment systems.

Payment Systems and GDP

There is a relationship between payment systems and economic activities. Payment systems in this case represent the value of transactions settled within a real time gross settlement system (RTGS) such as Namibia Interbank Settlement System (NISS) while economic activities are represented by the indicator called gross domestic product (GDP). The NISS system is more fully discussed in subsequent chapters. GDP refers to the value of economic activities produced in a country such as Namibia over a period of time such as on an annual basis.

BOX 1

GDP is a macroeconomic indicator that is used to measure the extent by which economic activities of a country have expanded. A decrease in GDP implies that the value of goods and services in a country has fallen while an increase tells that the same has increased. Countries are in favour of positive, high and sustainable GDP growth compared to negative, low and fluctuating GDP numbers. High GDP growth implies that a country is creating employment and serves as a good basis for measuring economic development. GDP growth or economic growth is a subset of economic development, which is a good measure of a country's standard of living.

There are several approaches to measuring GDP. The first one is the expenditure approach, which is the addition of consumption, investment, government spending and net export. Net export is export minus import. The value added or output approach is the other one and considers primary, secondary or manufacturing and tertiary industries in the calculation of GDP.

Correlation coefficient and coefficient of determination are the two statistical tools that were used to measure the degree of relationship between the two variables, that is, payment systems and GDP. Correlation coefficient with a symbol r measures the degree of association between the variables while coefficient of determination with a symbol r^2 enables us to calculate the total variation in y that is explained by the association between x and y. The correlation coefficient ranges from -1 to 1 and the coefficient of determination is found by squaring the correlation coefficient and multiplying the answer by 100 (Willemse, 2001).

The x and y above are taking the places of payment systems and GDP respectively. GDP is a dependent variable while payment systems denote an independent variable. An illustration can be used to explain the difference between dependent and independent variables. Consider a boy called Simataa who sat for Grade 12 examinations recently with an average score of A+ in all subjects. He says that the reason why he managed to record this high grade is because he put more effort during preparation. Exam results in this example are a dependent variable while effort is an independent variable. Consequently, an independent variable explains changes in the dependent variable. There is no way that the student was going to perform that well were it not for more effort on his side.

Results for the abovementioned variables for Namibia over a period of 2017 to 2021 show that r=0.54 and r^2=29 percent. There is positive correlation between payment systems and economic activities as the correlation coefficient is 0.54. The association is strong but not very strong as the figure of 0.54 is far away from 1. Coefficient of determination was recorded at 29 percent. This percentage implies that payment systems only explain or are responsible for 29 percent variation of economic activities out of the total variation. The remaining 71 percent is explained by other variables, other than payment systems, that are not part of the present analysis. An addition of other variables and expanding on the number of years compared to what was used in this example can improve these results.

The period in question can be reduced in the form of a line chart or figure as indicated below. Electronic payments, represented by retail and high values settled in NISS, increased over time during the 2017-2021 reference period. GDP also did the same with the exception of 2019 when there was a flat increase and in 2020 GDP fell compared to the previous year.

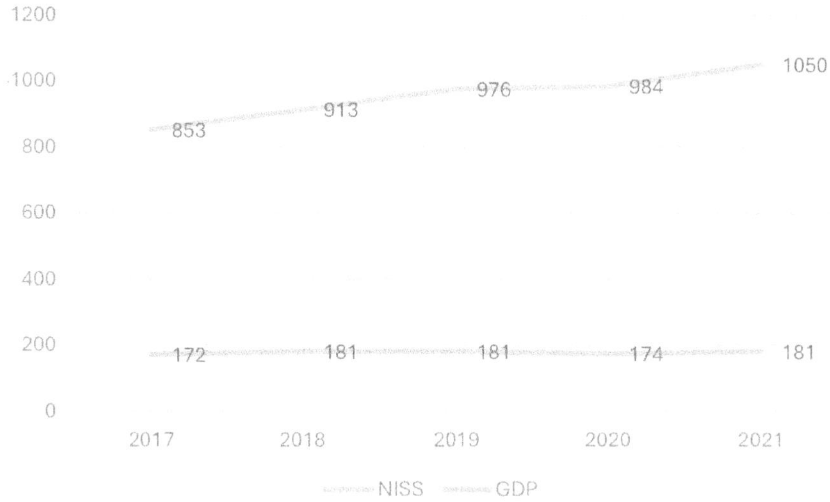

Figure 2.2. NISS and GDP

When electronic payments increased to NAD984 billion in 2020, GDP decreased to NAD174 billion in that year. This is not surprising. These payments have been shown to be resilient to the Covid-19 outbreak while GDP was not. The Committee on Payments and Market Infrastructures (2021) notes that the Covid-19 pandemic has boosted the use of digital and contactless payments. These indicators, electronic payments and GDP, showed an upward movement from the year 2021.

Chapter Summary

This chapter addressed the importance of payment systems. The chapter indicated that payment systems are important to our daily living and need to be protected from inherent risks to avoid a negative spillover into several markets in a country's economy. Payment systems have proved useful in several situations, including during the Covid-19 pandemic period. Consumers of financial services were able to buy goods and services using electronic means of payment during that time. Continuous reforming of these systems is key going forward to ensure that economic activities are not hampered.

Review Questions

1. Name and explain four types of markets in which payment systems play an important role.
2. Payment system reforms are important in several markets. Please motivate your answer.
3. Explain the following terms:
   a. Dependent variable
   b. Independent variable
   c. Economic growth
   d. Economic development

Selected References

Carstens, A. (2020). Shaping the future of payments. *BIS Quarterly Review*, 17-20. Retrieved from https://www.bis.org/

Committee on Payments and Market Infrastructures, (2021). *Covid-19 Accelerated the Digitalization of Payments*. Basel, Switzerland: Bank for International Settlements. Retrieved from https://www.bis.org/

HPS, (2024). *Keeping Up with the Pace: Modernizing Payment Systems*. Paris, France: HPS. Retrieved from https://www.hps-worldwide.com/

Lawack-Davids, V. (2012). The Legal and Regulatory Framework of Mobile Banking and Mobile Payments in South Africa. *Journal of International Commercial Law and Technology*, 7(4), 318-327. Retrieved from https://www.researchgate.net/

Willemse, I. (2001). *Statistical Methods for Business*. Cape Town, South Africa: Juta.

CHAPTER 3

Credit Card Payments

This is the first of the thirty-two core chapters on digital banking and payments for the banking professionals. The focus in this chapter is on credit card payments, which are when a cardholder uses a credit card for purchases of goods and services at any of the several delivery channels. Credit cards are part of the world of plastic money or non-cash payment instruments where the use of hard cash does not feature at all when considering pure credit card transactions. What makes credit cards such an important instrument for payments? What explains their continuous use especially in challenging economic times? These questions have challenged many and this chapter helps in finding answers.

Learning Objectives

By the end of this chapter, you should be able to

- explain the meaning of credit card payment and its different features;
- understand where you can use a credit card when purchasing goods and services;
- construct a payment schedule for credit cards;
- have a view of fees and charges associated with the use of a credit card;

- outline international card brands or circuits that have played an important role in the field of credit cards; and
- apply the concept of debt consolidation to credit cards.

Description of Credit Card

A credit card is part of the world of plastic money or non-cash payment instruments where the use of hard cash does not feature at all when considering pure credit card transactions. It is a physical plastic in rectangular form that is issued to you, the cardholder, accompanied by a line of credit up to a certain limit, to enable purchases of goods and services at delivery channels of your financial services provider or at delivery channels of other financial services providers. The limit on a credit card differs from customer to customer and is arrived at by a financial services provider taking into account factors such the income and expenses, current and long-term assets, and overall risk profile of a customer.

There are several financial service providers in a credit card industry. A cardholder can use a credit card at delivery channels of their financial service provider for on-us transactions and is able to use a credit card at delivery channels of other financial services providers for off-us transactions. On-us transactions are transactions where the cardholder and the beneficiary to a transaction all have accounts with the same financial service provider such as a bank. Off-us transactions are transactions where the cardholder and the beneficiary to a transaction have accounts at different financial services providers such as banks.

Credit cards can be divided into several categories. These plastic cards can be issued to *customer types* such as retail or individuals, business or commercial, and corporate or institutional customers. *Income* category covers silver, gold, platinum, and private levels. Silver can be associated with low income, gold with middle income, platinum with high income and private with ultra-high income. Cardholders can also be classified in terms of *when they settle credit card balances.* "Convenience users" view credit card as a means of payment that brings in convenience and such users tend to settle their outstanding balance at the end of each month. This is not the same with "revolvers" who do not wish to settle the outstanding balance at the end of each month, but instead prefer to roll-over what is due to the following month, and are happy to pay interest on the outstanding balance. The last category that can be considered is the *type of issuers*. These can be divided into banks and non-bank financial institutions. Banks are traditional issuers of credit cards while the entry of non-banks into the credit card industry can be seen as a result of a number of factors including profitability of the industry, need to diversify into new markets and products, and regulatory changes aimed at promoting financial inclusion.

Credit cards provide several advantages to the cardholder. Some key advantages that cardholders enjoy while in possession of a credit card payment instrument are the following:

- Access to funds at any point of time for withdrawals, purchases and transfers.
- Ability to transact via channels including those owned by account holding bank and those that are owned by other financial service providers.
- Opportunity to benefit from free interest period when the outstanding balance is settled in good time.
- Ability to roll-over the outstanding balance to the following month if not settled in full.
- Evidence of creditworthiness, with a good credit record, in the eyes of other service providers and merchants.
- Participation in reward programmes offered by a financial service provider.
- Access to certain services and facilities such as travel insurance, and discounts at selected service providers, airport lounges and accommodation establishments.

There are disadvantages that the cardholder needs to be aware of as well. Some key disadvantages that cardholders need to know while in possession of a credit card payment instrument are the following:

- Credit cards are associated with an unsecured line of credit and therefore the interest rate tends to be high.
- Failure to settle the outstanding amount on time leads to an increase in interest payments and by extension high short-term debt.
- There are additional charges associated with maintaining a credit card account.
- A high outstanding amount on a credit card implies a negative impact on a client's risk profile or credit score.
- Interest and principal payment associated with a credit card deprive a cardholder of much needed funds that can be channelled to pressing needs or emergencies.

Channels for Credit Card Payments

A channel is the first point of contact that a cardholder interacts with to consume various financial or banking services. The key channels in this regard include automated teller machine, speed point or point-of-sale (POS) terminal and e-commerce. *Automated teller machine* is the traditional channel outside a bank branch from which to withdraw physical cash for day-to-day use. These machines include traditional automated teller machines, deposit-taking machines and cash express machines. Traditional machines are what we are used to while deposit-taking ones allow a cardholder to deposit physical cash without visiting a branch. Cash express machines are also found in urban and peri-urban centres and provide limited services compared to the bigger machines.

The primary way a payment card comes into contact with an automated teller machine is through inserting a card into the card slot and then entering a personal identification number (PIN) on the keypad to authenticate a transaction. If the reason for entering a card was to withdraw cash, then cash is dispensed and the cardholder walks away.

There is a host of value-added services offered through an automated teller machine. Withdrawing cash by means of a physical payment card, at automated teller machines of our own banks and machines of other banks, is a service known to many of us. These machines are also used for advertising, including displaying fees and charges to be incurred for certain transaction types. Cardless withdrawals are also performed at an automated teller machine. This involves generating a once-off PIN through following a menu on your cellphone and using the code generated at an automated teller machine to make a withdrawal. What a cool service, especially in a situation where you have forgotten your card in the car or at home!

Major developments that have been witnessed in recent years as far as automated teller machines are concerned include reducing these machines at places where there is limited traffic or security. Value-added services, such as cardless withdrawals, are now common at these machines, as indicated above. Putting a chain of automated teller machines at big shopping malls, at bank branches, or convenient places is another key development. The move from brick-and-mortar to digital implies that some bank branches are being closed to reduce operational costs and automated teller machines are being enhanced to include more functionality to serve as many people as possible. Besides, the closure of bank branches has led to the migration of customers to automated teller machines resulting in long queues at some of these machines especially when people receive their salaries. Long queues at automated teller machines can also be explained by the fact that people are traditionally more comfortable withdrawing cash from machines owned by their bank and not of other banks to avoid incurring unnecessary charges. Which one is better? Is it standing in a queue for 30 minutes to 1 hour in front of a machine of your bank or incurring an additional fee or charge by withdrawing cash at a nearby and less congested machine owned by another bank? This is a personal question that you can think about and then try to answer.

Speed point or point-of-sale terminal is the second card channel that is considered. This is a machine that is owned by an acquirer and located at the point-of-sale of a specific merchant where a cardholder presents a payment card or similar instrument to a cashier when buying a good or service. There are key words that need to be explained in this definition of a speed point. An acquirer is a bank that has an account relationship with a merchant while a merchant is a business outlet such as a supermarket or any other establishment that sells goods and services to the general public.

There are three known ways a card comes into contact with a speed point. These are inserting a card into a slot, swiping a card on one side of the machine, and tapping or waving a card above the machine. While inserting or swiping a card are the most common, tapping a card is a more recent phenomenon.

Traditional ways of authorising card payments include signature and personal identification number (PIN). The use of a PIN is a recent development and is an added security step on top of a signature to ensure that customers are protected when making card payments. While some establishments in Namibia require both a PIN and signature at check-out, others do not, as long as a PIN is entered. This is where education for the benefit of merchants is key as check-out is negatively affected if these two forms are employed for each transaction.

Single acquiring is the most predominant method, as opposed to multiple acquiring. With "single acquiring", only speed points of a certain bank are found in a specific retail shop while with "multiple acquiring" one expects to find speed points of several banks in a retail shop. Multiple acquiring encourages the presentation of cards at speed points of the card issuer leading to processing of transactions within the same bank. On the other hand, single acquiring encourages the presentation of cards at speed points of other banks other than those of the card issuer, leading to interbank processing. Consequently, single acquiring is the most preferred arrangement and not multiple acquiring as the latter is associated with duplication of resources and likelihood of other devices remaining idle. The advantage of multiple acquiring – that of having some devices on standby in case other devices don't work – does not justify having this arrangement.

Other developments that have occurred in the speed point environment are worth mentioning. These include electronic wallet at till as well as cash-back. While electronic wallet at till involves redeeming value in the electronic wallet to physical cash at the speed point, cash-back refers to a situation where a cardholder receives cash at a speed point in combination with the purchase of goods or services.

The last card channel to consider is *e-commerce or online* as some in the industry prefer to refer to it. Let us stick to e-commerce to avoid confusing it with online banking. What is e-commence?

BOX 2

Maria is enrolled with a private university in Switzerland and was happy at the point of registration to do her studies with an international institution from a developed country. Her field of study is banking and she is confident that she will use her acquired knowledge for the benefit of the society, employer and industry after successful completion.

Her university periodically sends invoices for amounts due, payable by using a payment option of her choice that includes credit card, bank transfer or Swift. Swift stands for Society for Worldwide Interbank Financial Telecommunication. Maria opts to pay with a credit card. She logs onto an e-commerce site of the university, via a link powered by the payment processing service called PayPal and concludes the payment after entering credit card details. The student prefers this option as it is convenient, affordable and allows her to conclude a payment quickly.

Commerce or trading is the activity of buying and selling goods and services. This might be construed as referring to brick and mortar businesses. Electronic commerce (abbreviated as e-commerce) is a branch of electronic business and means the selling and buying of goods and services online or virtually. Maria in the above example does her card payments on an e-commerce site that is owned by her university.

E-commerce is not new and Bloomenthal (2022) indicates that e-commerce dates back to 1960s when companies used an electronic system called the electronic data interchange to facilitate the transfer of documents, with the first transaction having involved the sale of a CD between friends through a retail website called NetMarket. This form of trading has grown in size in terms of business models, payment gateways or payment processing services and payment options as well as online shops.

Although brick and mortar form of trading is still the most dominant in many countries at present, e-commerce can grow into a significant substitute going forward. Appetite from potential providers including start-ups, as well as investment in communication technology related fields, are some of the sources of growth likely to drive this form of trading in the future.

Card Charges

There are charges or fees that are associated with the use of a credit card or a credit card account. They are in most cases noticeable on your monthly statement. Please remember that a credit card is a facility that allows you to access your account. It is in your account itself where money, value or funds reside. Consequently, these charges are triggered because you have used the account or facility and usage in this case comes in a number of ways. These include transfers between a credit card and another account, purchases at a delivery terminal, and other usages.

The following are types of charges or fees related to the use of a credit card:

- Interest. This is levied because unsecured money has been loaned or lent to you. It is expressed in percent form, which is applied on the outstanding amount to arrive at the actual interest or interest charge.
- Monthly account fee. The charge is necessary to make sure that your account remains active for the foreseeable future. It is there to ensure that your account is properly managed on an ongoing basis.
- Value added tax (VAT). It appears on your credit card statement as well. The charge can be embedded in certain elements or shown as a standalone fee. This indirect tax is collected by a financial services provider on behalf of the government.
- Debit amount. This is the amount that needs to be debited to your account by the due date and it reduces the closing balance the following month if paid. Failure to pay this amount by the due date leads to an increase in interest and in the outstanding amount.
- Other charges. These take various forms and include but are not limited to card protection fee, over-the-limit-fee, card replacement fee, and personal identification number (PIN) replacement fee.

Multiple Credit Cards

It is common for cardholders to carry multiple credit cards. The question is: what leads to clients carrying or using multiple credit cards, and is there anything to worry about as a result of carrying multiple cards? There could be several reasons why clients can carry multiple credit cards. One is the need to have access to liquid and unsecured funds at all times. Another might be loyalty to a previous financial services provider, or reluctance to sever a relationship even if moving from one employer to another or from one country to another. Some employers allow selected employees to possess a corporate or business credit card. An entrepreneur can own a corporate credit card in addition to a personal credit card. Status also plays a role, as some might think that owning multiple credit cards is associated with overall net worth, whereby the higher the net assets, the higher the likelihood of owning multiple credit cards.

Owning multiple credit cards provides several advantages. It is a fact that one is able to have access to liquid and unsecured funds at all times. There are some drawbacks and these include costs incurred such as ongoing fees and charges, replacing cards if lost or stolen, card insurance, and other costs as discussed above. Fraud risk should not be ignored as well. The more cards you are carrying, the higher the chance of fraud through unauthorised access to your credit card account.

Market Size

There are several ways of looking at the size of the credit card market. One way is to look at the financial services providers providing card products to their clients. Other ways include but are not limited to the number of merchants accepting credit cards within their outlets, the number of transactions that are processed at delivery channels, the count of delivery channels themselves, and lastly the value of credit card transactions in relation to gross domestic product (GDP). GDP is the market value of goods and services produced in a given country over a period of time such as a year.

Establishing the size of a credit card market at country, regional and international level is not an easy exercise. This is because data might not be available. Where it is available, there might be some gaps in terms of the time period that is covered, and reliability in relation to the quality of published data. In another situation, the data might be available but not published for the general public to consume.

Data that is used to understand the size of the credit card market at a global level was collected from the Bank for International Settlements (BIS). The BIS is based in Basel, Switzerland and acts as a bank for central banks. It has several committees that support it in the process of carrying out its functions or mandate. These committees are the Basel Committee on Banking Supervision, the Committee on the Global Financial System, the Committee on Payments and Market Infrastructures, the Markets Committee, the Central Bank Governance Forum, and the Irving Fisher Committee on Central Bank Statistics.

The Committee on Payments and Market Infrastructures (CPMI) periodically collects and publishes red book statistics on payments and financial market infrastructures (PFMIs) related to member countries. Not all countries are members of the CPMI. Statistics as collected by the CPMI for selected years appear in the table below.

Table 3.1
Market Size for Credit Card

Year	Volume (mil)	Percentage (%)	Number of Cards (000)
2017	80,239	11.44	2,647,786
2018	88,858	11.74	2,864,994
2019	98,770	11.15	2,981,893
2020	93,813	-5.02	3,124,261
2021	100,285	6.90	3,256,335

Source: Committee of Payments and Market Infrastructures (2023)

It is evident from the above table that the credit card market has grown over the years during the reference period, which is from 2017 to 2021. The number of credit card transactions stood at 100 billion in 2021 and this represents 7 percent growth compared to the previous year. Besides, the volume of transactions shows a 5 percent fall in 2020 with the possible explanation for this being the Covid-19 pandemic. In terms of plastics, the number of cards stood at 3 billion in 2021 compared to over 2 billion in 2017.

Future of the Credit Card

Payment methods do come and go in a given country and even at a global level. This is ascribed to advancements in technology, prevalence of risks, and other forces that make one payment method less appealing to use compared to other means of payment. For example, the system of barter does not exist anymore. Barter involves the exchange of one good for another good to conclude a transaction. If one person has a Nokia cellphone and is looking for a Samsung mobile phone and the two individuals agree to exchange the devices, then a transaction has been concluded.

Is a credit card payment instrument still appealing to consumers of goods and services at present? What is the chance that a credit card product will continue to be demanded by clients of financial institutions going forward? It was noted earlier that credit cards provide a number of benefits or advantages to those carrying them. Some of the benefits noted include access to funds at any point of time for withdrawals, purchases and transfers, as well as the fact that a cardholder can roll-over the outstanding balance to the following month if not settled in full.

Foottit, King, Davy, Halpin, Gaida, Michnevic and Waldron (2019) note that the credit card will not disappear but will be supplemented by more targeted lending products that address the demands of the digital-first generation of shoppers. The conclusion that can be made from this finding is that a credit card as a payment instrument is here to stay, at least for the foreseeable future. Key words that can be deduced from the above include online shopping, digital savvy shoppers and targeted lending products. Consequently, the end of credit card as payment instrument is not imminent, owing to the need for online shopping and the convenience that the instrument provides to consumers of financial services.

Credit Card Statement

A credit card statement is an important document that a cardholder is expected to scrutinise periodically to make sure that the transactions shown are legitimate, having been authorised by the account holder. Illegitimate transactions need to be communicated to the financial services provider as soon as possible so that necessary adjustments or corrections can be made. The statement is distributed to an account holder periodically, showing purchases of goods and services as well as transfers in and out of the account. Means of distributing credit card statements include but are not limited to email, postal services, and other possible delivery channels.

Understanding elements on the credit card statement is vital. The account holder will be able to see clearly both the expense items and the receipts that were made during the previous month or period. Sound knowledge of the statement also helps the holder of the account to pinpoint if there were fraudulent activities on the account. The following are the more common elements that appear on the credit card statement:

Table 3.2
Elements on the Credit Card Statement

Name	Description
Date	This includes the statement and the due dates. Statement date is the date when the statement was compiled for distribution to the client and the due date is the date when the amount to be debited to the customer account is due.
Limit	This is the purchase / transfer limit loaded on your account. Purchases and transfers need to fall within the limit allocated to a cardholder.

Name	Description
Opening balance	The amount brought down from the previous month as at the statement date.
Usage	All the purchases of goods and services including transfers in or out of the account.
Fees and charges	These include interest and other fees and charges levied to the outstanding amount and to your credit card account.
Payment received	All the credits to the credit card account by the account holder.
Closing balance	This is the opening balance plus fees and charges minus the payment received by the statement date.
Overdue amount	This is reflected if the amount to be debited to your account is not collected.
Debit amount	This is the amount to be debited to your account.
Interest rates	Includes both interest on debit and credit card balances for a given year or period.
Contact details	Contact details of the financial services provider and card-holder are provided.

Example 1

A credit cardholder just received a credit card statement via email and is not sure how the amount to be debited to the account, closing amount and available balance on the statement were calculated. The following information is visible on the statement: opening balance NAD5000, card limit NAD6000, payment received NAD50, monthly management charge NAD20 (this includes value added tax of NAD5), interest NAD25. Consequently, calculations are shown below:

- Amount to be debited to the account

	NAD
Monthly management charge	20
Interest	25
	45

- Closing balance

	NAD
Opening balance	5,000
Add: interest and charges	45
	5,045
Less: payment received	50
	4,995

- Available balance

	NAD
Card limit	6,000
Less: closing balance	4995
	1005

Example 2

Another credit card holder, who is careful about his spending and would like to settle the outstanding or closing balance over a period of time, decides to reach out to the financial service provider to discuss a payment plan his friend advised him about. The friend gave him the idea of having the debit amount fixed at NAD45 and to increase prepayment by NAD50 each month, starting with NAD50 at the beginning of the year. This appeared to be palatable to the cardholder and the payment schedule starting with the opening balance of NAD5000 is depicted in the following table.

Table 3.3
Credit Card Payment Schedule

Month	Opening Balance (NAD)	Debit Amount (NAD)	Payment Received (NAD)	Closing Balance (NAD)
January	5,000	45	50	4,995
February	4,995	45	100	4,940
March	4,940	45	150	4,835
April	4,835	45	200	4,680
May	4,680	45	250	4,475
June	4,475	45	300	4,220
July	4,220	45	350	3,915
August	3,915	45	400	3,560
September	3,560	45	450	3,155
October	3,155	45	500	2,700
November	2,700	45	550	2,195
December	2,195	45	600	1,640

The payment plan worked to the benefit of the cardholder and by the end of December only NAD1,640 debt was outstanding on his credit card account. He thought about what to do next with three options before him. One option is to use the available balance to cover more pressing family expenses. The second option is to continue with the payment plan with the goal of clearing the outstanding amount, with the last option being to settle the closing balance the following month when he receives his salary. The cardholder is convinced that any of the options would be for the benefit not only for him but for his family as well.

Debt Consolidation

Debt consolidation is a major topic for discussion in finance circles. It follows that any material, book or guide that is related to finance should have a section focusing on debt consolidation. This stems from several perspectives. While some individuals are highly indebted with multiple loans or large amounts in debt outstanding, others tend to live within their means. There are those with multiple credit cards, implying more in debt outstanding, compared to those with one credit card in their possession. Besides, some stakeholders do not know where to seek help to manage their finances.

Kagan (2023) says that debt consolidation means taking out a new loan or credit card to pay off other existing loans or credit cards. There is a need to understand the advantages and disadvantages of debt consolidation. Advantages include a lower interest rate, reduction in monthly instalments, and channelling money for saving, investment and emergencies. Disadvantages include the total interest cost being more if using long-term debt to eliminate short-term debt; the overall principal amount outstanding does not change; and debt consolidation implies a new loan.

Example 3

Consider a customer with various short-term and medium-term loans amounting to NAD80,000 with associated interest rates. The lowest amount of these loans is NAD4,000 and the highest debt outstanding is NAD50,000. This customer has a home loan on which he owes NAD200,000 and has also managed to accumulate equity on the home loan amounting to NAD500,000. Home loan equity is the difference between the original amount of the loan at inception and what the client of a financial service provider has actually paid towards settling the loan. The customer has a large family and wants to sort out his financial affairs as instalments are having a negative impact on his income, saving, investment and saving for unforeseen situations. How should the customer go about consolidating his debts?

Table 3.4
Debt Consolidation

Debt	Balance Outstanding (NAD)	Annual Interest Rate (%)	Debt Limit (NAD)
Credit Card	5,000	18	10,000
Personal Loan	7,000	15	90,000
Clothing Account	4,000	22	15000
Cash Loan	8,000	25	50,000
Overdraft	6,000	17	20,000
Car Loan	50,000	13	300,000
Total	80,0000		Not applicable
Equity on Home Loan	500,000	11	700,000

The customer has several options to implement to consolidate the loans. One option is to increase the personal loan balance to NAD80,000 at an interest rate of 15 percent per annum and then take NAD73,000 out of this amount to settle other debts. An additional option available is to reach out to the personal banker to access NAD80,00 of the equity on the home loan and settle all short-term and medium-term loans. Interest that is going to apply in this case is 11 percent per annum.

International Card Brands

Look at the payment card, in this case the credit card, that your financial service provider such as a bank has issued to you. The name or logo of your bank appears on it. The name or logo of an international card network, circuit or brand is visible on the card as well. These institutions, circuits, brands or networks provide processing, switching, clearing and settlement of transactions that are done at various card-accepting channels across the world. The key enablers in connecting economic agents such as cardholders, merchants and financial institutions around the world are the international payment circuits (Pulina, 2011).

The well-known international card brands are American Express, Discover, Japan Credit Bureau, Mastercard, UnionPay, and Visa. These institutions are briefly outlined and described below.

- American Express. This is active in the *payments business* and was established in 1850, making it the oldest common international card brand. It is headquartered in New York City, New York, United States.
- Discover. This financial service provider can be traced back to 1985 and its mission is to '*help people spend smarter, manage debt better and save more so they achieve a brighter financial future*'. It is headquartered in Chicago, Illinois, United States.

- Japan Credit Bureau. It is an international payment brand that was established in 1981. *The main business areas includes credit card operations, financing, collection, gift and certificate issuing and sales.* It is headquartered in Tokyo, Japan.
- Mastercard. The payment processing company dates back to 1966 and *works with businesses and governments around the world in payments and beyond to improve the lives of people it serves.* It is headquartered in Harrison, New York, United States.
- UnionPay. This company was established in 2002 and provides cross-border payment services to cardholders. It is headquartered in Shanghai, China.
- Visa. The card payment services company has been in the world of *digital payments* since 1958. It is headquartered in San Francisco, California, United States.

Chapter Summary

This chapter was focussed on credit card payments. These are payments initiated by a credit card payment instrument at various channels domestically and internationally and are based on a predetermined credit card limit. Transactions that are attempted beyond the limit are rejected. You must know that a credit card is used to access an unsecured credit facility and consequently the associated interest rate tends to be relatively high. Using the facility more prudently for essential and emergency expenses only is key to minimise incurring avoidable interest costs.

Review Questions

1. Define what is meant by "credit card". What are the advantages and disadvantages of this payment instrument?

2. A credit card holder just received a credit card statement showing the following information: opening balance NAD2,500, card limit NAD3,000, payment received NAD100, monthly management charge NAD20 (this includes value added tax of NAD10), and interest NAD50.

   Required:

   a. Calculate the amount to be debited to the account, the closing balance and the available balance.
   b. Explain the terms opening balance, closing balance and credit card limit.

3. Name the most common international card brands that you have learned. What do you think these companies do?
4. Outline different charges that can be levied to your credit card account.
5. Discuss debt consolidation and different options available for consolidating short-term debts.

Selected References

Bloomenthal, A. (2022). *E-commerce Defined: Types, History and Examples.* New York City, New York: Investopedia. Retrieved from *https://www.investopedia.com/*

Committee of Payments and Market Infrastructures, (2023). *The Red Book Statistics for CPMI Countries.* Basel, Switzerland: Bank for International Settlements. Retrieved from http://www.bis.org/

Foottit, I., King, D., Davy, M., Halpin, J., Gaida, T., Michnevic, M & Waldron, M. (2019). *The Future of Credit Card – A European Perspective.* London, United Kingdom: Monitor Deloitte. Retrieved from https://www2.deloitte.com/

Kagan, J. (2023). *What is Debt Consolidation and When is it a Good Idea?* New York City, New York: Investopedia. Retrieved from https://www.investopedia.com/

Pulina, M. (2011). Consumer Behaviour in the Credit Card Market: A Banking Case Study. *International Journal of Consumer Studies*, 35, 86-94. https://doi.org/10.1111/j.1470-6431.2010.00939.x

CHAPTER 4

Debit Card Payments

Debit cards are an important payment instrument for the purchase of goods and services in our daily lives. When some people see the instrument in their hand or wallet they think that they have money at that particular point of time. However, a debit card in itself is not equivalent to money. It is a means to access money a person has at their disposal. What is a debit card? What has made this payment method such a highly treasured piece of plastic? How is it different from other payment instruments?

Learning Objectives

By the end of this chapter, you should be able to

- explain the meaning of "debit card" and its different features;
- understand where you can use a debit card when purchasing goods and services;
- appreciate the concept of hybrid card and related features;
- have a view of fees and charges associated with the use of a debit card; and
- analyse a current account statement.

Description of Debit Card

A debit card is a payment card that is issued for use at payment channels backed by available funds in a bank account. Have you ever tried to use a debit card at the speed point and the response was *insufficient funds*? This happens sometimes. Ideally, no payment should be processed if there are insufficient funds in the bank account. This differentiates a debit card from a credit card. The former enables access to your money in your current, cheque or transmission account while the latter makes it possible for you to access unsecured funds loaned to you up to a certain limit in a credit card account.

Debit cards are traditionally classified in different ways. Some of these are income or assets, age and customer type. "Income" in this case refers to how much one earns in terms of salary and "assets" refer to current and long-term assets. Categories such as classic or entry, gold, platinum, private and wealth are based on income or assets. Age matters as well. For example, individuals below or above a certain age get certain types of cards. "Customer type" in this case refers to individual, commercial and corporate or institutional customers. Sveriges Riksbank (2013) distinguishes between offline and online debit cards and notes that a payment using an online card can only be conducted if the card payment terminal is directly connected to the bank so that it is immediately possible to check whether there is sufficient money in the buyer's bank account. Online debit cards therefore eliminate the possibility of the merchant not being paid for goods and services that were sold to the cardholder.

A debit card, just like any payment card, can be easily recognisable. Important features that can assist you in identifying a debit card are the following:

- It has the logo of your financial service provider and that of an international card brand.
- Your signature appears on the back of your card. It is advisable to put a signature in the space provided.

- The card is named 'Debit Card' or similar on the front.
- There are both issue and expiry dates associated with the debit card.
- Your card should have a card number and other security features on the front and at the back as well.

Debit card payment instruments provide the following benefits:

- access to a demand deposit account;
- peace of mind as the source of funds for a transaction is your own funds;
- a traditional payment instrument acceptable at most delivery terminals;
- access to a wide range of customer groups; and
- lower interchange rates compared to credit and hybrid cards.

There are associated disadvantages related to debit cards as well. These are outlined below:

- lack of credit function for some cards;
- lower preference for online or e-commerce transactions compared to other card instruments; and
- need for prefunding of deposit account to avoid "insufficient funds" response at checkout.

Hybrid Card

Consumers have a choice to make about a payment instrument for purchasing goods and services at a particular point of time. In an environment where the supply of payment cards is adequate, making such a choice is not a challenge. The ability to make a choice is hampered in a market characterised by imperfect or oligopolistic market structures. These imperfect competitive structures have unwanted outcomes such as limited innovation, limited choices and high prices as well as eventual negative impact on consumption and overall economic performance.

Payment cards come in a variety of forms. Credit cards were discussed in the previous chapter while debit cards are described above. There is a payment card type that is less common, called a hybrid card. An example of the term "hybrid" can be taken from animal agriculture. The mule is a hybrid of a donkey and a horse, producing working animals that have various uses such as tilling the soil and carrying goods and people.

Like the mule, the hybrid card combines two useful elements: it is a payment card that has a *pay-now function* similar to a debit card, with connectivity to a deposit or checking account; and a *pay-later function* similar to a credit card, where transactions are processed as credit card sales with typical deferred payment programming (Kasavana, 2010). The hybrid card therefore provides the benefits of both worlds in a single card, that is, pay-now debit and pay-later credit card technologies.

A hybrid card presents a number of advantages as presented below:

- combines features of debit and credit cards;
- enhances customer experience owing to multiple elements in one card;
- adds more choices from a customer's standpoint; and
- meets the quest for innovation and modernisation in payment and settlement systems.

There are disadvantages related to hybrid cards and these are outlined as follows:

- attracts higher interchange (fee paid by the acquirer to the issuer for transactions done at a speed point in a four-party card model) compared to a debit card;
- might be expensive to develop and bring to market from an issuer standpoint; and
- is not easily distinguishable from a traditional debit card.

Channels for Debit Card Payments

The channels for debit card payments are the same as those for credit and hybrid card payments. Debit cards and hybrid cards are in this case used interchangeably. It is good to separate the two owing to different functions that are embedded in each card. The channels in question are automated teller machine, speed point and e-commerce. One of the channels, speed point, is illustrated in the following example.

Example 1

Let us look at the following figure, which shows two slips issued from different speed points at two shopping outlets:

Figure 4.1. Slips from two speed points

The first slip shows a debit card payment at a speed point owned by Nedbank and the merchant in question is KFC with the amount involved being NAD368.80. The second slip shows a debit card payment at a speed point owned by Bank Windhoek and the merchant is Windhoek Cash and Carry with the amount involved being NAD216.07. One debit card was used at the two shops on the same day, that is, 22 December 2022, within the space of 30 minutes.

What can be drawn from the above example? A debit card that is issued by a certain bank can be used at a speed point owned by another bank. In this example the debit card issuer is FNB Namibia and the card was used at speed points owned by Nedbank and Bank Windhoek respectively (the box below shows the number of commercial banks in Namibia). This is technically called card interoperability, which in our example is the ability of systems of different banks to communicate with each other in order to allow a transaction to be processed and concluded.

BOX 3

The Namibian banking sector has grown over the years in terms of the actual number of licensed banking institutions and type of products offered. There are currently seven commercial banks licensed to conduct banking business in Namibia. Banking business includes accepting deposits, lending money and payment services, to mention but a few. These commercial banks are Bank Windhoek, FNB Namibia, Nedbank Namibia, Standard Bank Namibia, Letshego Bank, Bank BIC and Banco Atlantico. While traditional banks have been in operation for a considerable time, the last three are relatively new participants in the banking sector.

Commercial banks offer a wide range of payment services and instruments to their customers in the national payment system. Both cash and non-cash payment instruments are offered and used across delivery channels such as branches, speed points, automated teller machines and electronic commerce. Customers of banks are now accustomed to electronic means of payments as paper-based payments instruments have been abolished in line with industry and regulatory requirements.

Card Charges

A debit card payment instrument has charges that are levied to cardholders. Just like any other payment plastic, these charges are levied by a card issuer to recoup production and other costs for delivering the product to the market. Some fees are charged to direct the behaviour of a cardholder to a required state. Fees that are associated with a debit card instrument, and other card types for that matter, are listed below.

- Card replacement fee. This fee type kicks in when your card needs to be replaced. An old card can be replaced with the new if it is lost, stolen or has expired.
- PIN replacement fee. Your PIN needs to be replaced if it is misplaced, forgotten or tampered with.
- Withdrawal fee. A cardholder can make withdrawals at various delivery channels such as their own bank's automated teller machines, other banks' automated teller machines, speed points, and branches.
- Protection fee. There are various types of protection around card payments that can be considered by financial services providers, such as insurance to cover the event of fraud or financial difficulties that may be experienced.
- Decline fee. This is related to withdrawals at a particular delivery channel and can be as a result of insufficient funds as an example.
- Purchase fee. This is one of the fees that can be levied especially for purchases of goods and services online or in-person.

Children, Youth and Senior Cards

Plastic payment cards are classified into segments as was noted already such as income, customer type and age. The last category requires a specific focus. Reference here is to children, youth and senior cardholders. These have certain needs that financial services providers have noted over the years. This relates to the need for all members of society to have access to financial services including banking and payment services. These customer groups represent a niche that requires attention from the standpoint of banks and non-bank financial institutions as the following table provides.

Table 4.2
Children, Youth and Senior Cards

Need	Children	Youth	Senior
Learn financial literacy from a very young age	X		
Tuition, hostel, meals and basic needs		X	
Pension benefits, household needs, professional / business services			X

From a very young age, children need to learn how cards work when they accompany their parents or older ones on a shopping trip. They can be taught how to use a card at a speed point and to withdraw money from an automated teller machine or any other cash dispensing machine. The youth are at high school or at university and are close to being independent. Visa Consulting and Analytics (2022) notes that a debit product with digitally advanced features such as parental controls and real-time notifications addresses concerns of parents who may be hesitant to hand a debit card to their children. There are specific expenses that children and the youth need to cover and they can only do that if payment cards are availed to them. Their sources of funds include parents, guardians, relatives and academic sponsors. Senior citizens might have retired from 9-to-5 jobs but still have expenses and responsibilities to provide for their families. The card fees they incur are likely lower than those of other age groups.

Current Account Statement

The current account is one of the important bank accounts one obtains in one's working life. It is available to individual, business and corporate customers. This account is a record of money coming in and money going out over a period of time such as a month. In other words, the account refers to a record of financial transactions conducted at delivery channels using a plastic payment card such as a debit card. Money coming into the account could be your salary and money going out of it could be fees and charges that you have incurred. There is movement in your bank account each time a debit card is used to buy goods and services.

What is important is to understand the types of transactions that are recorded on your current account statement. The following are the more common elements that appear on the current account statement.

Table 4.3

Elements on the Current Account Statement

Name	Description
Date	Statement date is the date when the statement was compiled for distribution to the client.
Purchases	This includes purchases at speed points or point-of-sale devices and online.
Opening and closing balances	This refers to the amounts at the beginning of the period and end of the period on your account.
Payments	These include payments done via mobile applications, internet banking payments / transfers, cellphone / unstructured supplementary service data (USSD), scheduled payments, and payments to a cellphone number linked to a bank account number.
Fees and charges	These include interest and other fees and charges levied to your account.
Withdrawals	Cardholders / account holders can withdraw funds from automated teller machines and speed points.

Name	Description
Deposits	Deposits can be made at deposit-taking automated teller machines and branches.
Collections	Reference here is to debit orders. You might see ENDO on your statement and this stands for enhanced debit order.
Other purchases	Items here include airtime, electricity and other purchases.
Send money	This refers to money sent to an electronic wallet or cellphone number.
Interest rates	This includes both debit and credit rates for a given year.
Contact details	Contact details of the financial services provider and cardholder are provided.

Chapter Summary

This chapter covered debit card payments, which are the payments that are initiated through the use of a debit card at various channels. These channels include physical and online channels. The concept of a hybrid card was discussed as was the current account statement. Cardholders need to review their current account statements closely to ensure that transactions that appear on the statement are all genuine. Fraudulent transactions need to be reported to their financial service providers.

Review Questions

1. Mention and describe different charges you are likely to incur when using a debit card at card accepting machines.
2. What is the difference between a debit card and a hybrid card?
3. What is a debit card? List the advantages and disadvantages of this payment instrument.
4. A cardholder just received a current account statement for the previous month via email and notes the following from the statement:

	NAD
Purchases at speed point	600
Withdrawal at ATM	2000
Cash purchases at till	1500
Online banking payments	200
Online banking transfers	500
Mobile App payments	300
Payments via USSD	170

Required:

a. Name the payment channels that are visible from the table.
b. Which payment channel does the cardholder prefer?
c. Which payment channel does the cardholder prefer the least?
d. Calculate all transactions that the cardholder completed electronically.
e. What is the proportion of cash and electronic transactions out of total transactions?
f. Comment on your answer in (e) above.

Selected References

Kasavana, M. L. (2010). Introducing Hybrid Payment Cards: Appealing to Customers will these Smart Cards change your Business. *Hospitality Upgrade*, 118-122. Retrieved from *https://www.hospitalityupgrade.com/*

Sveriges Riksbank, (2013). *The Swedish Retail Payment Market*. Stockholm, Sweden: Sveriges Riksbank.

Visa Consulting and Analytics, (2022). *Leading with Debit*. San Francisco, California: Visa. Retrieved from http://www.visa.cm/

CHAPTER 5

Reward, Gift and Store Cards

Reward, gift and store cards are worth considering in discussions around payment, clearing and settlement systems. The cards are still visible in the wallets of consumers and there is nothing on the horizon that suggests that the cards will be done away with anytime soon, so this book would be incomplete without reference to them. These cards are not payment instruments, but they should be viewed as complements to payment methods.

Learning Objectives

By the end of this chapter, you should be able to

- define reward, gift and store cards;
- understand how these cards are obtained; and
- comprehend how these cards work.

Reward Card

Reward or royalty cards allow you to earn points each time you purchase from your favourite store. Points accumulate over time and are converted into real currency on your card. The value accumulated can be used in two ways. You can use the value on your card to buy an item (for example, chocolate) within the available balance. Alternatively, you can use the value to reduce the amount you need to pay at the till. The following is an example of a reward card:

Figure 5.1. Reward card

Let us assume that the reward balance on your card is NAD100 and all the items you brought at the till from the shelves cost NAD890. Your net amount due to the shop becomes NAD790 after the reward amount is redeemed. The process to follow at the till if reward points need to be added to your reward card is the following:

- The cashier asks you if you have a reward card and if you do, the reward card is swiped at the appropriate terminal.
- Goods collected from the shelve are processed at the till. Points, based on the value of the items you bought, should have been added to your reward card at this point.

- The customer checks out using a payment card to complete the transaction. The till slip will usually reflect the points earned.

Gift Card

A gift card is based on the fact that a gift needs to be given to a person other than yourself. Anitsal, Anitsal and Brown (2013) note that besides the use of traditional credit cards, nowadays gift cards are becoming an established trend in the marketplace. The word gift refers to a present in the form of a good or service offered with no expectation of anything in return after the offer is extended to the beneficiary party. Gifts have traditionally been given during special seasons or occasions. For example, a couple that just got married might be offered free tickets for a honeymoon outside the country or at favourite location inside the country. However, there are many other reasons to give gifts. You might decide to buy stationery for a well-deserving student who comes from a less privileged household. A humble businessman offers to buy food and other items for a family whose house got destroyed in the flood recently.

Figure 5.2. Gift card

The abovc figure is an example of a gift card. It allows the purchaser of the card to load money on the card for the beneficiary to spend in the shop of the issuer. There is a need to keep the gift card in a safe location after value has been loaded to prevent it from falling into the wrong hands. The end-to-end process of a gift card is outlined below.

- Step 1. The gift card is given to a customer who intends to load value next time.
- Step 2. Value or money is loaded onto the card and is given to the ultimate beneficiary.
- Step 3. The beneficiary is free to spend the loaded value in the shop of the issuer.

Store Card

Imagine in a clothing shop after collecting goods from the shelves you walk over to check out. The cashier asks whether the transaction is cash or on account. This implies that you could use a store card. If the intention is to use a store card, then this card is presented at a dedicated point-of-sale. The transaction is then completed from end-to-end and you walk away with the items that you purchased.

Figure 5.3. Store card

The above figure is an example of a store card. This is a plastic shopping card that is issued by a shop or merchant to an individual who presents it at a point-of-sale to buy items on credit with the aim of settling the amount owing at a future date. There are both differences and similarities between a store card and a credit card. They are both consume-now-and-pay-later cards in the sense that consumption of items bought happens now, but settlement of indebtedness takes place at some point in the future – say after few days or a month. The cards are based on a preauthorised credit or spend limit. One of the differences is that a credit card is issued by a financial institution such as a bank while a store card is issued by a merchant such as a clothing retailer. In addition, a credit card can be presented at various payment channels or terminals while a store card can only be used at specific terminals within a shop or group of related shops.

The store card has been referred to by other names in the payments and banking literature; names such as private label credit card or white label credit card. De Teran (2023) says that private label credit cards, also known as store cards, are a type of credit card that can only be used at a specific retailer. A private label credit card is a card that is managed by a bank or commercial finance company for either a retail or wholesale manufacturer and does not carry a credit card network logo such as Visa or MasterCard (Kagan, 2021).

A private label credit card has some features of a pure credit card and pure store card. It is used at a particular store and it is issued by a bank with no card association logo. By comparison, a pure store card is issued by a store. The implication here is that private label credit cards can be issued either by a bank or by a particular store.

Merchants have procedures in place that they follow before they issue store cards to their customers. What is important in these procedures is the ability on the part of a customer to service the debt. There is no point in giving credit to a customer when a merchant knows full well that a customer cannot afford the repayments. This amounts to reckless lending, a practice that is regulated from a market conduct point of view.

BOX 4

Woolworths is a multinational retail company that also operates in Namibia and has different departments such as clothing, food and homeware.

The company offers a store card and has several branches in major cities of Namibia such as Windhoek, Oshakati, Swakopmund and Walvisbay. Windhoek is the capital city of Namibia while Oshakati is a capital city of the Oshana region. Swakopmund is the premier holiday city in Namibia with Walvisbay a coastal city that hosts the country's second international airport and is best known for fishing and recreation.

Shop owners, including Woolworths, use the following general process when deciding to issue store cards to their customers:

- A customer completes a credit application form and hands it to a specific merchant. Key documents such as payslip, bank statement and other documents are attached to the application. Included in the form is a debit order mandate, which gives a merchant authority to deduct a minimum amount periodically towards servicing the debt.
- Evaluation of the application follows. This important stage covers checking with a credit bureau and determining affordability.
- A credit decision is made in the form of allocating a specific credit limit to a customer if the application has passed the evaluation or screening process.
- The store card is then issued to a customer, entitling them to use the card by the next purchase at their favoured merchant or branch of the merchant.

Despite advantages that are associated with a store card, such as consume-now-and-pay-later, there are disadvantages to think about. The interest that is associated is often very high as it is an unsecured credit facility. Repayment can take a long time if a customer only pays a minimum of the amount owing. Customers should use their store cards frugally if they decide to take items on credit.

Chapter Summary

The present chapter covered reward, gift and store cards. These cards are not payment cards. They cannot be used to purchase goods and services like one does when using a traditional payment card. Such cards are used to complement plastic payment cards. As an example, a reward card is used to record points that can be redeemed in future, each time a customer checks out with a payment card at the point-of-sale.

Review Questions

1. Define what reward, gift and store cards entail.
2. The reward card can be used to lower the amount owing at the point-of-sale. Support or disprove this statement by using a simple calculation.
3. An MBA graduate has recently landed a new job and urgently needs clothing from your shop on credit. Outline the process to follow for granting a store card to the graduate.

Selected Refcrences

Anitsal, M.M., Anitsal, I., & Brown, A. (2013). Gift Cards and Gift Giving. *Journal of Applied Marketing Theory*, 4(1), 40-61. Retrieved from https://www.digitalcommons.georgiasouthern.edu/

De Teran, C.D. (2023). *Private Label Credit Cards are on the Decline: A Look at the Current Market*. Payments Journal. Retrieved from https://www.paymentsjournal.com/

Kagan, J. (2021). *Private Label Credit Cards: Overview, Benefits and Examples*. New York, NY: Investopedia. Retrieved from https://www.investopedia.com/

CHAPTER 6

Domestic Card and Other Card Payments

The card environment is a wide area that is often less studied by practitioners, researchers and analysts. This is because the field of digital banking and payment systems is relatively new compared to other well-established areas such as business management, accounting, agriculture, medicine and other fields of study. Several card types and related transactions were introduced to you in the previous chapters and these include credit, debit, reward, gift, and store cards. Consequently, the present chapter looks at domestic card and other card payments.

Learning Objectives

By the end of this chapter, you should be able to

- explain domestic card schemes and reasons for creating them;
- know the selected domestic card schemes including countries of origin; and
- understand other card payments.

Domestic Card

The demand for domestic card schemes is growing due to several reasons. This is in line with a need to have home grown solutions and payment methods. It is believed that domestic cards are cheaper compared to internationally branded cards. They are linked to regulatory expectations to promote financial inclusion. In addition, restrictions such as economic sanctions negate the use of international cards locally in several lands.

A domestic card is a payment instrument that is designed for use domestically in the country of issue. The issuer of a domestic card as well as the acquirer of that card all reside in the same country for end-to-end clearing and settlement. The understanding is that such a domestic card is not available for use outside the country of issue. Consequently, clearing and settlement of payment transactions happen within a country's borders.

There have been some developments in recent times in terms of whether domestic cards would remain concentrated domestically. The tides have changed. Some domestic cards have expanded beyond domestic markets and are being accepted in many countries around the world. This has to do with economies of scale. The gist of economies of scale is that average cost per unit goes down as more and more goods and services are produced and offered for sale. Domestic markets have become saturated and it makes economic sense to branch into other markets internationally to realise return on investment.

Domestic card schemes have been created in many countries around the world. The following table shows a list of national card schemes from selected countries:

Table 6.1
National Card Schemes from Selected Countries

Name of Scheme	Country	Year to Market	Motivation
Union Pay International	China	2002	Political policies. Not satisfied with domestic market.
Ru-Pay	India	2012	Decreasing cost of clearing and settlement.
Bankomat	Italy	1983	Domestic use.
Cartes Bleue	France	1967	Operate nationally.
Quick Teller	Nigeria	2018	Domestic use and then regionally.
MultiBanco	Portugal	2005	Domestic use.
Interac	Canada	1084	Cost saving and domestically run.
EFTPOS	Australia	2001	Lower credit card interchange fees.
MIR	Russia	2015	Politically imposed sanctions.
Troy	Turkey	2015	Domestic use, increase efficiency, fiscal policy and unbanked population.

Source: Kayaliderreden and Cetiner (2018)

While these schemes were created for domestic use, some later started to operate internationally. Key reasons why the schemes were created include domestic use, cost reduction or saving, international sanctions, government or political policies and financial inclusion from the perspective of the unbanked population (Kayaliderreden and Cetiner, 2018).

Co-Branded Card

Co-branding is a common practice not only in the marketing and communications industry but also in the banking and payments environment. The concept implies a situation where two related firms join forces and resources to deliver a product in the market, as opposed to a situation where only one firm introduces it to the market. Challenges that can hamper an organisation from taking the product to the market on its own include limited technical know-how and regulatory limitations, especially if there is no authorisation to issue a product. Co-branding therefore gives the opportunity to the issuer to introduce a product into a new market in which the partner-firm is already participating.

More narrowly defined, co-branding means the combination of two brands to create a single, unique product and from a customer standpoint this signals that the partners are committed to a long-term relationship (Leuthesser, Kohli and Suri, 2014). On their part, Guigui and Gores (2020) note that core-branded cards are partnership cards that allow an issuer and retailer to drive channel spend backed by a shared vision for the card, resulting in a win-win situation. The two partners in this case are the retailer and the issuer. It is the former that has the customer base, while the latter has the technology to issue a payment card. This example shows that the retailer realises an increase in purchases of goods and services via its outlets or branches while the issuer achieves its targets through fees and charges via the applicable channels being used at check out.

Smart Card

Smart cards have a long history and their coming to market is informed by a need to migrate from magnetic stripe technology to chip based technology. GoCardless (2021) note that smart cards were first launched in 1983 with a French card for pay phones, and used to make payments or to carry scannable information, with an integrated chip built into the card, making it unnecessary to contact a remote database for processing. The following table provides a list of the different types of smart cards.

Table 6.2
Types of Smart Cards

Type	Description
Contact smart card	Inserted directly into the smart card reader. A contact plate of the card connects to the reader's touchpoint for data to be sent or received.
Contactless smart card	Requires no physical contact with card reader. Card and reader connect using antennae and wireless radio frequencies.
Dual-interface smart card	Combines contact and contactless capabilities.
Memory chip-only smart card	Meant to provide a single function. Example: prepared phone cards that include a memory chip that stores, reads and writes data.
Microprocessor smart card	Includes both a memory chip and built-in microprocessor for increased function.

Source: GoCardless (2021)

These cards provide several benefits. First, the card is based on chip technology with no need to contact a database when a transaction at the point-of-sale is in progress. Second, migration from magnetic technology to chip based technology is a sign of modernisation in a given industry. Third, some smart cards have a contactless capability, thus leading to improved check out at the point-of-sale. Fourth, a smart card is one of the solutions that can be implemented to address financial inclusion challenges. The box below provides an overview of the history of smart card technology in Namibia.

BOX 5

Non-bank financial institutions (NBFIs) have been instrumental in the introduction of payment methods in Namibia. Such efforts complement what the traditional banking institutions have been doing over the years. One of the NBFIs is Namibia Post Limited (NamPost). NamPost was established in terms of the Posts and Telecommunications Establishment Act, 17 (Act No. 17 of 1992) to provide postal services, courier services and supplementary services. These supplementary services cover the savings bank and money transfer services.

NamPost was the first entity to introduce smart card technology in Namibia in 2006, in association with Net 1, to replace the savings book technology. This partnership resulted in the creation of a joint venture company called Smart Switch Namibia that was tasked with the processing of transactions arising from the utilisation of the payment method. The closed loop system was praised by regulatory authorities and decision makers as a step forward in addressing financial inclusion. Given the limitation of the previous smart card product, NamPost made some enhancements that led to the introduction of a Visa branded smart card transactional payment instrument in 2019. The product provides services such as withdrawals, purchases of goods and services, and transfers.

Chapter Summary

There are other card types in a given payments industry in addition to traditional payment instruments. Traditional payment instruments include credit and debit cards. This chapter provided a description of domestic and other card payments. Domestic cards have emerged to answer some of the challenges associated with international card brands. Co-branded cards have resulted in institutions partnering to introduce cards into markets. Smart cards are one of the recent innovations that have proved useful in addressing financial inclusion challenges.

Review Questions

1. Explain and differentiate domestic cards, co-branded cards and smart cards.
2. Outline and explain different types of smart cards.
3. Consider the following table and match each payment scheme to the country of origin (provide your response in the space below):

Scheme	Country	Student Response
Union Pay International	India	
Ru-Pay	China	
Bankomat	Turkey	
Quick Teller	Portugal	
MultiBanco	Nigeria	
Troy	Italy	

Selected Rcferences

GoCardless, (2021). *What is a Smart Card?* London, United Kingdom: GoCardless. Retrieved from https://www.gocardless.com/

Guigui, U., & Gores, S. (2020). *Strategy in Payments: How to Improve Profit in Existing Retail and Partnerships.* London, United Kingdom: Monitor Deloitte. Retrieved from https://www2.deloitte.com/

Kayaliderreden, D., & Cetiner, M. (2018). Monitoring National Payment Scheme: Some Global Practices and Turkish Payment Scheme – Troy. *Journal of Business in the Digital Age,* 1 (2), 67-75. Retrieved from https://dergipark.org.tr/

Leuthesser, L., Kohli, C., & Suri, R. (2014). A Framework for using Co-branding to Leverage a Brand. *Brand Management*, 11 (1), 35-47. https://doi.org/10.1057/palgrave.bm2540146

CHAPTER 7

Cheque Payments

Let us walk down Memory Lane to recount what we know about the usage of cheques especially in Namibia in the past. Let us assume you are working right now. When you started working, how did you receive your first salary? Was it in the form of cash or cheque, or was your salary paid into your account electronically? It is most likely that some people were paid in the form of a cheque when they received their first salary, with the payments thereafter received via electronic means, say after a few months.

What do you think is happening right now in the Namibian banking environment? There is another assumption to make. You have just graduated from college and recently secured a job as a cashier at China Town in Windhoek. How do you think your employer is likely going to pay you at the end of the month after your hard work? There are only two options available: you will receive cash or be paid via electronic means. Please note that electronic means in this case may include a salary being paid into your bank account and getting paid via electronic wallet. Sometimes it takes time to open a bank account, hence the possibility of being paid in hard currency. With respect to established employers however, the general practice is to request a new employee to furnish banking details before the first payment is made via bank account.

Learning Objectives

By the end of this chapter, you should be able to

- define cheque as a payment instrument and different types of cheques you are likely to find in some markets;
- understand where cheques are presented for cash or for purchases of goods and services;
- know the advantages and disadvantages of using a cheque as a payment method;
- appreciate major developments in the usage of cheques globally, as well as some approaches to phasing out cheques in a market; and
- describe the concept of cheque truncation and the benefits associated with it.

Description of Cheque Payments

What is a cheque? You might have written a cheque in favour of someone in the distant past and this person in most likelihood deposited it with their bank. If it was an on-us cheque, meaning you and the beneficiary having a relationship with the same bank, clearing and settlement of funds happened immediately; otherwise, in the case of an off-us cheque, the requirement was to wait for a few days before funds were to reflect in the payee's account

A cheque is essentially a non-cash, paper-based pull payment instrument that instructs the payer's bank to pay the stated amount of money to the beneficiary either immediately or by the date specified on it. The beneficiary can be someone banking with the same bank as the writer of a cheque, someone having a banking relationship with another bank, or even the writer of the cheque themselves. A cheque is a non-cash instrument meaning it is not cash but a means or vehicle that enables one to get hold of cash or hard currency.

The above definition is not too different from other writers in the field. Quinn and Roberds (2008) state that a cheque is a written order to a bank by a depositor at that bank (known as the drawer or maker) and the order instructs the bank to pay a third party (known as the payee) a certain sum of money from the depositor's account when the cheque is presented to the bank. This definition identifies key parties in a cheque transaction, which include the depositor who is referred to as an account holder; the payer's bank; and the payee. The payee's bank or collecting bank is also key even-though the entity is not mentioned in the description.

Different Types of Cheques

There are different types of cheques that are found in some markets. While certain cheques are widely known, others are not, but it does not imply that they are non-existent. As an example, "post-dated cheque" is a familiar term to many people, which is not the case with "banker's cheque", which is not that common. Paisabazaar (2022) provides a useful list of different types of cheques as per the following table:

Table 7.1
Different Types of Cheques

Type	Description
Bearer Cheque	This cheque is paid to the bearer of the cheque or whose name the cheque carries.
Order Cheque	The printed word "bearer" is cancelled thereby making it payable only to the person whose name is written in the place of drawee.

Crossed Cheque	It contains two parallel transverse lines and no matter who presents it, the transaction is made into the account of the person named on the cheque.
Open Cheque	This is an uncrossed cheque and is payable to the person presenting it.
Post Dated Cheque	A cheque bearing a later date than the one on which it is actually issued and whose value only appears in the payee's account by the date written on the cheque.
Stale Cheque	A stale cheque is past the validity period and cannot be encashed.
Traveller's Cheque	This is meant for travellers either to be encashed abroad or upon arrival from the trip.
Self-Cheque	The cheque is written by the account holder for themselves in order to withdraw cash from the bank.
Banker's Cheque	It is issued by the bank on behalf of the account holder to make a payment of a specified sum to another person or party.

Source: Paisabazaar (2022)

Channels for Cheque Payments

Well, your debtor has passed on a cheque instrument to you! The person is indebted to you and has attempted to honour their obligation by settling the debt. You have the cheque in your hand now. The next point is to deposit it with your bank so that your account gets credited with the value on the instrument. There are various points of contact you could use. One is a branch and others include point-of-sale and automated teller machines.

Creditors were able to deposit their cheques at branches in Namibia before the phasing out of the instrument. One had to walk or travel to the nearest branch to do just that. You did not mind about the cost, effort and time it took to head to the branch. However, cost is one of the factors taken into consideration by the industry before deciding to discontinue cheques in Namibia. Total costs included transport, processing costs, and other elements that might be a challenge to quantity. While at the branch you queue up and hand over the paper to the cashier who enters all the required details in the computer system or programme. Next is the waiting period before value hits your account and you receive and can spend what was due to you.

You could write a cheque while in the queue at a supermarket in Namibia! Let us assume the total cost of your items after scanning is NAD2500. You write a cheque issued to the supermarket or merchant for that amount. The holder of the cheque deposits it with their bank and eventually the value is credited in their account.

With the advancement in technology, depositing cheques through automated teller machines is now common in mature markets. Mitic (2022) notes that many banks and credit unions offer their customers the opportunity to deposit personal cheques at automated teller machines: after inserting the card in the card slot, you follow the instructions on the screen. Once again, there is a waiting period before the value written on the cheque is credited to an account. One was able to deposit a cheque at automated teller machines in Namibia with the use of an envelope. This service was later discontinued.

Advantages and Disadvantages of Cheques

Cheques, like other payment instruments, are associated with certain advantages and disadvantages. They are useful in some situations but not in others. While a cheque might be useful in a situation where it is the only available payment method, it is less of importance if the account holder has other means of payment.

The following are the advantages that are related to a cheque as payment instrument:

- Cheques are associated with prestige as the holder is perceived to be trustworthy and responsible in handling money.
- There is a measure of safety in carrying a cheque compared to carrying real money.
- It is useful in the reconciliation process as a counterfoil remains after the actual cheque has been detached to settle a transaction.
- Cheques as payment instrument appeal to senior citizens and juristic entities, especially in an environment where electronic means of payment are not widely adopted.

The following are the disadvantages that are related to a cheque as payment instrument:

- There is a high risk of fraud as some details on a cheque can be amended by fraudsters.
- There is an increasing cost of printing, transportation and processing of cheques. The further the distance from the collection or collation centre to the clearing hub, the higher the cost.
- There is a possibility of insufficient funds at the point of presenting a cheque.
- There are associated delays at checkout if a cheque is used as a method of payment.
- It is less appealing to young people who are more comfortable with electronic means of payment.

Discontinuation of Cheques in Namibia

No doubt you are aware that there are no more cheques circulating in Namibia. You might have seen this at the time when cheques as payment instruments were removed from the market, with signs in shops like, "No more cheques allowed, by order of Management", or "Cheques are not accepted here, by order of Management". What followed was a process of stakeholders getting used to the fact that cheques were no longer accepted as means of payment in Namibia, given the more efficient and safe payment methods available in the market. These payment methods include internet banking, cellphone banking or USSD, mobile payments via app, debit cards, credit cards, and electronic wallets.

Cheques were discontinued in Namibia as from 30 June 2019 due to fraud risks, declining volume of transactions, inefficiencies or high costs associated with the instrument and availability of alternative payment methods (Bank of Namibia, 2019). Fraud is an operational issue that includes altering the amount written or errors that can be made on the cheque. Falling volumes of transactions lead to diseconomies of scale, as per-unit cost tends to go up. The key challenge therefore is for all stakeholders to embrace conducting payments through electronic means, given the efficiencies associated with such alternative instruments.

International Trends in Cheque Payments

There are three sets of countries one finds when a discussion around international trends for cheques comes up. First, there are countries where cheques have been eliminated. Second, there are countries where the usage of cheques is falling. Third and last, there are countries where the usage of cheques is increasing.

Let us tackle the first one. We have just seen that cheques have been discontinued in Namibia at a domestic level. What happens at an international level? There are no cheques circulating in the Southern African Development Community (SADC). This regional bloc consists of Angola, Comoros, Kingdom of Eswatini, Madagascar, Mauritius, Namibia, South Africa, Zambia, Botswana, Democratic Republic of Congo, Kingdom of Lesotho, Malawi, Mozambique, Seychelles, United Republic of Tanzania, and Zimbabwe. Just like in Namibia, the phased-out cheques include customer cheques, travellers' cheques, and bank drafts.

Matongela (2016) notes that the usage of cheques is falling in the Committee of Payments and Markets Infrastructure (CPMI) countries, which are those for which the Bank for International Settlements (BIS) normally collects payments, clearing and settlement figures. However, the United States of America is still highly dependent on the usage of cheques. The following table says it all.

Table 7.2

Volume of Cheque Transactions for the United States of America

Year	Volume (million)	%
2016	16,738	(7.72)
2017	15,346	(8.32)
2018	13,937	(9.18)
2019	12,528	(10.12)
2020	11,216	(10.47)

Source: Committee of Payments and Markets Infrastructure (2021)

Cheque use in volume of transactions in the United States stood at 17 billion in 2016 and 11 billion in 2020 with associated negative growth rates at 8 percent and 10 percent respectively. These figures indicate that although cheque use in the world's largest and most advanced economy is high, the numbers have been falling over time (Committee on Payments and Markets Infrastructure, 2021).

Digital Check (2018) notes that there is a small number of countries in Southeast Asia and the Indian subcontinent displaying cheque usage trends opposite to what we have come to expect, with the number of cheques written remaining steady, or even rising, at a time when the global trend is for a steady decline. This is a surprise indeed, given what happens around the world in Namibia, SADC and CPMI countries. Is the increasing and steady trend going to continue? It is not easy to tell at this point. Besides, although there are some pockets of countries seeing an increase in the usage of cheques, the move to electronic means of payment is like a high tide that is a challenge to reverse or block.

Approaches to Phasing Out Cheques

Phasing out or eliminating cheques in a given market, be it domestic, regional or international, is a process that can last several months or even years as can be seen from the following figure.

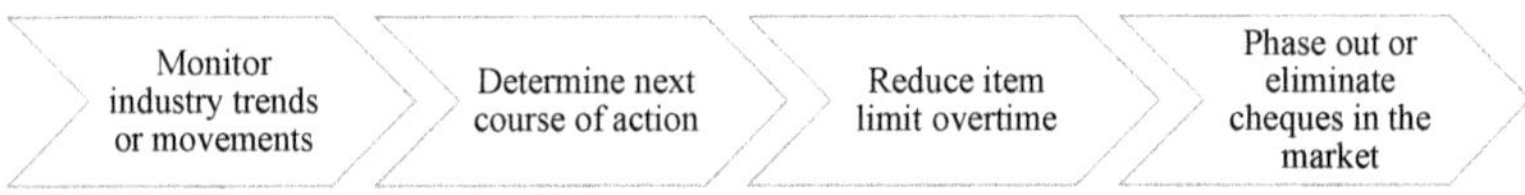

Figure 7.1. Approaches to phasing out of cheques

Trends need to be monitored to make informed decisions on the next course of action. Some variables need to be analysed as part of trend analysis and these variables include cost, level of fraud, and perception and extent of trust of the payment method in the market. There are two main outcomes from trend analysis: either the number of cheque transactions is increasing or it is decreasing. A fall in the number of cheque transactions warrants a reduction in the item limit over time, while an increase in the number of cheque transactions can lead to the introduction of efficiencies such as cheque truncation. An item limit is the maximum amount that is allowed to be written on a cheque. There is no way a customer can write an amount of NAD250,000 on a cheque if the item limit is NAD100,000.

There are various stakeholders that need to be consulted, involved or informed before cheques are finally removed from the market. In addition, a piece of regulation or notice needs to be issued to enable the phasing out of cheques. Stakeholders in this case include banking institutions, regulatory authorities, associations, merchants, consumers, service providers, government entities, and semi-government entities and other organisations. A regulation, which in most cases passes through a parliamentary process, is supposed to outline reasons for phasing out of cheques, compliance expectation, penalty for non-compliance and a deadline for compliance or when cheques are required to go out of the market.

Cheque Truncation

Some advantages and disadvantages of a cheque as a payment instrument were outlined above. One of the disadvantages of cheques in the market is the increasing cost of printing, transportation and processing. It was stated that the further the distance from collection or collation centre to the clearing hub, the higher the cost. This cost can only increase overtime as a result of several independent variables including the cost of fuel. When the fuel price goes up, especially in times of war or weak currency, there is a ripple effect on economic activity.

There are different ways a cheque reaches the collecting bank or financial institution. The collecting bank is the financial institution of an account holder where a cheque is deposited or cashed. One way is to deposit a cheque via a payment channel such as an automated teller machine, from which it then gets collected by officials at a certain point of time for processing. Another way is for the beneficiary to deposit it at a branch of their banking institution. Details on a cheque need to be captured after which the paper is transported from the collection point to the automated clearing house in case of off-us cheques, whereby the writer of a cheque has an account with another banking institution. Transporting cheques is associated with cost. There are other risks as well such as fraud. Cheque truncation tries to minimise these costs.

There were some efforts to introduce cheque truncation in Namibia, but these efforts did not last due to the cost involved and the fact that cheque usage was falling. Cheque truncation involves a situation where the deposited cheque is truncated or remains at the collecting bank with only its image transmitted to the automated clearing house for clearing. The automated clearing house will still do the necessary validations by liaising with the respective banks that are involved in the transaction. Capturing the details of a cheque and sending these through electronic means to the automated clearing house, after which the actual cheque or paper follows, is not cheque truncation as the paper has not remained at the collecting banking institution.

BOX 6

Bank of Zambia is the central bank of the Republic of Zambia. It was established to take over from the Bank of Northern Rhodesia in 1964. Its vision is to be a dynamic and credible central bank that contributes to the economic development of Zambia, while its mission is to achieve and maintain price and financial system stability to foster sustainable economic development. One of its functions is to manage the banking, currency and payment systems operations of the Bank of Zambia.

In its circular, CB circular number 13/2012, dated 7 August 2012, the Bank of Zambia directed all commercial banks to introduce a cheque truncation clearing system in Zambia. The initiative was made possible with the collaboration with the Bankers Association of Zambia (BAZ) and Zambia Electronic Clearing House Limited (ZECHL). According to the Bank of Zambia (2012), some of the benefits of cheque truncation include the elimination of the cumbersome physical presentation of cheques and time and cost saving associated with handling physical cheques; and that the clearing period will be shortened and standardised across the country to one clearing day.

There are advantages and disadvantages associated with cheque truncation. Disadvantages include costs associated with implementing the new system, and implementing such a system in an industry where the number of cheques is decreasing is not advisable as doing so leads to a rise in the cost per unit.

Advantages of cheque truncation have been noted especially in countries with significant or increasing transactions. The Bank of Zambia (2012) notes several benefits associated with cheque truncation:

- Elimination of the cumbersome physical presentation of cheques and saving time and costs associated with handling physical cheques.
- Shortening and standardisation of the clearing period across the country to one clearing day (T+1).
- Improvement in the velocity of cash flow between transacting parties in the economy owing to reduced clearing periods.
- Reduction in risks associated with manual handling and physical movement of cheques
- Reduction in the incidence of cheque related fraud.
- Introduction of efficiency in the work processes for banks as truncation will reduce the work time and manpower required at the branches manning these tasks.
- Encouragement of the wider use of cheques in the settlement of payment.

Clearing Cycle of Cheques

A cheque clearing cycle is the time period it takes, usually in days, for a beneficiary to receive value in a bank account after a cheque has been deposited via an applicable payment channel. The goal of regulatory authorities is to reduce the clearing cycle to a reasonable level. A high clearing cycle leads to a delay in the beneficiary receiving value arising from a cheque transaction and a low clearing cycle has the opposite effect. In other words, a high clearing cycle is associated with high float or uncleared effects, a situation that has a negative effect on economic activity.

Consider the case of Namibia before cheques were eliminated from the market. Reduction of the cheque clearing cycle to five days was a welcome development in the country given that the clearing cycle used to be 21 days. Imagine you as a creditor depositing a cheque and having to wait 21 days for your item to go through the clearing and settlement process before value hits your account! The delay in clearing and settlement has a negative effect on both production and consumption.

Chapter Summary

A cheque is one of the debit-pull payment instruments used for purchases of goods and services. It is used to instruct the payer's bank to pay the stated amount of money to the beneficiary either immediately or by the date specified on it. There are advantages associated with cheque payments such as appealing to senior citizens who have not widely adopted alternative payment methods, and prestige associated with carrying a cheque. Disadvantages include the cost of transporting cheques, and risk of fraud as details on a cheque can be amended by fraudsters. Regulatory authorities and industry players across the world have introduced measures to deal with the level of cheques and such measures include cheque truncation, managing the clearing cycle and elimination of cheques.

Review Questions

1. Define the following terms that are associated with the processing of cheque payments:
    a. Cheque truncation
    b. Cheque clearing cycle
    c. Cheque as a payment instrument

2. Outline advantages and disadvantages of cheque payment method.
3. A certain country is experiencing a decline in the number of cheques that are written by individuals and institutions. Discuss different approaches that can lead to the total elimination of cheques in a country.
4. The Bank of Zambia introduced cheque truncation in 2012 in collaboration with Bankers Association of Zambia and Zambia Electronic Clearing House Limited. Outline the key benefits that were noted by the central bank.
5. Outline different types of cheques that you have learned.

Selected References

Bank of Namibia, (2019). *Media Statement on the Phasing Out of Cheques as a Payment Instrument within the National Payment System.* Windhoek, Namibia: Bank of Namibia. Retrieved from https://www.bon.com.na/

Bank of Zambia, (2012). *Introduction of Cheque Truncation Clearing System in Zambia.* Lusaka, Zambia: Bank of Zambia. Retrieved from https://www.boz.zm/

Committee on Payments and Markets Infrastructure, (2021). *Red Book Statistics for CPMI Countries.* Basel, Switzerland: Bank for International Settlements. Retrieved from https://www.bis.org/

Digital Check, (2018). *The reappearing cheque – why cheque usage is actually on the rise in developing countries.* Northbrook, IL: Digital Check. Retrieved from https://www.digitalcheck.com/

Matongela, A.M. (2016). Analyzing Trends Towards Phasing Out of Cheques in the Namibian Banking Sector. *Journal of Information Engineering and Applications*, 1-8.

Mitic, I. (2022). *Depositing a Check at an ATM: How and Where I do It.* Retrieved from https://www.fortunly.com/

Quinn, S. & Roberds, W. (2008). *The Evolution of the Check as a Means of Payment: A Historical Survey*. Federal Reserve Bank of Atlanta Economic Review, 4, 1-28.

Paisabazaar, (2022). *What are the Different Types of Cheques Issued by Banks?* Gurugram, India: Paisabazaar. Retrieved from https://www.paisabazaar.com/

CHAPTER 8

Credit Transfer Payments

What is the central idea when it comes to credit transfer or online payments? These payments can easily be confused with other payment types. Let us begin with examples. Suppose you owe an individual some money. In this example you are a debtor and the other person is a creditor. What different options are there for you to settle the debt? You can push money to the creditor through the use of different channels. Another option is to agree with your counterpart that they deduct money from your account at a certain time through their bank. The former option is addressed in this chapter, while the latter is discussed in the following chapter.

Learning Objectives

After the end of this chapter, you should be able to

- know how to describe credit transfer payments;
- understand the types of and channels for credit transfer payments;
- appreciate key concepts that are associated with credit transfer payments; and
- comprehend fees and charges related to credit transfer payments.

Description of Credit Transfer Payments

One could say that credit transfer payments are those payments done via electronic means to settle an obligation one has with another person, counterpart, or institution. These payments can also be referred to as credit push payments. Credit transfer payments are done via a credit transfer system, which is a funds transfer system through which payment instructions or orders move from the payer's bank or originator's bank to the receiver's or beneficiary's bank (Bedell, 2013).

Let us return to the example in the introductory paragraph to illustrate what credit push payments are all about. Suppose you owe an individual some money. In this example you are a debtor and the other person is a creditor. There are different options to use to push money to the creditor through different channels. Internet banking or a banking application can be used to pay the other party to whom you owe money. This is what is called a credit push. Other terms that are normally used include online payments, direct credit, standing order or electronic funds transfer (EFTs). Sub-classifications of these transactions include once-off, recurring, same-day and dated payments. Consequently, there are different use cases you can think about with respect to credit push payments, such as settling your invoice, paying for children's school fees, sending money to family or loved ones, settling statutory obligations, and grants or payments done by government to individuals or institutions.

Types of Credit Transfer Payments

There are different types of credit transfer payments as the following table shows (reference here does not include self-payments or transfer between accounts of the account holder):

Table 8.1
Different Types of Credit Transfer Payments

Type	Description
Direct deposit	A good example is a payment of a salary by an employer to an employee's or recipient's bank account.
Direct payment	This takes place where a debtor initiates a payment to settle indebtedness for goods or services provided.
Once-off payment	This is the opposite of a recurring payment whereby there is no future commitment once indebtedness is settled at a particular point of time.
Recurring payment	This is the opposite of a once-off payment whereby there is a commitment to pay a certain amount of money repeatedly over a certain period of time or indefinitely.
Scheduled Payments	These are payments that are scheduled, booked or diarised now but where actual settlement happens at some point in future. Examples include one-day, two-day and dated transactions.
Split payment	This is the practice of dividing a payment into smaller payments, typically with the aim of circumventing a limit that is placed by a banking institution or regulatory authority.
Stop order payment	A stop order is a recurring payment instructing your banking institution to pay a certain amount of money to a specific beneficiary say every month.

These payments are classified according to the direction of payment, timing or frequency of payment, and location of the account of the beneficiary. The location of the account of the beneficiary can be within the same banking institution as the payer and this is commonly called on-us payment. Where the location of the account of the beneficiary is with another banking institution and not the payer's banking institution, this is commonly called off-us payment.

Channels for Credit Transfer Payments

What channels can one use to initiate credit transfer payments? Which one of these have you used before? Among the channels that you used which one do you prefer? These questions can only be answered by you. These channels include internet banking, cellphone banking, and mobile application.

Internet banking is what many people are aware of. For some, this is the first channel they have used for their credit transfer payments as other channels are more recent innovations. Internet banking is also called online banking or web banking and allows bank customers or users to carry out credit push and other financial transactions using desktop applications provided by their bank or other financial service providers on the internet. All that a customer needs to do to start using this channel is to register for it, say at a bank branch, coupled with getting a password and username. Prerequisites for registering for internet banking do vary and include having a bank account, the payment card of your primary account and other personal particulars that your financial service provider or bank may require.

It is better to do internet banking at home or work than in public places using public wi-fi or internet to avoid unauthorised access by criminals to your hard-earned money. Besides, internet banking provides convenience as it allows you to do a host of transactions such as transfers, payments, view balances, amend card limits, notice of withdrawal, and other transactions. The channel might not be practical if you are on the go, due to portability issues related to your desktop computer or other machines you cannot move around with.

Cellphone banking is the second channel for online payments that needs to be considered. Terms associated with cellphone banking include but are not limited to mobile banking and unstructured supplementary service data (USSD) banking. Cellphone banking allows the provision of banking or financial services to customers via cellphone or mobile phone powered by an appropriate technology such as USSD. Hanouch and Chen (2015) state that USSD is a communication service or infrastructure that is controlled by mobile network operators (MNOs) and enables customers to send instructions to the mobile financial service (MFS) providers along with a personal identification number (PIN), while enabling the MFS provider to send responses to clients to confirm transactions. Advantages of this service include low usage cost and the ability to function on the majority of phones, while a notable challenge is the possibility of USSD sessions being dropped thus affecting customer experience (Hanouch & Chen, 2015).

There are some terms in the above definition that require clarification. Examples of MNOs are mobile telecommunication operators while MFS providers can be banks and non-bank financial institutions (NBFIs). Cellphone banking should not be confused with using a mobile application, which is a separate channel to be described ahead.

Most people, as the below box shows, are aware of USSD when they do certain transactions via their phones.

BOX 7

USSD is one of the channels for credit transfer payments available to customers of mobile financial service providers. One key issue that requires attention is USSD sessions that are dropped before a transaction is completed. Consider a customer who dashes to a shopping mall on the outskirts of the city on a busy day. The customer has multiple bank accounts and does not check ahead of time as to which one should be used at checkout.

The customer is now in the front of a queue at a shopping mall with insufficient funds in one of the accounts, coupled with inadequate mobile data. He then reasons that the only way out is to transfer funds from one account to the preferred account. What follows is that he pulls out his phone and follows the USSD menu, only for the session to be dropped multiple times, to his frustration and that of many in the queue. The customer checks out in the end though. This is definitely inconvenient and the customer is hopeful that challenges like this one can be promptly and jointly addressed by relevant authorities and providers of financial services.

These transactions include payments, transfers, buying electricity or airtime, sending money, viewing mini statements or balances, creating beneficiary profiles and a host of other transactions that can be performed. USSD works with a dial string and some of these dial strings can take the form of *number*number# (such as *111*111#). There is a menu that needs to be followed after keying in the string until a transaction is completed. A PIN needs to be entered to authenticate a user.

Mobile application, or mobile app or banking app for short, is the last channel we are considering. Consider a job interviewee for a payments position who is asked by one member of the interview panel to state which channel he uses most: mobile app or USSD. The interviewee says he uses both but mostly the mobile app. "Usage is situational," the interviewee says. This implies that "availability of data and purpose of a session one is engaged in are some of the key factors to consider on the type of technology to use at each particular point of time".

A mobile app or banking app is a software programme designed to assist a customer of a financial institution (typically a bank) to do certain payment instructions. Payment instructions include those done via USSD plus advanced payment types. One can say that payment transactions one can do via internet banking can be done via a mobile app as well. The implication here is that a banking app mirrors the services of internet banking, including services such as adding a beneficiary, sending money, amending the transaction limit, and many more.

How does one get hold of a mobile or banking app? Your personal banker or branch will tell you to download it from a certain online store such as Google Play, and can help you to do so. Many banking apps come with several layers of authentication. You will be required to key-in a username and password each time you transact on the app. It is highly possible that you will also be expected to authenticate certain sessions with a one-time password (OTP). All this is done to ensure that you have maximum security anywhere and anytime while doing your banking transactions on the go.

The banking app might require more data to use compared to USSD. Irrespective of whether you use a banking app or USSD, the fact remains that they are all mobile channels that are being promoted by banking institutions. Gupta (2013) states that most banks believe that the mobile channel will help them reduce transaction costs as well as increase customer engagement and retention. Consequently, load enough data on your phone or use wi-fi to do your transactions. Again, be careful if you opt to use public wi-fi as there is a possibility of intruders getting to your personal details and eventually siphoning money you worked hard for.

Fees and Charges

There are fees and charges that are associated with credit transfer payments. These are levied depending on which channel is used at particular point of time. For example, airtime and electricity purchase fees are incurred when accessing these services using cellphone banking or mobile apps. The rest of the fees and charges are depicted in the table below:

Table 8.2
Fees and Charges

Type	Description
Stop order fee	This can be for setting stop order or for ongoing transactions.
Unpaid fee	This refers to a situation where a credit transfer payment is not successful.
Airtime purchases fee	The item relates to airtime top ups.
Electricity purchases fee	This is the purchase of electricity through your bank from an electricity service provider.
Beneficiary or 3rd party payments	This relates to payments to beneficiaries or third parties.
Instant payments fee	Some retail payments need to be settled as soon as possible, say within one minute, and there is a fee that is associated with that.
Payment recalls fee	This is incurred when a payment is recalled before value is credited to a beneficiary's account.

Chapter Summary

This chapter covered credit transfer payments. These payments can also be referred to as credit push payments that are done via electronic means to settle an obligation one has with another person, counterpart, or an institution. Types of these and channels through which they are done were also addressed. While some transactions are suitable through internet banking, others can preferably be done via cellphone banking or mobile application. The key is for customers of financial services to carry out credit transfer payments in a secure environment to avoid unauthorised access by criminals to their hard-earned money.

Review Questions

1. Outline and explain different types of credit transfer payments that you have learned.
2. Discuss the channels for credit transfer payments. State which one you prefer by motivating your answer.
3. State the pros and cons of each channel for credit transfer payments that you covered in your course.
4. Explain the following fees and charges:
    a. Payment recall fee.
    b. Unpaid fee.
    c. Instant payment fee.

Selected References

Bedell, D. (2013). *Payment Instruments – Credit Transfers*. New York, NY: Global Finance. Retrieved from https://www.gfmag.com/

Gupta, S. (2013). The Mobile Banking and Payment Revolution. *The European Financial Review*, 3-6.

Hanouch, M. & Chen, G. (2015). *Promoting Competition in Mobile Payments: The Role of USSD*. Washington, DC: CGAP. Retrieved from http://cgap.org/

CHAPTER 9

Debit Transfer Payments

Debit transfer payments fall within the same family of electronic funds transfer payments. This means that electronic funds transfer payments can be divided into two main categories; that is, credit transfer payments and debit transfer payments. These payments can be further divided based on a threshold amount to differentiate the type of payments that are of low value and those that are regarded as high-value payments. Credit transfer payments were discussed in the previous chapter, while the current chapter covers debit transfer payments.

Learning Objectives

By the end of this chapter, you should be able to

- describe what debit transfer payments are all about;
- outline different types of debit transfer payments;
- know what a direct transfer mandate means; and
- understand the difference between a stop order and a debit transfer.

Description of Debit Transfer Payments

Debit transfer is another form of electronic funds transfer payments. Do you own a car? Is your car covered by short-term insurance? Is there an amount that gets deducted from your account on a monthly or periodic basis by a short-term insurer? If the answer is yes then you participate in a debit transfer scheme. Other terms associated with debit transfer include direct debit and collection, either of which are suitable to use in daily conversation.

Debit transfer is a debit pull payment instruction initiated by a creditor through their bank to claim money from your account for services rendered or products consumed. Direct debit is a payment service whereby the payee and payment sender agree on automatic payment debiting of the payer's bank account (Sveriges Riksbank, 2013). Please remember that you are the debtor and your service or product provider is the creditor in this payment instruction. The key difference between this form of payment instruction and credit transfer is that the former is a *debit pull* and the creditor initiates a payment instruction while the latter is a *credit push* and the debtor initiates a payment instruction.

Types of Debit Transfer Payments

There are use cases for debit transfer schemes. The following are the typical use cases for or types of debit transfer payments.

Table 9.1
Types of Debit Transfer Payments

Type	Description
Regular bills for variable amounts	Regular bills can cover your municipal, mobile and fixed-line telephone bills.

Fixed subscriptions or memberships	These include recurring payments like magazine subscriptions or gym membership.
Paying on account	Some organisations provide direct debit as an option for spreading your costs or paying on account. Included here can be payment for a clothing account.

Source: Hooper (2023)

The above list of use cases covers both the variable and fixed types of debit transfer payments. Variable elements can change within the contract period by informing the account holder as such ahead of time. Fixed use cases are considered fixed during the contract period with a likelihood of variation after the initial contract period.

Advantages and Disadvantages of Debit Transfer Payments

Debit transfer as a payment method provides unique advantages to parties in the payment scheme and these are outlined below.

- It gives the debtor peace of mind knowing that the creditor will deduct money from the primary account for services rendered or product consumed.
- The creditor has peace of mind as well, as payment is unlikely to be missed.
- A simple mandate form is completed.

There are associated disadvantages as well for the debit transfer payment method and the ones worth mentioning are listed below:

- customer complaints owing to deduction of wrong amount by some creditors even when a mandate authorising what to deduct exists;
- variability of premiums as indicated in the mandate;
- challenges in cancelling mandates owing to contract restrictions; and
- better payment methods available to debtors for settling indebtedness.

Channel for Debit Transfer Payments

Channels for electronic funds transfer payments include internet banking, cellphone banking, mobile application, and online collection platform. While the first three are commonly used by individual customers as well, well established businesses are known to use internet banking as well as online collection platform. Consequently, the channel for debit transfer payments is the online collection platform. The online collection platform makes it possible for the mandate to be created, submitted and executed.

Debit Transfer Mandate

There is one principal aspect to note when it comes to the validity of debit transfer payment instructions. This is called a mandate. It is an agreement between a debtor and creditor for the latter to deduct a certain amount of money from the former's account by the particular date each month when the payment is due. Information that appears on the mandate about the debtor includes name, address, bank account details, amount to be deducted, and deduction date. The absence of a mandate renders a payment instruction invalid when presented by a creditor for collection and it is consequently dishonoured by the respective banking institutions that form part of the transaction. It is therefore important that a mandate exists to confirm that the creditor has authorisation to deduct money from the debtor's account going forward.

How does the creation of a mandate work? It is simple process, which is depicted in the following figure.

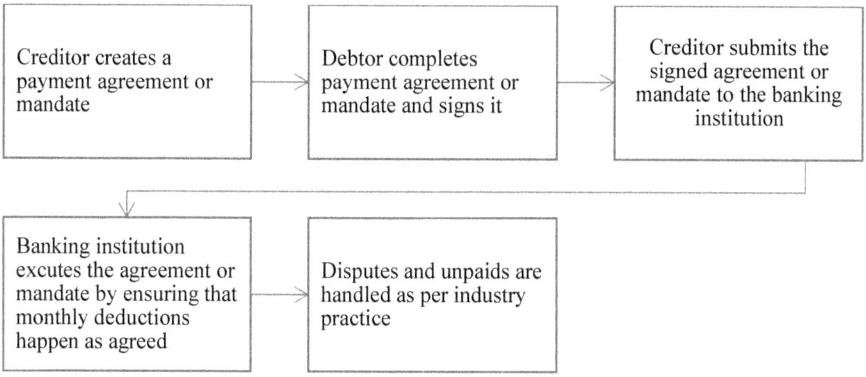

Figure 9.1. Debit transfer payments mandate process

The process starts with the creditor creating a form that the debtor needs to complete and sign. This form is handed or submitted to the creditor either physically or via electronic means for onward submission to the creditor's or collector's banking institution. Money can now start to be collected from the customer's account repeatedly and periodically going forward as per the signed agreement or form.

Have you experienced a situation whereby an entity deducts money from your account without the permission or mandate to do so even when there is no service or product being consumed? The right thing to do is to reach out to your bank or regulatory institution, informing them of the situation and requesting a permanent solution, including claiming back funds that were wrongly deducted from your account, as that constitutes a fraudulent payment instruction.

BOX 8

Take for example a couple who expressed an interest in subscribing to membership to access a certain service on a monthly basis. Key was to provide contact and banking details with the expectation that each debtor was to be debited separately. Amounts to be deducted and dates when deduction has to happen were shared with the creditor as part of the normal mandate creation process.

The process enabling the customers to use the service began well. However, an issue soon arose: instead of each account being deducted separately, one of the accounts was being double deducted. This happened a few times and the matter was reported to the creditor accordingly. Laxity from the creditor in resolving the issue was the order of the day.

Debit Transfer and Stop Order

There is both similarity and difference between debit transfers and stop orders. They are all part of the family of electronic funds transfer payments. A debit transfer is a pull payment, while a stop order is a push payment; the debit transfer is initiated by the creditor, while the stop order is initiated by the debtor. Stop order payments can be for on-us and off-us payments.

Chapter Summary

This chapter looked at debit transfer payments to build on what was discussed in the previous chapter. Debit transfer is a debit pull payment instruction initiated by a creditor through their bank to claim money from your account for service rendered or product consumed. Key matters that were discussed include types of debit transfer payments and the payment agreement or mandate. Debit transfer mandate is important in making sure that only legitimate transactions are processed by creditors as well as both the beneficiary and paying banking institutions.

Review Questions

1. Outline and explain different types of debit transfer payments.
2. Write short notes on the debit transfer mandate process that you have learned.
3. Outline the advantages and disadvantages of debit transfer payments.

Selected References

Hooper, C. (2023). *What is Direct Debit? A Guide for Payers.* London, United Kingdom: GoCardless. Retrieved from https://www.gocardless.com/

Sveriges Riksbank, (2013). *The Swedish Retail Payment Market.* Stockholm, Sweden: Sveriges Riksbank.

CHAPTER 10

Electronic Wallet Payments

A researcher and his family travelled to Waterberg Resort for a holiday during the festive season. Waterberg Resort is situated about 60 kilometres east of Otjiwarongo in the Waterberg Plateau Park of Namibia. The park is endowed with a wide range of species including birds and animals. The place is a must-see if your interest is in hiking, sightseeing, swimming or just going out with your friends, family and loved ones.

After the holiday, while the family was checking out, the researcher thought of putting fuel in the car. He had no physical cash on him and decided to use a payment card to complete the transaction. Unfortunately, the transaction could not be completed owing to network issues. The attendant indicated that card payments do work although there is a network issue in the area. Payment via electronic wallet was the last option as the wait now seemed to be taking long. The researcher pulled out his phone, saved the attendant's details, keyed in the dial string, entered the transaction details and eventually the recipient confirmed that the transaction had gone through and the family drove out of the resort. The electronic wallet is one of the greatest innovations the industry has witnessed in recent times.

Learning Objcctives

By the end of this chapter, you should be able to

- describe what electronic wallet payments are all about;
- appreciate that there are channels for electronic wallet payments; and
- understand the meaning, foundation and technical models for interoperability.

Description of Electronic Wallet Payments

Have you ever been sent money via electronic wallet (e-wallet)? Have you heard a friend saying they need to walk to the automated teller machine to withdraw money that was received through a "blue wallet" or "easy wallet"? Have you heard that there is mobi-money as well? These are common brands in the market and the chance is high that you are aware of some or all of them.

BOX 9

Electronic wallets in Namibia at this point can be said to be like vegetable gardens or plots. Vegetables in the backyard garden can be planted on raised beds. These raised beds are separate from each other such that if you irrigate one bed, water is not going to spill over to the other raised bed but rather be retained in the first bed to enable vegetables or plants to grow in that bed. In the same way, the brands in the market do not talk to each other; they are in a closed loop, not an open loop, from a technical standpoint.

Electronic wallets are issued by both banking institutions and non-bank financial institutions (NBFIs) in Namibia. Payment systems or channels of these issuers are not interconnected or interoperable with respect to electronic wallets. Let us assume you want to send money to your relative at the farm. Your relative will have to withdraw money via a channel such as an automated teller machine that is owned by your bank and not another bank's automated teller machine.

There is however light at the end of the tunnel. Challenges related to lack of interoperability or closed loop systems can be addressed over time for the benefit of consumers of financial services including those at the farm who have to walk or travel to the nearest access points to consume financial services. The local payments industry in Namibia is working hard to bring about interoperability – doing away with closed loop systems – as far as electronic wallets or money is concerned, at some point in the future.

What do you think an electronic wallet is all about? An electronic wallet is better known as electronic money (e-money) in the banking or payments literature. It is viewed as both a verb – "James ewalleted Tom

NAD200 yesterday" – and a noun – "There is available balance in the easy wallet account" – in everyday interactions.

Electronic money is a payment method that fulfils elements such as: being issued based on the value of money deposited in advance to the issuer: the value of money is stored electronically on a media sever or chip; and the value of electronic money managed by the issuer is not deemed as a deposit (Iswara, Wialdy & Sihombing, 2019). The above definition implies that electronic money is that virtual money that is converted from physical or deposited money and sent to someone via a cellphone or channel for encashment at an alternative channel such as an automated teller machine.

Electronic wallets can be issued by banking institutions or non-bank financial institutions to their customers. There is a collaboration approach as well whereby a bank and a non-bank can work together to issue such an instrument to the general public. Approaches to issuing electronic wallets therefore include bank-led, non-bank led or a combination of these. The mixed approach might be appealing as each entity needs to leverage on what the other entity has in terms of resources. In one situation, a bank might be endowed with infrastructure while a non-bank has the customer base and in the other situation, the opposite is true, leading to some form of collaboration between the two entities.

A trust account or pooled account is key for the business relationship between a bank and non-bank financial institution to work successfully. The trust account is opened with a bank in the name of a non-bank financial institution solely to honour transactions from transacting customers. Money or funds converted into virtual money are stored and ringfenced in the trust account. There are regulatory requirements that need to be met for the opening, operation and closing of a trust account.

Channels for Electronic Wallet Payments

All the channels that have been discussed can be used to send money to your friends, family members or loved ones. These channels are mobile app, internet banking, USSD, automated teller machines, and point-of-sale devices. While mobile app and USSD are available while on the go, the others, that is, internet banking, automated teller machines, and point-of-sale devices, are not.

A mobile app is accessed via your phone after you have downloaded it as advised by your bank branch and once you have keyed in the relevant credentials. You need to have data or be connected to wi-fi to access your banking app. USSD is accessed via a dial string after which you follow a menu to complete a specific transaction. Internet banking can be accessed through your personal computer while at home and at the office. Automated teller machines can be used to send and receive electronic wallets. Point-of-sale devices are a recent phenomenon. These devices or speed points as they are sometimes called can be used for cashing out money received via electronic wallets.

Which of the above channels is better as far as electronic wallets are concerned? They are all important, depending on the transaction at hand. What if you are out there walking in the street during lunch time and urgently need to call someone at the farm to find out if animals and crops are fine? You are probably going to use either USSD or a mobile app to buy airtime to make the call.

Sim Card Registration

Imagine this situation. You received a message via SMS that someone mistakenly sent you NAD2000 through an electronic wallet, and that you need to pay the money back. There is no time to think and there is more than enough money in your back account. The next thing you do is to get your mobile phone, save the number appearing in the message and then send the same amount of money to the number that you just saved. Later on, you realise that the request was fake and you have been robbed. Several attempts to reach the owner of the number are made to no avail and the money you worked hard for becomes irrecoverable as it is a challenge to trace and identify the person you sent the money to.

The above scenario touches on the need for sim cards to be registered. There are different views that have been made with respect to sim card registration. While some may view sim card registration as an attempt to dive into the private affairs of the general public, others are positive enough and say that sim card registration helps to mitigate fraud, especially when it comes to payments and other important matters. Where do you stand on this? How are you going to feel if the scenario described above relates to you?

Mandatory sim card registration in Namibia, aimed at facilitating the investigation of crimes committed with the aid of mobile devices and ensuring a safe digital environment, is to commence on 1 January 2023 and end on 31 December 2023 with unregistered sim cards due to be deactivated thereafter (Namibia Economist, 2022). Registration requirements vary from one mobile service provider to the next, but generally these include a valid sim card, personal identification and a need for the sim card holder to visit a registration outlet or point in person. Personal identification can include both a physical document and a picture of the sim card holder, especially for online registration. The initiative needs to be commended and one wishes that all stakeholders will support it to ensure that all sim cards go through the registration process going forward. You have a role to play in this as well by ensuring that your sim card is registered with your service provider.

Interoperability of Electronic Wallet Payments

Interoperability in electronic wallet payments is important for a number of reasons. It is a public policy objective as it enjoys attention from regulators;

there is a need by the general public to access payment channels and services; and it is a springboard for innovation on the part of providers of financial services. The net effect of interoperability is therefore increased consumption of financial services, investment required in the provision of these services and economic growth.

The word interoperability should be clearly understood. Interoperability is normally associated with open loop payment systems, while intraoperability, a less common term, can imply closed loop payment systems. Indradjaja (2020) indicates that without sufficient interoperability in the market, where both the merchant and the consumer are still confined to using the same digital payments provider, uptake of digital payments is low and as a result, merchants who are trying to broaden their base of consumers must adopt numerous digital payment systems and consumers frequently find themselves unable to pay for items at merchants that are not on the same digital payment networks as them. This definition implies that interoperability is the condition in the market in which payment systems interact with each other while at the same time avoiding parallel systems in order to bring about the required access to financial services irrespective of the service provider a customer is associated with.

Interoperability from the perspective of electronic wallet payments is realised if the recipient of an electronic wallet is able to cash out at any channel irrespective of the issuer of that electronic wallet. For example, there are two banks, A and B, to the transaction, as well as Tom, the payer, who banks with bank A and Sarah, the beneficiary, who banks with B. Interoperability in this illustration is realised if Sarah is able to cash out at a channel belonging to her banking institution well.

Models for Electronic Wallet Payments

Ensuring successful implementation of interoperability in electronic wallet payments is a vision or goal that can resonate well with key stakeholders in payment, clearing and settlement systems. This is so because the overriding objective is the realisation of financial inclusion for the benefit of all stakeholders. The foundation for implementing interoperability therefore is the involvement of all stakeholders, sound industry and government structure, a regulatory framework if moral suasion or co-petition does not work, selection of the correct technical model, and the choice of competent solution providers via a transparent process.

Nautival and Navarro (2020) provide four technical models for interoperability which are outlined below:

- Bilateral agreement model. This implies that interoperable participants connect to each other via one-to-one connections.
- Aggregator model. It refers to a situation where a third party that is already integrated with multiple ecosystem players in a market helps to establish payments interoperability between participants.
- Mobile hub model. The model means that mobile operators set up a central entity that acts as a hub to connect them inter-operably.
- Global payments hub model. This takes place where an entity that is not a mobile operator sets up a central hub that enables digital financial services providers to be interoperable.

The above technical models all have advantages and disadvantages. Some models are applicable for growing markets while others are suitable for advanced markets. There are some models that resonate well with regulatory authorities. As an example, the payments hub model allows banks and non-bank financial institutions to point their systems to a central clearing entity for all clearing participants. Bilateral agreement and aggregator models are not suitable if the number of participants is high, while the mobile hub model is more relevant to mobile network operators and not other participants.

Chapter Summary

This chapter looked at electronic wallet payments. Electronic money is that virtual money that is converted from physical or deposited money and sent to someone via a cellphone or channel for encashment at an appropriate channel. Interoperability in electronic wallet payments is critical for financial inclusion. This is the condition in the market in which payment systems interact with each other while at the same time avoiding parallel systems in order to bring about the required access to financial services irrespective of the service provider a customer is associated with.

Review Questions

1. Define the following concepts that are related to electronic wallet payments:
   a. Interoperability
   b. Electronic wallet
   c. Trust account
2. Name and explain four technical models for interoperability which are associated with Nautival and Navarro, as you have learned.
3. Write short notes on the motivation for sim card registration in Namibia.

Selected References

Indradjaja, B. (2020). *Business and industry updates – The accelerating digital payments landscape in Indonesia.* Jakarta, Indonesia: Deloitte. Retrieved from https://www2.deloitte.com/

Iswara, G.T., Wialdy, K., & Sihombing, S.O. (2019). Predicting the relationship of antecedent variables of intention to use: Empirical analysis on e-money application. *Journal Dinamika Manajemen*, 10(2), 256-268.

https://doi.org/10.15294/jdm.v10i2.20443

Namibia Economist, (2022). Communications Regulator Clarifies Mandatory Sim Registration Commencement Dates: Namibia Economist. Retrieved from https://www.economist.com.na/

Nautival, A., & Navarro, A. (2020). *The many paths to mobile interoperability – Selecting the right technical model for your market.* London, United Kingdom: GSM Association. Retrieved from https://www.gsma.com/

CHAPTER 11

Cash Payments

How often do you pay with cash when buying goods and services in a given week? How much in cash do you carry in your physical wallet? What do you think the use of cash will be like, say five to ten years from now? These are useful questions that tell you about the current and future state of the usage of cash in our local economy or even at an international level. No one knows to what extent cash will be in use in the distant future. We can only estimate based on the current reality.

The likelihood is high that a majority of people especially in cities and towns conduct their purchases of goods and services using payment cards, with the situation being possibly different in rural and peri-urban settings. Besides, for some the chance is high that they carry more receipts in their physical wallet than physical cash or currency. This is because there are more alternatives to cash during this present time compared to how payment for goods and services used to be done in the past. Society has moved slowly away from cash by adopting electronic payment instruments, subject to the need for more education on alternative forms going forward. This is not to say that cash is not needed. It is very much required, especially for smaller payments in cities and towns and with the majority of payments in rural and peri-urban areas.

Learning Objectives

By the end of this chapter, you should be able to

- explain what cash payments are all about;
- outline advantages and disadvantages of cash payments;
- understand where you can use cash for payment of goods and services; and
- know about cash in circulation and displacement of cash.

Description of Cash Payments

There are two points to note as far as the description of cash payments is concerned. The first is to understand what cash is all about and the second is to know what it means when we say cash payments. Cash includes all the notes and coins that are in circulation and having been issued by the responsible authority. In Namibia, the Bank of Namibia, the central bank, is the only entity that is responsible for issuing currency in line with the applicable legislation. Bank notes and coins in Namibia include 5c, 10c, 50c, NAD1, NAD5, NAD10, NAD20, NAD30, NAD50, NAD100 and NAD200.

The South African rand, commonly referred to as ZAR, is a legal tender in Namibia on a one-to-one basis. This means that the NAD1 that you have in your pocket is equivalent to a ZAR/R1 viewed from the Namibian perspective, but the opposite is not true viewed from a South Africa perspective. Your local currency in Namibia needs to be converted if you are in South Africa as the Namibian dollar is not a legal tender in that country. It follows that your NAD1 in Namibia is not equivalent to the ZAR1 in South Africa owing to the conversion or exchange process that applies.

Cash payment therefore is any transaction that is concluded with physical cash rather than alternative or non-cash payment instruments such as card, online and cheque payment methods. Kapana is considered as staple food especially in cities such as Windhoek. One can travel to Katutura open market by the single quarters or other places in Windhoek to find this delicious food in the form of pieces of meat that are cut for you when you buy. Reaching for NAD100 in your wallet to pay for kapana at the open market is considered a cash payment as physical cash is involved in the payment process.

Advantages and Disadvantages of Cash Payments

Cash payments have advantages and disadvantages just like other payment methods. These other payment methods are called non-cash payment methods. Advantages of cash payments are outlined below:

- Settlement of transactions happens in real time.
- No need to worry about possibility of insufficient funds compared to account based transactions.
- Associated peace of mind knowing that amount owing is settled immediately.
- Suitable for small transactions.
- Ideal for face-to-face payments.

There are disadvantages of cash payments that need to be understood and these are the following:

- Not suitable for large transactions.
- Possibility of soiled notes or notes that have been tampered with by criminals, which holders of bank notes need to be careful of.
- Possibility of using cash that is stolen.

Channels for Cash Payments

One simplifying assumption can be made. This is that a buyer of goods or services has cash, be it notes or coins, on hand. Currency in this case might have been obtained from various access points such as automated teller machines, bank branches or at point-of-sale terminals. The money at hand is ready to be spent. What are the touch points where physical cash can be spent?

Physical cash can be spent at the *point-of-sale* or at *check out*. Let us assume the items at the check-out are worth NAD50. What follows is that you get out your wallet to pay for the items, and if you use NAD100 to pay, the cashier will give change as well.

Vending machines are other areas where you can pay physical cash to get goods or services. There is a wide range of services that are available at vending machines, including but not limited to airtime and electricity. Notes and coins that a vending machine can handle are normally displayed on the machine itself. The process involves one selecting a product to buy followed by inserting the correct amount in the allocated slot before proof of a service bought is dispensed. Cash is also used at certain *parking areas*. A machine dispenses a parking ticket at the point of entry that is later inserted at check-out in order to make payment and exit the parking area.

Currency in Circulation

What is the best term for money that is in the hands of the general public? It is *currency in circulation*. This is part of a narrowly defined money supply, technically referred to as M1. The assumption therefore is that the money you have in your wallet is part of currency in circulation. Consequently, the lower the currency in circulation the lower is the money available for purchase of goods and services by the general public.

Table 11.1
Currency in Circulation

Year	Value (NADm)	%	Volume (m)	%
2017	4659	6.0	643	5.8
2018	4521	(3.0)	675	5.0
2019	4518	(0.1)	693	2.7
2020	4712	4.3	723	4.3
2021	4759	1.0	739	2.2

Source: Bank of Namibia (2018, 2019, 2021)

The above table shows a general decrease in currency in circulation in value and volume terms over a five-year time frame. There were negative growth rates in value terms in 2018 and 2019. Currency in circulation was not spared from the Covid-19 pandemic. Growth rates in value and volume terms were 1 percent and 2.2 percent respectively in 2021 compared to the previous year.

Cash Displacement

Cash still has a role to play in our society. It is physical money consisting of notes and coins with a number of functions. These functions include medium of exchange, store of value, unit of account and standard for deferred payment. Money in our bank and other accounts fulfils these functions as well. The point is that although the volume of cash in circulation might be going down over time, physical cash still has a role to play.

Why is the debate around cash lite or displacement so significant? Cash lite is a reduction of the usage of cash over time, transferring to an alternative electronic means of making payments. There are advantages and disadvantages related to cash. The functions of money or currency are noted above. Cash is essential for low-value payments although there is no strict definition of what is meant by "low-value" payments. Is it possible to adopt a definition that is being used in electronic payments circles? From an electronic payments point of view "low value" means any amount that is below NAD5 million. This threshold can be applied to cash payments as well whereby payments in cash can be limited to NAD5 million.

Cash also provides for instant settlement of debt without the need for a clearing and settlement process. All that is required is to scan the goods being bought or consume the service and once this is done cash exchanges hands and final settlement happens at that moment.

There are disadvantages related to cash such as the high likelihood that it may be stolen. The loss can be significant if the amount involved is a large sum of money. Imagine you left your car unlocked and your wallet with a sizeable amount of money is in there and a thief snatches it. Or imagine someone breaks into your safe and a lot of money is stolen. It is a huge loss indeed. Consequently, the benefit of electronic means of payment is that they obviate or avoid money being stolen in its physical form. This is not to say that there is no fraud related to online payments. The argument is that one is more prone to theft with cash payments compared to online payments.

The industry's position therefore on cash-lite economy especially from Namibia's standpoint is highly commended. Digital transformation, which is basically the need to embrace electronic means of payments and move away from paper, is a journey worth pursuing. Does it mean that just because cheques have been eliminated then physical cash or currency should be shown the door as well? Not necessarily so. Cash will still remain for the foreseeable future unless there are policy changes. One expects cash to be around especially for low-value payments despite alternative payment methods that are available.

There are developments on an international front as well. Payment cards are ubiquitous. The drive to electronic means of payment is not a myth; it is real and being felt. Is it right to travel to the United States with a wad of cash in your pocket or just carry a payment card? From a security standpoint, it is better to have it all on your card and possibly a small amount on hand in your pocket. There is no need to swipe your card at the point-of-sale for a small packet of sweets, but instead present foreign currency if at your disposal. The box article below shows the strategy of the Central Bank of Nigeria on the displacement of cash in Nigeria.

BOX 10

The Central Bank of Nigeria (CBN) can be traced to the 1958 Act of Parliament as amended over the years. CBN is charged with the responsibility of administering the banking institutions and non-bank financial institutions with the aim of ensuring high standards of banking practice and financial stability through its surveillance activities and promotion of efficient payment system.

In its *Nigeria Payments System Vision 2025*, the Central Bank of Nigeria (2022) mentions five key drivers to accelerating the switch to electronic payments and these include: interoperability and the exchange of cash for digital counterparts in emerging payment systems; the mobile first generation who are more inclined to instant access to funds and averse to long queues in traditional banks but prefer to transact digitally; responding to the concerns of the informal economy – to ease the difficulty in meeting tax obligations and increase transparency in business transactions; continued adoption of mobile and digital wallets; and enabling frictionless payments, that is, removing the need for a one-time password (OTP), based on the amount of security available at the initiating terminal.

Chapter Summary

Cash still has a role to play in our society. It is physical money consisting of notes and coins with a number of functions. These functions include medium of exchange, store of value, unit of account and standard for deferred payment. Cash payment therefore is any transaction that is concluded with physical cash other than alternative or non-cash payment instruments such as card, online and cheque payment methods.

Review Questions

1. Mention five key drivers to accelerating the switch to electronic payments as mentioned in the *Nigeria Payments System Vision 2025* of the Central Bank of Nigeria.
2. Write short notes on the following concepts:
    a. Cash displacement
    b. Cash payments
    c. Currency in circulation
3. What are the advantages and disadvantages of cash payments?

Selected References

Bank of Namibia, (2018). *Annual Report 2020.* Windhoek, Namibia: Bank of Namibia. Retrieved from https://www.bon.com.na/

Bank of Namibia, (2019). *Annual Report 2018.* Windhoek, Namibia: Bank of Namibia. Retrieved from https://www.bon.com.na/

Bank of Namibia, (2021). *Annual Report 2020.* Windhoek, Namibia: Bank of Namibia. Retrieved from https://www.bon.com.na/

Central Bank of Nigeria, (2022). *Nigeria Payments System Vision 2025.* Abuja, Nigeria: Central Bank of Nigeria. Retrieved from https://www.cbn.gov.ng/

CHAPTER 12

High-Value Payments

Why are some payments classified as high-value payments and others as low-value payments? It is because some payments can only be processed by certain payment systems; it is a control mechanism for payment systems risks; and it is an industry practice. Consequently, categorisation of payments into low value and high value is something that is warranted.

Think about a corporation or other institution that would like to process a payment of about NAD10 million in favour of another party. How should it go about it? What channels are available to conclude this payment? Remember that a channel is the first point of contact for a payment to be made. There are payment channels that are available for processing these types of payments as this chapter will highlight.

Learning Objectives

By the end of this chapter, you should be able to

- describe what high-value payments are all about;
- indicate the channels for high-value payments; and
- understand the term "straight-through processing".

Description of High-Value Payments

High-value payments need to be understood from a number of perspectives. Description of these payments therefore centres around types of payments, the settlement process that is involved, and money for settlement. Areas that we covered thus far such as card, cheques and others are all referred to as low-value payments. Given that we have covered low-value payments already, there is therefore a need to comprehend high-value payments as well.

High-value payments are given this name because there is a threshold that industry players have subscribed to. In Namibia, high-value payments are transactions with a settlement value that exceed NAD5 million. Consider a company that intends to procure computers and related accessories worth NAD5,200,195.00 from a local supplier in order to set up a laboratory. It arranges for settlement of this amount via its bank for the benefit of the supplier, who banks with another bank. This is a high-value payment as it is above the predetermined threshold or transaction limit. Such payments are normally done by a wide range of stakeholders including financial institutions, corporations, traders, and the government and its agencies.

The settlement process for high-value payments is different from how low-value payments are settled. High-value payments are not channelled via a payment clearing and settlement operator (PCSO). They are transmitted to the settlement system operator for settlement or discharge of a payment obligation under principles of finality and irrevocability. The settlement operator is typically a central bank. The system that is used for settlement of high-value payments in Namibia is called the Namibia Interbank Settlement System (NISS), that is owned and operated by the Bank of Namibia. Low-value payments can also be settled directly via the NISS settlement system, but the issue is cost, relative to the amount of each transaction to be processed. It is for this reason that many customers do not use this settlement system and instead prefer to use close substitutes such as internet banking, cards and other alternatives. Payments that are channelled via NISS are settled closer to real-time. In Eswatini, the equivalent system is called Swaziland Interbank Payment and Settlement System (SWIPSS) as the following box article shows.

BOX 11

The Central Bank of Eswatini can be traced to 1974 through the Monetary Authority of Swaziland Order of that year. Part of its mandate is to facilitate the development and operation of an efficient national payment system.

In view of the above, the Central Bank of Eswatini (2020) details the ownership, participants and performance of Swaziland Interbank Payment and Settlement System (SWIPSS), which provides real time gross settlement (RTGS) for high-value critical payments. The system is owned and managed by the Central Bank of Eswatini and serves the Ministry of Finance and four commercial banks including First National Bank, Standard Bank, Nedbank and Eswatini Bank.

Settlement money for high-value payments is called central bank money. This essentially means that settlement goes via the banks that directly have settlement accounts in the NISS systems such that the paying bank's account needs to be debited for the value of the transaction and the account of the receiving bank is credited for the same value. It is a long-held belief that a central bank will always honour its obligation compared to banking institutions that can fail. Failure of a banking institution that acts as a settlement bank can have negative ripple effects on the banking system and the economy at large. The need to avoid the risk of contagion or a domino effect is what makes real time settlement systems (RTGS) such as the NISS settlement system of utmost importance for the settlement of high-value payments.

Channels for High-Value Payments

How do high-value payers interact with their financial institutions to make sure that instructions are initiated and eventually concluded? There are two important channels that customers or payers need to consider. These are online or internet banking, and visiting or contacting their branch.

Online banking is not only for individuals but for businesses that are involved in buying and selling goods and services as well. Business transactions are complex, while one expects front end payment systems for individuals to be less complex in terms of transaction types, by comparison. An onboarding process needs to be concluded for an entity to start using online banking.

What if a business entity has not signed up or onboarded for online banking? There could be other situations preventing an entity from being onboarded to an online banking solution. One way is to *visit or contact a branch* in order for a banker to assist in processing a payment manually through completing certain forms or following a due diligence process. A payment can finally be processed once all formalities have been concluded, leading to the payer settling their debt and the beneficiary receiving what is due to them. Manual payments are discouraged, given the migration of customers to online channels to minimise the impact on operational teams.

Straight-Through Processing

Let us look at a possible scenario. You estimate that you will arrive at your destination for your important appointment within 30 minutes. Alas, it starts to rain, visibility is impaired, and all of a sudden traffic picks up. Instead of arriving at your destination within 30 minutes, you arrive only after 45 minutes. Consequently, the appointment is rescheduled, leaving you disappointed. In this situation, unfavourable events on the road led to the cancellation and rescheduling of the appointment.

Straight-through processing (STP) needs to be seen in that light. It is key to high-value payments, given that these payments are intended to be settled immediately without unnecessary delays or bottlenecks. What do you expect when you want to send money through your bank to a beneficiary of another bank? Your interest is seeing the beneficiary or creditor receiving value immediately. Besides, you do not expect anything, including manual intervention from both the paying and receiving sides, to negatively affect the movement of the payment instruction that you initiated.

Investopedia (2020) points out that STP is an automated process done purely through electronic transfers with no manual intervention involved, with the benefits being increased efficiency and speed of payments domestically and globally. It is noted from this definition that an automated process leads to speed of payment while manual intervention has a negative impact on the speed of payment. The challenge for financial institutions and related stakeholders is to look into their processes and identify weak points and automate these with the view of speeding up processing of payments for the benefit of end users.

Access and Participation

Access and participation in payments, clearing and settlement systems is a goal that has received the attention of policy makers over a number of years across jurisdictions. This is because there are several associated benefits. Access and participation in this connection does not refer to individual customers of financial services, but rather entities that provide these services and that want to participate in the clearing and settlement systems. Benefits associated with widening participation in these systems include but are not limited to the playing field being levelled, opportunity to clear and settle in own name, reduction in clearing and settlement costs, opportunity to modernise payment systems, and likelihood of lower costs to end users.

Notable changes have been made to bring about equity in the access to and participation in the national payment system from Namibia's perspective. The Determination on the Criteria on Authorisation of Participation in the Clearing and Settlement Systems or Payment System Determination number 6 (PSD 6) provides for direct and indirect participation with the non-bank financial institutions (NBFIs) able to open settlement accounts in the NISS system at the Bank of Namibia (Bank of Namibia, 2013).

Some observation can be made on PSD-6. Participation in clearing and settlement systems is now open to all entities, subject to the approval process that needs to be followed. The more the participants in the systems, the more the likelihood of lower processing and end-user costs, viewed from a microeconomics standpoint. It is one's wish that more entities that are interested in participation in the system can do so knowing full well that there is an authorisation process that needs to be observed.

Chapter Summary

High-value payments are called that because there is a threshold that industry players have subscribed to. In Namibia, high-value payments are transactions with a settlement value that exceeds NAD5 million. Straight-Through Processing is an automated process done purely through electronic transfers with no manual intervention involved, with the benefits being increased efficiency and speed of payments domestically and globally. It is key to high-value payments as well, given that these payments are intended to be settled immediately without unnecessary delays or bottlenecks.

Review Questions

1. Explain the term "straight-through processing" and "state associated benefit".
2. Explain the following terms related to high-value payments:
   a. High-value payments
   b. Access and participation of payment systems
   c. Central bank money
3. Briefly outline channels for high-value payments.

Selected References

Bank of Namibia, (2013). *Determination on the Efficiency of the National Payment System (PSD-7).* Windhoek, Namibia: Bank of Namibia. Retrieved from https://www.bon.com.na/

Central Bank of Eswatini, (2020). *CBDC Diagnostic Study – Phase 1 Findings.* Mbabane, Eswatini: Central Bank of Eswatini. Retrieved from https://www.centralbank.org.sz/

Investopedia, (2020). *Straight Through Processing (STP): Definition and Benefits.* New York, NY. Retrieved from https://www.investopedia.com/

CHAPTER 13

Clearing of Payments

Have you ever wondered about the key difference between cash and non-cash payments? This can be extended to the difference between on-us and off-us payments. Let us assume that this crossed your mind before. Just to recap: non-cash payments include electronic transfer payments such as credit transfers and direct debits and card payments such as those arising from the use of debit and credit cards at channels such as automated teller machines, speed points as well as online or electronic commerce. On-us transactions are payments where both the payer and the payee have account relationship with the same bank. The payee and the payer bank with different banking institutions with respect to off-us transactions.

The key difference between cash and non-cash payments is that the former does not require clearing whereas this is required for the latter. In addition, off-us transactions require clearing while on-us transactions do not require clearing.

Learning Objectives

By the end of this chapter, you should be able to

- understand the concept of clearing;
- comprehend the basic clearing model; and
- know how different non-cash payments are cleared and processed.

Description of Clearing

The foregoing provided a basis for the clearing of payment instructions. There are a number of considerations for clearing to take place. First, any payment that needs to be cleared has to be an off-us payment. An off-us payment is an instruction where a payer and a payee have account relationships with different banking institutions. Second, the payment involved should have been initiated through the use of a non-cash payment method such as credit card, debit card, credit transfer or debit transfer. Third, an institution that needs to submit payment instructions for clearing should be an indirect or direct participant in the automated payment clearing house. Lastly, a payment needs to be validated once it is in the process of clearing.

The clearing of a payment instruction therefore refers to the exchange of payment instructions, calculation of payment obligation and the submission of an obligation of each participant for settlement. The above definition requires unravelling. Each participant of a payment clearing and settlement operator submits a list of payments it has generated from its customers for a given day. It is the duty of a payment clearing and settlement operator to determine which bank needs to pay another bank to settle the indebtedness. There are a number of validations that happen to arrive at the total obligation for each bank or participant. The end result of these validations is the submission of a settlement file for settlement within the books of the settlement operator.

Clearing in Namibia is performed by an entity called NamClear. This organisation is a not-for-profit that is owned by members. NamClear has been authorised to perform the service of clearing of payment instructions for its members or participants. It falls under the regulatory oversight of the Bank of Namibia.

The fact that there is currently one clearing entity in Namibia has to do with the size of the market. The payment clearing and settlement operator generates its revenue through the budget process and the volume of payment instructions becomes critical in the calculation of potential revenue. Diseconomies of scale can result, characterised by limited volume and high cost per unit should there be more clearing houses than the market requires.

Basic Clearing Model

The clearing process starts with the submission of input files to the automated payment clearing house as per the following diagram. These files can be for card or electronic funds transfer instructions. The clearing house performs a number of functions in the clearing process, including: data authentication; switching services; calculation of payment obligations; management of limits and cut-off times; monitoring performance of participants; and enforcement of rules and expected service levels.

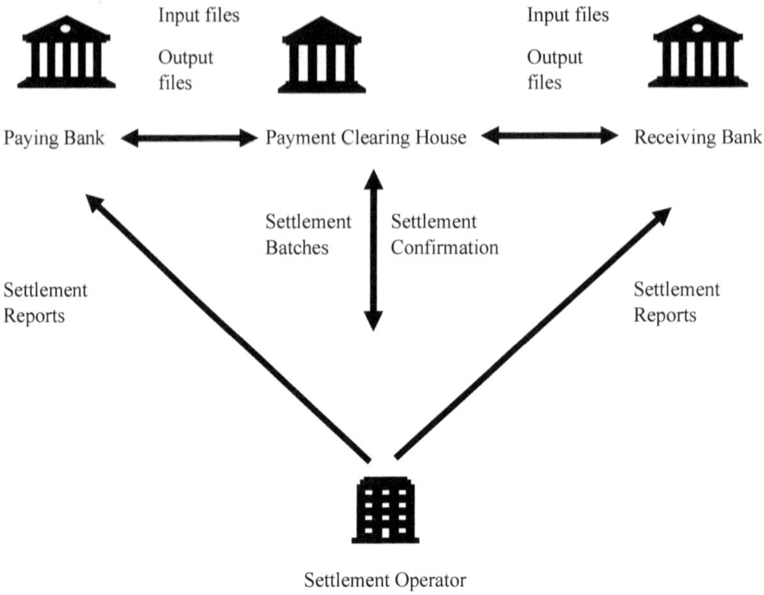

Figure 13.1. Basic Clearing Model

Once authentication with all the banks involved in the transaction is done, what follows is the submission of output files to the respective banks and the sending of settlement batches for settlement in the settlement system of the operator. Settlement confirmation is provided to the payment clearing house after settlement in the books of the settlement operator has taken place. Settlement reports are sent to the respective banks to confirm settlement. The following box article provides additional information of the domestic clearing and settlement operator (DCSO) for Namibia.

BOX 12

NamClear is the domestic clearing and settlement operator (DCSO) for the Namibian payments industry. It was established in 2003 and fully localised card, cheques and electronic funds transfer (EFT) processing environments in 2013 (Bank of Namibia, 2019). This entailed ensuring that clearing of Namibian payments happens locally away from the South African environment as a risk mitigation measure. The company is currently overseen by the Bank of Namibia.

The DCSO performs the clearing of domestic transactions just like any other operator. Traditional clearing functions include exchange of financial messages, validation of payment instructions, calculation of settlement obligations, and submission of settlement file to the Bank of Namibia for settlement. Cheques have since been phased out in Namibia and consequently clearing is happening for card and EFT at present. There are developments in the domestic retail environment that might have an impact on the scope of clearing in future.

Card Payments

Let us consider an example of a cardholder, Maria, using her card at Nedbank Namibia. How do you think the merchant – in this case KFC, which uses Nedbank – claims money from the cardholder, who banks with FNB Namibia? This requires an understanding of the authorisation, clearing and settlement process, as given in the following figure and explanation.

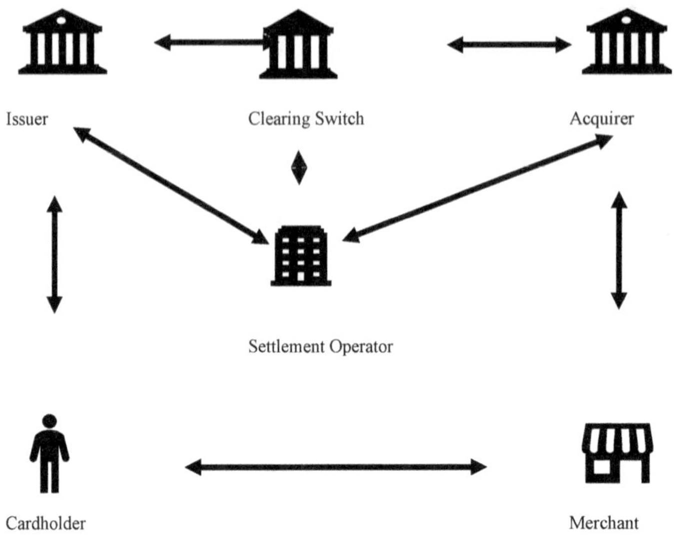

Figure 13.2. Clearing of Card Payments

The above four-party or corner model consists of key stakeholders such as cardholder, issuer, acquirer and merchant. Once the cardholder has presented a payment card at the merchant, an authorisation message is relayed from the speed point by the acquirer, the merchant's bank, to the issuer, the cardholder's bank, via the switch, to check if there is money in the account of the cardholder. Consequently, the cardholder (Maria in our example) walks away with her meal if there is money in her account and at that point the amount for the purchase is deducted from her account.

The merchant then begins the process of claiming the funds deducted from the cardholder's account. Details of Maria's transactions and other transactions for that day are sent to their bank, the acquirer, for clearing at an automated clearing house. The clearing house plays the role of a middleman to validate account and transaction details at the respective banks, calculates settlement obligations between the two banks, and eventually sends settlement obligation to the settlement operator to action. Please note that the payment clearing house operator in Namibia is NamClear, which is owned by participant banks, and the settlement operator is the Bank of Namibia. NamClear uses a system for clearing of card transactions called NamSwitch and Bank of Namibia uses a system for settlement of transactions called Namibia Interbank Settlement System (NISS).

Once the account and transaction details are validated and settlement obligation is calculated, the clearing operator sends the settlement batch file to the settlement operator to move funds from the account of FNB Namibia to the account of Nedbank Namibia at the settlement operator. The two banks have settlement accounts at the Bank of Namibia. What follows is that FNB Namibia's account is debited and Nedbank Namibia's settlement account is credited with the equivalent amount. Nedbank Namibia consequently credits the account of its merchant in its own books with the right amount. Where there are bank charges that apply these are applied, after which the net amount is credited. KFC at this point should have received money for the chicken meal that Mari bought.

The above might seem to be a long and complicated authorisation, clearing and settlement process. However, this is how an interbank card transaction, where the two banks are involved, works. Maria's account was deducted at the point of purchase while the account of the merchant was credited the following day. Consequently, it cannot be said that this is a long and complicated process as card transactions have advantages including lessening the need to carry cash all the time and doing transactions in a secure manner within the speed point environment.

An interbank card transaction is different from an intrabank card transaction. Interbank transactions are what was explained above where the cardholder uses a certain bank and the merchant has a relationship with another bank. Intrabank transactions mean both the cardholder and the merchant have a relationship with the same bank. Processing intrabank transactions is instantaneous within the same bank as there is no authorisation, clearing and settlement process that takes place. The entire process happens and is concluded within the same bank.

Four-party open loop model, which consists of main players such as cardholder, issuer, merchant and acquirer, discussed above, is the most common card scheme. There is a three-party model as well, although this is less common in the local payments industry. This closed-loop scheme consists of the main parties such as cardholder, merchant and issuer also acting as an acquirer. Diners Club and American Express are examples of the three-party arrangement.

Cheque Payments

The following figure illustrates how a cheque payment instruction is processed, cleared and settled. These terms should be familiar to you by now. All starts when the writer of the cheque, sometimes called the drawer, completes the payment details on a cheque, detaches it from the chequebook (leaving a counterfoil) and hands it over to the payee or beneficiary of the cheque. Our assumption here is that payer and payee have account relationships with different banking institutions or commercial banks.

What follows is that the payee walks over to their bank branch or collecting bank and deposits it via the counter into a bank account. Depositing via self-service terminals such as automated teller machines is possible. All the requisite information as it appears on the cheque is entered into the system by the cashier.

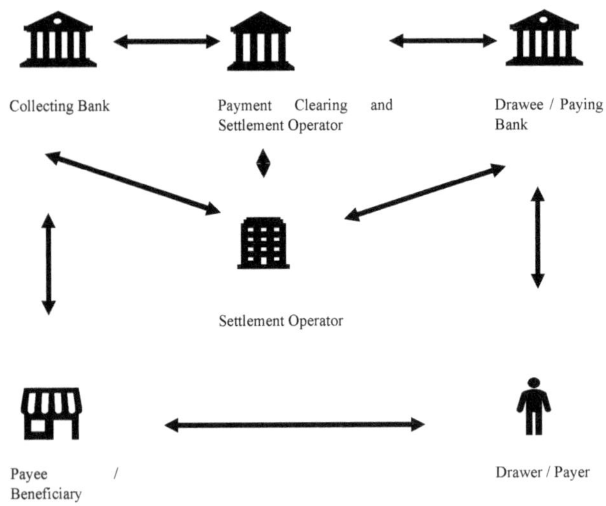

Figure 13.3. Clearing of Cheque Payments

On its part, the collecting bank has to collect all the cheques deposited across its branches country-wide with the view to having these taken to the payment clearing and settlement operator (PCSO) for clearing. A courier service company can be used to collect; and it is possible for all cheques to pass through a collection centre for sorting and other activities before they are transported to the PCSO.

The PCSO does the usual clearing such as validating account details, checking the legitimacy of the cheques, and a host of other activities, and if all is fine, the settlement obligation with respect to the paying bank is calculated and a settlement file is submitted to the settlement operator. Consequently, the account of the paying bank is debited in the books of the settlement operator and that of the collecting bank is credited and at this point the payee should have received value in their account.

Credit Transfer Payments

Consider a payer who bought building materials from a local dealer. The dealer only accepts payments through internet banking, so the payer agrees to settle the amount first before the goods are collected from the shop. This leads to the payer logging onto internet banking, creating a beneficiary profile in favour of the shop and settling the amount, after which an email is sent to the shop owner to confirm payment. Goods bought are now released as both the paying and beneficiary banks have confirmed availability of funds and that all account details are correct.

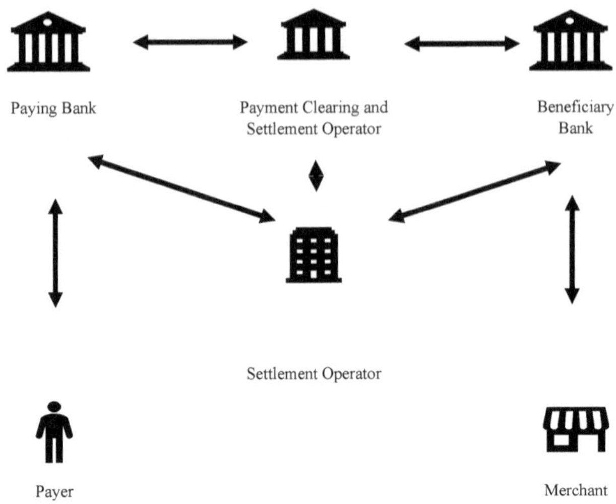

Figure 13.4. Clearing of Credit Transfer Payments

Please note that the shop owner or merchant has not received the money yet but only proof of payment. The paying bank sends payment details of the payer together with payments made by other customers for clearing at the payment clearing and settlement operator (PCSO), who engages the two banks to validate payment details. Consequently, the PCSO sends a settlement file to the settlement operator, normally a central bank, for settlement. This results in the account of the paying bank, in the books of the settlement operator, being debited and the account of the beneficiary bank credited. The beneficiary bank then passes the credit to the merchant. It is possible that the merchant can receive value in its account before the settlement process is completed and this results in credit risk, which we will tackle in the appropriate chapter ahead.

Debit Transfer Payments

Several use cases for debit transfers were outlined before. These include paying for short-term insurance such as car insurance, paying for long-term insurance (commonly called life cover), providing for investment obligation, and payment for services like gym membership. Let us use gym membership as an example. Where do you go to exercise? Let's assume that you go to one of the established fitness clubs like Virgin Active, Nucleus Health & Fitness Club, or somewhere similar, and this club has a different banking relationship compared to your own and that you have signed both membership agreement and mandate. The fitness club is called a user, collector or beneficiary. In the mandate you agree that a certain amount needs to be collected from your account, on a certain date, monthly.

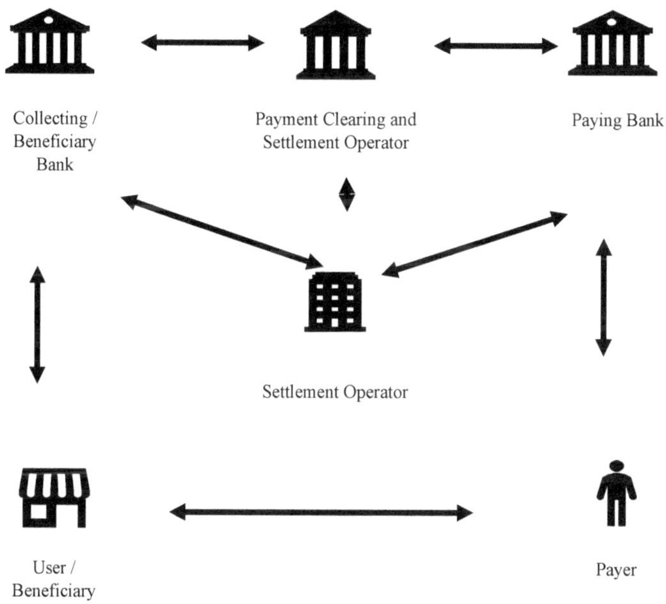

Figure 13.5. Clearing of Debit Transfer Payments

The beneficiary institution approaches its bank to collect say NAD800 from your account as a payer going forward (this amount can vary depending on the state of the economy and internal variables or costs). What follows is that the collecting bank needs to take money from your account with the paying bank via the PCSO. Once the account and payment details are confirmed the collecting bank sends your transaction details and details of other payers to the PCSO operator, which compiles a settlement file to the settlement operator. In turn, the settlement operator debits the account of the paying bank and credits the account of the collecting or beneficiary bank. Consequently, the beneficiary's account with the collecting bank is credited. Both the beneficiary and the payer will be able to see the transaction details in their respective bank statements. These parties will be expected to inform their banks, within a reasonable period of time, if there are entries on the statements they disagree with.

Electronic Wallet Payments

How do you think the payment, clearing and settlement process for electronic wallet transactions work? Which parties are involved in the transaction? Just imagine for a moment that you are about to e-wallet or blue wallet some money to a friend, family or loved one. This is the process that needs to be unravelled. The e-wallet industry is less developed than some other payment schemes and the transaction under discussion is a closed-loop one where only one issuer is involved. Automated teller machines of the issuer, in our case a bank, are used to withdraw or cash out money. Only a person-to-person transaction is involved in the model. In addition, the payee has a banking relationship with another bank other than that of the payer, as per the following figure.

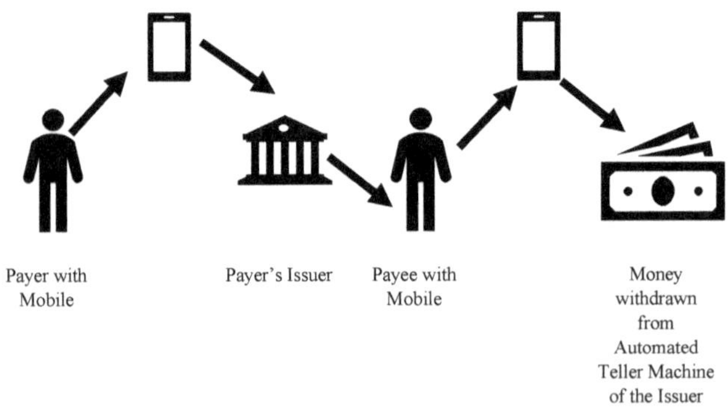

Figure 13.6. Clearing of Electronic Wallet Payments

In the above model, the payer has a banking relationship with the issuer and in our example the issuer is a bank, which has a closed-loop wallet scheme for its customers. The payee – friend, family member or loved one – asked for NAD500 to buy few personal items. This prompts the payer to log onto his mobile phone, entering all credentials, and request the bank or issuer to send the money for the benefit of the payee. The payee receives a message via the mobile phone with the message containing a voucher number and a secret code that expires after a few hours.

At the automated teller machine of the issuer or bank of the payer, the payee withdraws the money after entering the credentials received via the mobile phone. While on the machine, the payee struggles a bit and luckily a security guard is nearby to assist. Consequently, the recipient gets hold of the money from the automated teller machine, gives a tip to the security guard who was so helpful and dashes to the supermarket to purchase a few personal items.

Later that day, the payee in our example wonders why he could not withdraw money from the automated teller machine of his own bank, rather than having to use the ATM of the payer's bank. He then recalls a friend telling him about some challenges facing the domestic payments industry related to such things like interoperability and closed-loop arrangements, and reasons that maybe that is the issue and he will be able to withdraw money from his own bank if he were to face a similar transaction in future.

Cash Payments

By this point you should be familiar with how the clearing process for other retail payments works. Retail payments that we have discussed include card, online and cheque payments. Card payments involve swiping a card at a speed point or withdrawing currency at another bank's automated teller machine, before a merchant and acquiring bank receive what is due to them. You have seen how credit and debit transfers work. A payment instruction moves from a payer to a payee for credits while a payment instruction moves from a user or beneficiary to a payer for debits before settlement happens. Cheque payment instructions work the same way as direct debit. The clearing and settlement process for the above non-cash retail payments involves the use of a domestic clearing and settlement operator and the settlement system.

Cash clearing and settlement is different. It is instantaneous as it happens right there and then requiring no interbank clearing and settlement. Just to recap: the interbank clearing and settlement process is related to non-cash transactions where the payer and payee have a relationship with different banking institutions. Let us sketch a scenario. You walk into Kentucky Fried Chicken (KFC) in Windhoek to get a bucket of chicken, handing over the required amount to the cashier. The good you order is provided to you and the money is given to the cashier. Indebtedness has been settled in this case with no further action required as the whole idea about settlement is that money needs to exchange hands.

Chapter Summary

The present chapter covered clearing of non-cash retail payments. Clearing refers to the exchange of payment instructions, validation of payments, calculation of payment obligation and the submission of an obligation of each participant for settlement. Cash clearing and settlement is different because this is instantaneous as it happens right there and requires no interbank clearing and settlement.

Review Questions

1. Outline four traditional functions of a domestic clearing and settlement operator.
2. Explain the following concepts as they relate to clearing of payments:

   a. Clearing
   b. Settlement
   c. Four-party open-loop model
3. Illustrate diagrammatically how clearing of the following transactions happen:
   a. Card
   b. Credit transfer payments
   c. Debit transfer payments
   d. Electronic wallet payments
   e. Cheque payments

Selected References

Bank of Namibia, (2019). *Understanding the Namibian National Payment System.* Windhoek, Namibia: Bank of Namibia. Retrieved from https://www.bon.com.na/

CHAPTER 14

Settlement of Payments

Imagine that you are in a queue at a supermarket waiting for your turn at the cashier to pay for your goods or groceries. In this example, you and the merchant each have a relationship with a different bank. What follows is that you hand in your payment card, your personal identification number is entered and possibly you may be requested to sign a slip. The payment is processed and you walk away knowing full well that you have paid for the goods. Is this what is called settlement? It is good to pause at this moment and ponder over what settlement is all about.

Settlement of payment instruments is one of the key objectives in payment, clearing and settlement systems as far as non-cash payments are concerned. By this point you should be familiar with the fact that much of the focus in the settlement of payments is on non-cash and not cash, as the settlement with respect to the latter is instant while the former requires a settlement process to be followed end-to-end, especially where different banks are involved.

Learning Objectives

By the end of this chapter, you should be able to

- understand the settlement process;

- know the difference between commercial and central bank money; and
- calculate system utilisation ratio.

Description of Settlement

What does settlement of payments mean? The opposite of this question can also be asked. What should the definition of settlement of payments not include? Settlement is the final discharge of someone's or an entity's indebtedness, resulting in the beneficiary's account being credited. This implies that the originating debtor's account is debited and the creditor's account is credited at this point of the payment process from the perspective of non-cash payments.

Bank of Namibia (2023) says that settlement means the act of discharging obligations in respect of funds transfer from one system participant to another system participant in the settlement system. This definition refers to "system participant", which is an entity that is authorised to have a settlement account in the settlement system that is operated by a settlement operator for the discharge of payment instructions. In Namibia, the settlement system is called the Namibia Interbank Settlement System (NISS) and it is owned and operated by the Bank of Namibia. A participant's settlement account is debited for payments to other participants or banks and it is credited for receipts from other participants or banks.

There is a need to clarify the word *settlement* even further. Final settlement takes place when the paying account is debited and the receiving account is credited for the transaction value. Sending a proof of payment to the creditor when value has not reflected is not considered final settlement. What if there is a communication breakdown, interception of the payment message, payment is discovered to be fraudulent, or the creditor's account is suspended or closed? All these bottlenecks can result in the creditor keeping on asking about the whereabouts of what is due to them. Simply saying funds have been deducted from the account and proof of payment sent via email does not convince the beneficiary in this regard that settlement has taken place.

We always assume that the creditor has received value as soon as the proof of payment is sent. There is nothing wrong with this. In fact, it shows the confidence that the general public has in the payment, clearing and settlement process. However, the right thing to do after you have made a payment and sent proof of payment is to ask the beneficiary if they received money in their account.

Settlement System

Settlement is triggered by the indebtedness of one participant to another in the settlement system as indicated above. This means there has to be settlement between the two entities. Settlement can involve high-value or low-value transactions. Do you still remember the difference between high-value and low-value payments? High-value transactions are those with value that is greater than NAD5 million while low-value transactions are those below this amount (this distinction may differ from one country to another).

Each participant in the settlement system has an exchange settlement account. Items such as balance brought down, receipts during the day, loans extended by the settlement operator under a repurchase scheme and outgoing payments are all recorded in each participant's settlement account. A settlement account is like a normal T-account you have learned in your introductory finance or accounting course, consisting of incoming payments on the left-hand side and outgoing payments on the right-hand side, depending on the book that you read or how you were taught. This can be illustrated below, where the debit side receives and the credit side gives (amounts are in Namibian dollars or NAD).

Table 14.1
Settlement account for bank A

Debit		Credit	
Balance at start of day	200	Payments to participants	800
Receipts from participants	400	Surplus end of day	200
Loan from system operator	200		
Interest received from system operator	200		
	1000		1000

The above table shows that bank A has received about NAD1000 in its settlement account during the day and part of it was used to settle its obligation to other participants amounting to NAD800. There is a surplus in the settlement account of about NAD200 with options available on how to handle the available balance. This amount can remain in the account for the following day or be swept somewhere within the books of the settlement operator to generate interest. Option three is to invest the money overnight in the market to generate interest.

Just to recap: final settlement is arrived at when a participant's settlement account is debited and another's account is credited with the same amount. This is what is called settlement under the principle of finality and irrevocability. This implies that what has been settled cannot be undone or unwound as it is done and dusted. What follows then is that the ultimate beneficiary's account is credited with the same amount.

Other countries have implemented real time gross settlement systems (RTGS) as well. As an example, the Central Bank of Lesotho operates the Lesotho wire system as the following box article shows.

BOX 13

The Central Bank of Lesotho can be traced to 1978 and fulfils functions ordinarily performed by a central bank in terms of the Central Bank of Lesotho, 2000 (No. 2 of 2000). One of the objectives of the Central Bank of Lesotho is to promote the efficient operations of the payments system.

Payment system reform initiatives led to the implementation of the Lesotho wire system (Central Bank of Lesotho, 2006), which has several features: payments settled via the system are final and irrevocable; banks and the central banks are participants in the system; and payments resulting from the clearing of various payment streams are settled through the wire system.

Matters and Issues Post Settlement

Although the goal of any payment, clearing and settlement process is the ultimate settlement of transactions, it is important to note that there are issues that do arise after actual settlement has happened. This section looks at issues such as reports, queries, reconciliation, and disputes, as well as reversals and recalls.

There are different types of *reports* that are made available post settlement. Typical reports include settlement or performance reports that should show payments that were settled, opening balances, transfers from one account to the other, incoming payments, outgoing payments, transfers to the settlement operator and other items that are important. These reports are available as per the agreed frequency in line with an agreement between a settlement operator and a participant in a settlement system.

Queries can come from different sources. These sources include participants in the settlement system or customers of participants in the settlement system. Participants in the settlement system can find out if their settlement account has been debited with a certain amount. The reverse is also true: participants in the settlement system can find out if their settlement account has been credited with a certain amount. A customer of a participant in the settlement system can request for a certain transaction to be traced or to find out the whereabout of a certain pending transaction.

Reconciliation is a key activity in payment, clearing and settlement systems. The term reconciliation in this context means checking external reports, arising from the settlement operator, with internal records to find out if there are discrepancies. This activity is traditionally common before settlement but after clearing. There is nothing that prevents reconciliation being done post settlement as well, as the probability can be high that issues can be picked up after settlement too. Mark-off files and obligation or transactions reports are important tools in the reconciliation process especially prior to settlement. Automation of reconciliation is important given the high volume of transactions to be reconciled.

A *dispute* arises when two entities that are involved in a transaction cannot agree on a particular issue. Consider a situation where settlement could not happen due to technical issues on the side of one participant. The innocent party tries to claim interest, while the one in the wrong disagrees with the claim, resulting in a dispute. There is a set procedure leading towards a resolution of a dispute. Steps that are involved include the need for the two entities to agree. When they are unable to agree it follows that mediation can be considered, with arbitration being the next step if mediation does not work. It is important that agreement is reached between the two entities before the other options can be considered, to avoid incurring unnecessary costs in the form of time and money.

Recalls and reversals are related concepts. The key difference is that a recall is experienced before clearing while a reversal typically happens after clearing. It was indicated above that settlement is the final discharge of someone's or an entity's indebtedness, resulting in the beneficiary's account being credited. A need to reverse a transaction after settlement would imply an initiative by a receiving bank to initiate a totally different payment instruction albeit for the same amount but subject to conditions agreed on by the two entities involved. Aspects to consider may include costs that are incurred in the reversal of a transaction and this is likely to have an impact on the original amount.

Commercial and Central Bank Money

What is the difference between commercial and central bank money in payment systems? Which one of these is preferred, given the need to eliminate inherent risks? Are there practical examples to demonstrate the existence of the two ways of settling payment instructions? These are questions worth considering and elaborating upon.

Commercial bank money is used in the settlement of payment instructions in a situation where a central bank is not involved in the settlement process. Consider how payments of an indirect participant in clearing and settlement systems are processed and settled. An indirect participant maintains a settlement account with a direct participant who in turn has a settlement account with the central bank. Crediting and debiting of a settlement account of an indirect participant is the responsibility of a direct participant. A correspondent banking arrangement for international payments is another example where commercial bank money plays a role. With correspondent banking, a debtor bank uses the service of another local bank to channel the funds to the creditor bank in another country for ultimate transmission to the beneficiary. There is no involvement of a central bank in this process.

There is also settlement in central bank money. While with commercial bank money settlement of payment instructions happens in the books of another commercial bank, central bank money involves the settlement of payments in the books of the central bank. This process starts when a commercial bank or banking institution has a settlement account in the settlement system owned and operated by a central bank.

Ideally, settlement of payment instructions needs to happen in the books of a central bank. This is because the probability of a central bank failing is close to zero compared to the potential failure of a banking institution. Consequently, settlement in central bank money helps in the prevention of systemic risk, which is the risk of other entities being affected as the result of problems or failure of a fellow participant in the settlement system.

Optimal System Utilisation

Optimal or efficiency utilisation of a settlement system is key for any functioning economy. The greater the number of transactions that are settled via a settlement system the better is the contribution towards economic performance; and the opposite to this is true. One of the ways of measuring the extent to which a settlement system is efficiently used is the optimal utilisation ratio. The Central Bank of Eswatini (2020) says that optimal utilisation ratio is expressed as processed digital transaction value to nominal gross domestic product (GDP).

Table 14.2
Optimal system utilisation

Year	Total value settled in NISS	Nominal GDP	Utilisation Ratio (times)
2018	913	181	5.0
2019	976	181	5.4
2020	984	174	5.7
2021	1050	184	5.7
2022	1131	206	5.5

Source: Bank of Namibia (2022), Namibia Statistics Agency (2023)

It can be seen from the above table that the utilisation ratio for the Namibia Interbank Settlement System (NISS) was close to 5 times during 2018 and 2019. The utilisation ratio picked up to close to 6 times during the periods 2020, 2021 and 2022.

Chapter Summary

Settlement of payment instruments is one of the key objectives in payment, clearing and settlement systems as far as non-cash payments are concerned. Settlement is the final discharge of someone's or an entity's indebtedness, resulting in the beneficiary's account being credited. Settlement has also been described as the act of discharging obligations in respect of funds transfer from one system participant to another system participant in the settlement system. Besides, settlement typically happens in central bank money to minimise inherent risks. Central bank money involves the settlement of payments in the books of the central bank and this process starts when a commercial bank or banking institution has a settlement account in the settlement system owned and operated by a central bank.

Review Questions

1. Explain the following concepts as they relate to settlement of payments:
   a. Settlement account
   b. Recall
   c. Reversal
   d. Optimal utilisation ratio
2. Explain the difference between commercial bank and central bank money.
3. Outline steps that are involved in resolving a dispute in the context of payment, clearing and settlement systems.

Selected References

Bank of Namibia, (2023). *Annual Report 2022.* Windhoek, Namibia: Bank of Namibia. Retrieved from https://www.bon.com.na/

Bank of Namibia, (2023). *Understanding the Namibian National Payment System.* Windhoek, Namibia: Bank of Namibia. Retrieved from https://www.bon.com.na/

Central Bank of Eswatini, (2020). *CBDC Diagnostic Study – Phase 1 Findings.* Mbabane, Eswatini: Central Bank of Eswatini.

Retrieved from https://www.centralbank.org.sz/

Central Bank of Lesotho, (2006). The Launching of Lesotho Wire System: Prospects for the Economy. *Economic Review,* 72, 1-4.

Retrieved from https://www.centralbank.org.ls/

Namibia Statistics Agency, (2023). *Annual National Accounts 2022.* Windhoek, Namibia: Namibia Statistics Agency. Retrieved from https://www.nsa.nsa.org.na/

CHAPTER 15

Participants in Payment Systems

Participants in a national payment system come in various forms. They are called participants because they are actively involved in the processing of payment instructions. Think of soccer players. Soccer players are not like spectators whose responsibilities include watching a game on a field of play and giving the required moral support to the "boys". The players are, in association with a goalkeeper, deeply involved in directing a soccer ball to the right target in order to win a game. Participants can also be viewed in the same light. There is more to think about than what meets the eye.

Learning Objectives

By the end of this chapter, you should be able to

- know the role of participants; and
- comprehend types of participants in a national payment system.

Description of Participants

How can one tell that a particular entity is a participant in clearing and settlement systems? In the example of a soccer team, a soccer player puts on the attire of that team with a team position number written at the back of their jersey. It then becomes easy to identify that the person belongs to a particular team when on a field of play.

The above analogy can be used to identify participants in clearing and settlement systems. Participants are authorised (through a letter to commence business, letter of no objection or certificate of membership) to participate in such systems by a principal regulator of the national payment system. Authorisation is a process that requires a number of factors to be considered before any entity is admitted as a participant in such an environment. There should be an expression of interest first. That then leads to a series of steps that need to be completed before the required authorisation is given. Full authorisation implies that an entity is now able to submit its transactions for clearing and settlement in the applicable clearing and settlement systems.

There are other participants as well. These are identified because of what they do in the national payment system. This shows that participants in the national payment system should not necessarily be those that own transactions to be routed for clearing and settlement. Participants discussed in this chapter include banking institutions, non-bank financial institutions, direct and indirect participants, system operators, service providers, central banks, and vendors.

Role of Participants

Participation in the national payment system bestows on an entity both rights and responsibilities. Rights are the obligations of others on an entity in question and responsibilities refer to actions an entity is supposed to carry out as per expectation from the industry. The responsibilities of a soccer player on a field of play include respecting the rules of the game, sticking to one's position when the game is in session, not keeping the ball to oneself but sharing with fellow players and, if given an opportunity, scoring a goal so as to help the team to win.

There is an expectation that participants play a certain role in payment, clearing and settlement systems. Doing so not only assists regulators in fulfilling their functions but also contributes towards safety and efficiency in the systems in which they operate. The following is true about the role of participants in these systems:

- Participants from payments perspective are expected to observe the legal and regulatory framework so as not to introduce risks into the national payment system.
- They are expected to ensure that their systems are stable enough for payment instructions to be processed unhindered at all times through doing annual and periodic testing of systems.
- Participants need to put national interests ahead of their own as the best way to contribute towards the modernisation of the national payment system.
- These entities are expected to assist both the principal and self-regulatory authorities in the management of the national payment system.
- In addition, participants are required to provide reports, statistical information and comments on specific matters as per expectation from the authorities.

Types of Participants

Banking institutions are licensed to conduct banking business that includes accepting deposits, lending, savings and investments, as well as providing payment services. They are the primary participants in the national payment system through participation in the whole payment value chain that includes payment, clearing and settlement processes. These institutions have settlement accounts in the books of a settlement entity, typically a central bank. Consequently, they clear and settle payment instructions in their own name.

Direct and indirect participants imply that participation in clearing and settlement is a gradual process that is informed by the volume of transactions an entity has at its disposal. Direct participants, typically banking institutions, clear and settle payment instructions in their own name. Relatively small banking institutions classified by volume of payment instructions can clear and settle payment instructions through direct or established participants under a sponsorship arrangement. A direct participant carries all the risks in this arrangement on behalf of an indirect participant.

Central banks are also participants in the clearing and settlement process. They act both as overseers and as participants. As overseers or supervisors, they make sure that the national payment system is sound and stable so as to avoid any form of systemic risk in the system. Systemic risk is a risk of one participant failing, leading to the failure of other participants. Central banks participate in clearing and settlement systems, given their role as banker of government, in addition to their own transactions.

Non-bank financial institutions are not banking institutions. Some of these entities accept deposits, have savings and investment schemes and provide payment services, but they are not licensed to lend money in the true sense of the word from a banking supervision standpoint. It is only banking institutions that are expected to do full banking business. Other non-bank financial institutions are in the field of micro-loans including term or periodic loans. Payment instructions of these institutions are processed for clearing and settlement through banking institutions.

System operators play a key role in the national payment system. A clearing operator provides switching and clearing services on behalf of its members across payment streams. These streams include card and electronic funds transfer for low-value transactions. The result of clearing is a settlement file that is submitted to the settlement operator. The settlement operator provides settlement services to direct participants or banking institutions.

Service providers are also under the category of non-bank financial institutions. An example of a service provider is a third-party payment service provider that provides payment intermediation services to its customers as a traditional form of business. They link payers and beneficiaries outside the banking sphere. Terms of service are with these providers and not with a banking institution. The description of service providers differs from country to country and this may include banking institutions in some markets as well.

Vendors are found towards the inner core in the payment system environment. Their role is to sell software products or solutions to banking institutions, system operators and other participants in the national payment system. Traditionally there are service level agreements between participants and the vendors to make sure that provision of services meets a particular level. Non-performance on the side of a vendor has severe implications in the national payment system as a whole. The implication here is that participants need to be careful at all times in terms of the kind of vendors they are supposed to do business with. Selection of certain vendors is done as per an industry predetermined approval process before commencement of business.

The participants in payment, clearing and settlement systems listed above have an important role to play in the proper functioning of these systems. Such a list is not exhaustive and differs from country to country. As an example, the following box article outlines key participants, stakeholders and users of payment systems in Ghana.

BOX 14

The Bank of Ghana was established by the Bank of Ghana Ordinance 1957 (No. 34 of 1957) as part of the journey towards political independence in Ghana. One of the functions of the Bank of Ghana is to promote, regulate and supervise payment and settlement systems.

There are three participants, stakeholders or users of payment systems (Bank of Ghana, 2023). The central bank is an overseer, operator and a participant of the payment system. Commercial banks participate in the system by making and receiving payments on their own behalf or that of their customers. Service providers are the printers of payment instruments and telecommunication companies who provide the infrastructure arrangements for the payment system.

Common Ground

Interaction of participants is essential to realise a common good. This can be made clear with the illustration of a sectional title scheme. The scheme separates an entire property into exclusive ownership and joint ownership. Buying a property in a sectional title scheme entitles the buyer to own a section of the entire property with the right to use a common ground and this common ground can be reserved for driving through, general parking, playground and gardening. All residents have an obligation to maintain the common property through paying mandatory levies to a managing agent.

The above is a useful illustration of participants in payment, clearing and settlement systems whereby, although the players are expected to compete, there are matters they need to work together on. Participants can compete in the provision of goods and services from their vantage points through setting their own pricing and being responsible for supplying quality goods and services to differentiate themselves from competition. There should be a spirit of co-operation as well so as to collectively achieve some milestones that need to be delivered. Collaboration and competition are what has become commonly known as co-petition. Participants can collaborate through discussing issues of mutual concern, jointly coming up with relevant agreements, and striving to modernise the environment in which they operate.

Levelling the Playing Field

Broader participation of a variety of stakeholders in payment, clearing and settlement systems is key from a competitive market structure point of view. Basic microeconomic theory shows that more supply of goods and services leads to a fall in the price per unit. Increased supply of goods and services in this case is made possible due to new entrants in the market. The lesson from the foregoing is that the field is required to be levelled to bring about the entry of other non-traditional players in the market so as to bring about more choices to customers of financial services.

There is a drive globally to ensure access to these systems by non-bank financial institutions. It was indicated that some of these entities accept deposits, have savings and investment schemes and provide payment services, but they are not licensed to lend money in the true sense of the word from a banking supervision standpoint. In Namibia, entry into the national payment system, especially by non-bank financial institutions, is being made possible by the *determination on the criteria for authorisation of participants in the clearing and settlement systems* (Bank of Namibia, 2013).

Chapter Summary

This chapter covered participants in payment systems. It was noted that participants in a national payment system come in various forms and that they are called participants because they are actively involved in the processing of payment instructions. Sectional title scheme was used as an example to show how participants interact as they try to realise a common good. In addition, broader participation of a variety of stakeholders in payment, clearing and settlement systems is key from a competitive market structure point of view with the result being increased supply of goods and services and lower price per unit.

Review Questions

1. Outline the role of participants in payment, clearing and settlement systems.
2. Name and explain different types of participants in payment systems that you have learned.
3. Use the illustration of a sectional title scheme to illustrate how participants in payment systems need to work together towards modernisation of these systems.

Selected References

Bank of Ghana, (2023). *Participants of Payment Systems*. Accra, Ghana: Bank of Ghana. Retrieved from https://www.bog.gov.gh/

Government of the Republic of Namibia, (2013). *Determination on the Criteria for Authorization of Participants in the Clearing and Settlement Systems (PSD-6)*. Windhoek, Namibia: Government of the Republic of Namibia. Retrieved from https://www.bon.com.na/

CHAPTER 16

Risks in Payment Systems

Risks are ubiquitous and know no borders. They are prevalent in banking in general and payments in particular. It is not about the quantum or the need to fear risks that matters but to what extent measures are put in place to manage perceived or known risks. No wonder organisations spend a great deal of financial resources to make sure that risks are adequately managed. These organisations spend money on acquiring relevant systems and upskilling human resources to better manage risks they face.

Learning Objectives

By the end of this chapter, you should be able to

- know what risk is all about;
- understand different types of risks; and
- comprehend risk management framework.

Description of Risk

The word risk is described in everyday conversation as the possibility of something bad happening. Consider climatic conditions and their associated impact. In a situation where weather patterns are unpredictable, if the rain does not occur during normal rain seasons, farmers face a challenge in terms of figuring out the best time to cultivate their fields. The risk is that the rain does not appear as expected, resulting in a chain reaction of drought, low yields and hunger.

In payments, risk can be defined in a number of ways. One way is to look at risk as a possibility of a payment instruction not being processed due to technical or operational events or causes. A payment cannot be processed if there are technical issues on the side of a participant that is to send an input file to the automated clearing house. Additionally, a payment can fail to be processed if there are insufficient funds in the account of an individual or that of a participant in their settlement account. Controls are therefore important to make sure that payment instructions are processed at all times to prevent unnecessary risks.

Types of Risks

There are several risks that are common in payment, clearing and settlement systems. Core risks that are inherent in these systems are listed in the following table and include credit risk, legal risk, liquidity risk, operational risk, reputational risk and systemic risk. Each risk is described and possible controls for each risk type are provided.

Table 16.1
Types of Risks

Risk ID	Risk Name	Risk Description	Possible Controls
R1	Credit risk	Risk that a participant is unable to settle obligations now or anytime thereafter	Due diligence at the time of onboarding; continuous monitoring of a participant; collateral
R2	Legal risk	Risk of uncertainty in a piece of legislation thus negatively affecting compliance. Sometimes referred to as compliance or regulatory risk	Review of legal and regulatory framework; adequate consultations during the process of drafting legislation or sub-ordinate legislation
R3	Liquidity risk	Risk that a participant is unable to settle obligations now but can do so sometime later	Prefunding of settlement account; collateral; borrowing from the settlement operator or market
R4	Operational risk	Risk due to processing errors, failed processes, untrained human resources or technical malfunction	Training; disaster recovery planning and testing; review of operational processes; risk framework
R5	Reputational risk	Risk of a bad name due to negative publicity or failure to comply with regulatory framework	Media and environment scanning; compliance to legal and regulatory framework

R6	Systemic risk	Risk that can arise from other risks leading to a domino effect whereby a failure of one entity can lead to other entities failing as well	Liquidity monitoring; continuous oversight/ supervision of participants; failure to settlement arrangements

Consider this scenario, which is a true story. A buyer in one country sends an email to a seller, a major public company in another country, with the intention of buying a storage container. The email is intercepted by a fraudster, who misrepresents himself as being employed by the seller, working in a business unit responsible for shipping storage containers. What follows is that the buyer requests an invoice and the fraudster provides attractive details including a low price for the item. The buyer then compares details on a public company's website to those appearing on the invoice, and notes major, surprising differences. The phone number is wrong; uniform resource locator (URL), internet address or web address has errors and is not secure; invoice price is too low; and the public company has a banking relationship with a digital bank. Traditionally, a digital bank is a financial institution that does not have a physical retail location such as a bank branch but rather a kiosk or an open venue for customer queries and support. Consequently, the buyer drops an email to the digital bank and the public company to establish authenticity and no feedback is received in good time. This is a typical example of potential operational risk or payment fraud.

Finding a way to manage inherent risks is an important consideration. Controls need to be reviewed from time to time to ensure that they are still relevant. There is a need to isolate risks in terms of low, medium and high, and consequently to channel resources to more pressing or important risks. Proper management of risks can prevent systemic risk from happening, which is the risk that failure in one entity can lead to other entities failing as well.

Risk Management Framework

It is one thing to identify risks that are common in payment systems and quite another to make sure that the identified risks receive the attention they deserve from senior management and key stakeholders. A framework brings to mind a structure within which something ought to be done to achieve the desired outcome. Relating this to risk management, it implies that a risk management framework is a structure for managing risks that were identified, to bring about safety and efficiency in a given payment, clearing or settlement system.

The Board of the Federal Reserve (2023) notes that a risk management framework is the set of objectives, policies, arrangements, procedures and resources that a system employs to limit and manage risk (as depicted in the figure that follows). This definition implies that a risk framework is not just a document that meets the eye nor is it just a document that lists all the risks that need to be controlled. It is a total system that needs to be fully employed to minimise all inherent risks in the environment of payments. Resources – be they human, financial or other – need to be put together to better manage such risks and without that, any risk management endeavour becomes a pipe dream.

Identify risks clearly and set sound risk managment objectives.	• Risks, as well as the objectives and strategies for minimising the identified risks, need to be identified.
Establish sound governance arrangements to oversee the risk managment framework.	• It is the responsibility of boards at a system operator or participant level to ensure that risk management framework is implemented and relevant information is shared for decision making.
Establish clear and appropriate rules and procedures to carry out the risk management objectives.	• Rules and procedures should be clear on responsibilites of key stakeholders, crisis management and settlement failure procedure.
Employ the resources necessary to achieve the system's risk management objectives and implement effectively its rules and procedures.	• Availability of competent staff to assist in achieving risk managment objectives is key.

Figure 16.1. Risk management framework

Risk management is one of the objectives of central banks across the world. Central banks have a vested interest in ensuring the safety and efficiency of payment, clearing and settlement systems. This is so because of the negative impact that arises if such systems are not well managed. Consider a situation where liquidity or settlement risk is not properly addressed. The end result is system risk that can have a devastating effect not only on the financial system but also on the real economy, thus disrupting the circular flow of income. This is where a policy on payment system risk becomes important as shown is the box article below, and the Fed is one of the central banks that have put in place such a policy.

BOX 15

The Federal Reserve System or the Fed for short is the central bank of the United States and was established in 1913. It performs five functions to promote the effective operation of the United States economy and the public interest. Three entities falling under the Fed are the Board of the Governors, 12 Federal Reserve Banks, and the Federal Open Market Committee. One of the functions of the Fed is that it fosters payment and settlement system safety and efficiency through services to the banking industry and the United States government that facilitate United States dollar transactions and payments.

In an effort to ensure proper functioning of payment and settlement systems, the Fed has put in place the policy on payment system risk. The policy addresses the risks that payment, clearing, and settlement activities present to the financial system and to the reserve banks and contains a risk management framework with four elements as depicted in the above picture (Board of Governors of the Federal Reserve System, 2013).

Knowing the scope of risk management and the type of measures to employ with the view to minimise risks is important. The SADC Committee of Central Bank Governors (2002) notes that risk management measures are aimed at reducing the risks faced by individual national payment system participants, and minimising risk in the national payment system; and these measures are divided into five types as follows:

Table 16.2
Risk Management Measures

Measure	Description
Prefunding of all payments	Settlement of transactions is based on availability of funds.
Exposure limit	Involves placing bilateral and multilateral limits on the values settled between participants.
Collateralisation	Refers to posting assets that can be liquidated to guarantee settlement or advancement of funds for settlement.
Loss-sharing	Applicable in net settlement systems whereby surviving participants agree to share loss among themselves if one of the participants fails to settle obligation.

Shortening of time lags in settlement	Real time gross settlement systems (RTGS) allow for prompt final settlement, while with deferred net settlement systems (DNS) settlement is delayed at end of day.

Source: SADC Committee of Central Bank Governors (2002)

Each measure is listed with its associated description. Consider collateralisation as an example. It is a measure that is used in exceptional situations. Where there are sufficient funds in the settlement account of a participant, none of the assets that were posted can be used as collateral to access funding, while the opposite is true if there are insufficient funds and settlement of transactions needs to take place.

Chapter Summary

Risks are ubiquitous and are prevalent in banking and payments. The word risk refers to a possibility of a payment instruction not being processed due to technical or operational events or causes. This is where risk management framework becomes important. Risk management framework is a structure for managing risks that are identified to bring about safety and efficiency in a given payment, clearing or settlement system. Central banks around the world have put in place risk management frameworks to assist in containing inherent and emerging risks.

Review Questions

1. List and explain key payment system risks that you have learned.
2. Outline and explain four major elements of the risk management framework that you are familiar with.
3. Explain the following terms:

   a. Risk
   b. Collateralisation
   c. Risk management
4. Discuss five important measures that are aimed at reducing risks in the national payment system.

Selected References

Board of Governors of the Federal Reserve System, (2023). *Policy on Payment System Risk*. Washington, DC: Federal Reserve System. Retrieved from https://www.federalreserve.gov/

SADC Committee of Central Bank Governors, (2002). *Guide to Developing a Strategic Framework for Payment System Modernization*. Pretoria, South Africa: Southern African Development Community. Retrieved from https://www.sadcbankers.org/

CHAPTER 17

Financial Inclusion

Financial inclusion is a key public policy objective not only in Namibia but also around the world. This is because of the positive impact on society if the measures around financial inclusion are implemented. What does this mean? Does it mean that some financial services should be offered for free? If it is true that some financial services need to be offered for free, what about some goods and services that you buy from local shops or merchants? It is possible for some of these services and products to be offered for free as well? These questions are left for you to ponder.

Learning Objectives

By the end of this chapter, you should be able to

- understand the meaning of financial inclusion;
- know how to measure financial inclusion; and
- comprehend how financial inclusion is being promoted across the world.

Description of Financial Inclusion

Financial inclusion is one of the most studied areas in banking and payment systems. Several meanings have been advanced. One of these is that financial inclusion is a goal by governments and regulatory authorities that entails offering affordable financial services to unbanked and underbanked members of the society in urban, peri-urban and rural areas. The assumption is that members of the society in urban areas are relatively well off compared to those in rural and peri-urban areas. Financially excluded individuals in most cases do not have normal bank accounts as basis for accessing financial services.

The term "broad financial services" normally includes savings, credit, remittances, insurance and payments. These broad financial services that are key for financial inclusion are described below.

- Savings. This financial service allows the account holder to put money aside out of disposable income to cover future known and unpredictable expenses. Investment is related to saving, with the difference being that the former is about putting money away for a long term while the latter deals with putting money aside for a short time. The duration is a matter of interpretation.
- Credit. The key here is the availability of financial assistance to certain sections of society such as small and medium enterprises and individuals at affordable cost. This capital is made available with the view to investing in income-producing activities and attending to essential necessities. The issue of collateralisation needs to be looked into as part of the quest to make credit available to as many stakeholders as possible.
- Remittances. This financial service covers sending money from surplus units to deficit units using non-traditional payment methods within a country or across nations. Additionally, this medium of sending money is meant to cover underbanked and unbanked

members of society, for example through sending money from one cell phone number to another.

- Payments. The two services, that is payments and remittances, are similar. Payments entails more than remittances and includes other affordable payment methods and cash-in and cash-out services to make challenges around accessibility to cash at alternative channels a thing of the past.
- Insurance. There are short-term and long-term insurance products. Short-term insurance covers a car and building while long-term insurance covers life. For example, if there is a geyser burst at home, the short-term insurance product is triggered to cover the claim whereas if someone dies, a long-term insurance claim is made accordingly. Insurance therefore is viewed as a necessity and not as a luxury from a financial inclusion standpoint.

Consider insurance as a financial service at this point. Is it possible to conclude that insurance products are widely accessible by many people to the extent required? One person might say "Yes" and another might say "May be". One can also reason along the same lines by looking at savings, credit, remittances, and payments. Strides have been made though that are worth reflecting upon around these components of financial services.

There is no way a discussion around financial inclusion can be concluded without touching on financial literacy. The goal of financial literacy is to ensure that the general public is educated or informed on matters related to financial services so that they can make informed decisions. One person can make good financial decision around insurance simply because they understand and have been briefed on how insurance products work. The other way around is true as well: someone else can make an unwise financial decision around insurance simply because they do not understand and have not been briefed on how insurance products work.

Measuring Financial Inclusion

Measuring financial inclusion is important to inform any policy intervention required to achieve this public policy objective. The implication is that it is a challenge to address something that cannot be measured. This is in line with the SMART principle: Specific, Measurable, Attainable, Realistic and Time-bound. Any attempt to address this objective therefore can be done using this principle as a basis.

There have been attempts to measure financial inclusion at a global level, using several techniques, in core areas mentioned above such as savings, credit, insurance, remittances, and payments. Techniques that can be used to arrive at financial inclusion targets include surveys and algebraic methods. Surveys are administered by researchers or analysts to collect data in the field, which then needs to be sorted, analysed, organised, summarised, presented and published. Algebraic methods involve keying in the data in certain predetermined formulas to arrive at desired targets.

Alliance for Financial Inclusion (AFI) is one of the leading organisations that are active in the space of financial inclusion. It is headquartered in Kuala Lumpur, Malaysia and is committed to financial inclusion and poverty reduction. AFI has come up with techniques for measuring financial inclusion and these have been applied by policy makers across the world. This organisation has developed a formula called the number of access points per 10,000 adults, as shown below (Alliance for Financial Inclusion, 2019):

$$\text{Access Points} = \left(\frac{Total\ number\ of\ access\ points}{Total\ number\ of\ adults}\right) * 10{,}000$$

Access points in the above formula refer to the physical points of contact or delivery channels that consumers of financial services can interact with to consume financial services. Some examples of these are automated teller machines, point-of-sale devices and alternative channels like agents for cash-in and cash-out. Data on access points can be obtained from financial regulatory authorities. The number of adults are those falling within the range of the start of the working age and the end of the working age before an individual reaches pension age or immediately after pension age. National statistical agencies normally provide a definition of an adult. The 10,000 that is shown in the formula is a given number. Regulatory authorities normally put a target point per 10,000 they would like to see in their jurisdiction. A number below this target is concerning, with improvements required to reach the target, while a number equal to or above the target is pleasing to regulatory authorities from a financial inclusion standpoint. As an example, the Bank of Namibia provided targets for access points across channels for the years 2015 to 2020 (Bank of Namibia, 2015).

Example 1

Consider country A with a total number of automated teller machines of about 5,500 and an adult population of 400,000. The regulatory target for access points is 130 per 10,000 adults. Using the above information, the number of access points per 10,000 adults is calculated as follows:

$$\text{Access Points} = \left(\frac{5{,}500}{400{,}000}\right) * 10{,}000$$

$$\text{Access Points} = (0{,}1375) * 10{,}000$$

$$\text{Access Points} = 138$$

The above answer shows there are 138 access points per 10,000 adults in the country in question. This is above the regulatory target of 130 access points per 10,000. The financial regulatory authority should therefore be pleased with the result as this implies satisfactory progress towards financial inclusion.

BOX 16

Finmark Trust was established in 2002 and is based in Johannesburg, South Africa. It has been active in the financial inclusion environment over a number of years. Its mission is making financial markets work for the poor by promoting financial inclusion and regional financial integration. Information on its website shows that it pursues its vision through the creation and analysis of financial services demand-side data to provide in-depth insights on both served and unserved consumers across the developing world, and systematic financial sector inclusion and deepening programmes to overcome regulatory, supplier, and other market-level barriers hampering the effective provision of services.

Demand-side data has been created or collected via FinScope consumer survey, which is regarded as dynamic, and the content is evaluated by syndicate members to ensure that the most recent financial market trends are being addressed and taken into consideration (Finmark Trust, 2011).

Promoting for Financial Inclusion

Promoting financial inclusion entails finding ways to reduce exclusion so that the unbanked or underbanked members of society form part of the mainstream financial sector as well. There is no point in talking about financial inclusion when the majority of a particular society are still outside the mainstream financial sector. This is what many authorities across the world have tried to address.

Measures taken by authorities to promote financial inclusion include the introduction of basic bank accounts, information sharing, financial inclusion projects, and allowing certain entities to participate in payment, clearing and settlement systems. A basic bank account with an affordable fee structure is meant for individuals with limited income as well as for small enterprises. The general public can make informed decisions if they are informed on aspects around fees and charges that apply across the banking sector. Self-help projects can go a long way in assisting members of the public to generate income for themselves and their loved ones. The inclusion of more participants in payment, clearing and settlement systems has a positive impact on fees and charges for end users as well.

Matsebula (2023) lists concrete actions on how financial inclusion can be leveraged to systemically eradicate poverty and such actions include leveraging digital transformation and technological innovations; prioritising financial literacy programmes; encouraging collaborative efforts; and developing and supporting microfinance institutions. All these measures can assist in ensuring financial inclusion and reducing poverty and unemployment.

Chapter Summary

This chapter looked at financial inclusion, covering topics such as describing, measuring, and promoting financial inclusion. Financial inclusion is a goal by governments and regulatory authorities that entails offering affordable financial services to unbanked and underbanked members of the society in urban, peri-urban and rural areas. Measures taken by authorities to promote financial inclusion include the introduction of basic bank accounts, information sharing, financial inclusion projects, and allowing certain entities to participate in payment, clearing and settlement systems. All these measures can assist in ensuring financial inclusion and reducing poverty and unemployment.

Review Questions

1. Name and describe five broad financial services that are key for the realisation of financial inclusion.
2. Define the following terms:
   a. Financial inclusion
   b. Access points
3. List and explain two techniques that are important for measuring financial inclusion.
4. Consider country B with a total number of point-of-sale devices of about 5,000 and an adult population of 350,000. The regulatory target for access points is 150 per 10,000 adults. Calculate the number of access points per 10,000 adults using the formula that you have learned.

Selected References

Alliance for Financial Inclusion, (2019). *Alliance for Financial Inclusion Policy Model: AFI Core Set of Financial Inclusion Indicators*. Kuala Lumpur, Malaysia: Alliance for Financial Inclusion. Retrieved from https://www.afi-global.org/

Bank of Namibia, (2015). *Namibia National Payment System Vision 2020*. Windhoek, Namibia: Bank of Namibia. Retrieved from https://www.bon.com.na/

FinMark Trust, (2011). *FinScope Consumer Survey Namibia 2011*. Johannesburg, South Africa: FinMark Trust. Retrieved from https://www.finmark.org.za/

Matsebula, (2023). *Financial Inclusion: A Pathway to Eradicating Global Poverty*. Cape Town: South Africa. Payments Afrika. Retrieved from https://www.paymentsafrika.com/

CHAPTER 18

Regulation

Two businessmen were in conversation: 'Have you heard that another regulation was recently issued? It is only six months since the last one was issued!' The speaker seemed worried, and his friend seemed to feel the same: 'That is true, it is like our job is to focus more on regulatory aspects than our core strategies for moving the business forward!' The other person wondered and touched on the relevance of regulation.

Conversations like these are common today. They raise certain questions that require consideration. Why are regulations issued in the first place? If regulations are not issued, what is the chance that the market can self-correct? What are the benefits and costs of regulations viewed from authorities and regulated institutions? These are very important questions that this chapter will answer. As you read, please imagine a market with regulations that have been put in place and another market where there are no regulations at all for a certain portion of the market.

Learning Objectives

By the end of this chapter, you should be able to

- understand the description of regulation and types of regulations;
- differentiate between regulation and supervision;
- know the regulatory bodies; and
- appreciate the tools for enforcing compliance to regulations.

Description of Regulation

There is no way a definition of "regulation" can be fully understood without knowing the objective of regulation. This implies the notion of having an end in mind when explaining what regulation is all about. The payment system regulatory environment can be divided into four regulatory areas and the objective of regulation therefore is to reduce or mitigate payment system risks as much as possible without stifling market development and innovation (Cooper, Hougaard, Perez, Loots, Peter, Ferreira & Dunn, 2018). These regulatory areas, that include prudential oversight, market development, consumer protection and anti-money laundering (AML) / combatting the financing of terrorism (CFT), are outlined and described in the following table:

Table 18.1
Payment system regulatory areas

Regulatory Area	Description
Prudential oversight	Prudential requirements need to be proportional to the level of systemic risk associated with the respective firms and the type of services they are providing.
Market development	Regulation should create a competitive space for payment service providers to operate.
Consumer protection	Regulation should require payment service providers to make every effort to ensure that consumers understand products in the market, procedures for logging complaints, complaints handling, risk apportionment and the extent to which personal data can be used.
AML / CFT	AML / CFT legislative framework needs to detail the extent to which financial service providers ought to understand the identity of their customers to help detect and monitor potential financial crimes and this is known as consumer due diligence (CDD).

Source: Cooper, Hougaard, Perez, Loots, Peter, Ferreira and Dunn (2018)

Consequently, regulation refers to putting in place legal and regulatory framework with the aim of reducing or mitigating payment system risks while at the same time not stifling market development and innovation. Market development and innovation have a positive impact on economic growth and development.

The above needs to be elaborated upon. Regulation can be used as a verb or as a noun. As a verb, it refers to the process of actually putting in place an instrument of regulation. As a noun, it implies the secondary instrument, of a law, that has been put in place. This chapter covers both uses of the term "regulation".

Types of Regulations

Regulations can take various forms. These instruments are secondary or subordinate instruments that are formulated or written under a principal piece of legislation or law. There are several reasons why regulations are drawn up and some of these are: to expand on a clause in a legislation; to provide for gaps in a law; to make a law more enforceable or operational; and to bring clarity to payment system matters. Common types of regulations related to payment, clearing and settlement systems are outline below.

- Directives. These are meant to encourage or discourage a practice; once an objective has been achieved, the directive in question can be withdrawn or is no longer valid. A practice that has a positive impact in the market is encouraged while one with a negative effect is discouraged. For example, a directive can be issued to require local transactions being processed by international card schemes to be processed locally.
- Determinations. While directives might be short lived, a determination can last for a long time – as long as there is a need for it in the market. It provides for requirements that need to be met in a given regulatory area going forward into infinity. As an example, a determination can be issued on how data needs to be shared by payment service providers, and associated sanctions that are involved if the requirement is not followed.
- Position papers. A position paper is a product of research on a particular topic of relevance to the regulators or regulated institutions.

It can serve as a basis for a regulation to be issued in future or can be used to highlight an aspect within an existing regulation.

- Other types of regulations. Other types of regulatory instruments that are worth mentioning include guidelines, circulars, standards, specifications, orders, guidance notes or formal communiques. These are meant to clarify certain aspects of regulations or seek the attention of regulated entities on a given subject matter.

Regulation and Supervision

The terms regulation and supervision mean different things to different people including analysts. While the two might be different, sometimes they are used interchangeably. This should not be surprising because the objective of the two is to ensure stability of any system that is being taken care of or looked after. Consequently, the objective of regulation and supervision in payment systems is to ensure stability in the payment and settlement systems so that the flow of transactions between surplus and deficit units is not hindered at all. Surplus units in this case are debtors and deficit units are the creditors.

Regulation can be a process or the end of that process. The goal of a regulatory process is to come up with a regulation or sub-ordinate legislation that is used to bring in controls for a particular sector to function the way it is supposed to function. The implication therefore is that the word regulation has a double meaning. It can refer to a sub-ordinate regulatory instrument that is aimed at inducing certain changes that are desirable for the benefit of the society as a whole. Suppose users of a mobile services operator complain now and again of calls being dropped during a transaction process. This can warrant a regulation being issued to address the issue at hand. The mobile services operator in this case is expected to put in place required system changes to ensure that the matter is addressed once and for all. Regulation can also be viewed as that process that is followed to put in place a regulatory instrument for the benefit of all stakeholders.

Supervision takes the regulatory process further. It is the application of a regulatory instrument to make sure that all the required changes as outlined in the regulatory instrument are implemented. Monitoring of compliance to a certain regulation that has been put in place is a supervisory process and not a regulatory process. Regulation therefore stops when a regulation has been issued, while supervision kicks in by using a published regulation to demand observance of a regulatory instrument. There is no need to be too strict as these terms are sometimes used interchangeably.

The principal regulator or supervisor of payment, clearing and settlement systems in Namibia is Bank of Namibia. It has issued a number of key regulations over the years, including determinations and directives. These regulations that were issued over the years were used and are being used to bring about desired changes in the systems with the view to achieving safety, efficiency and effectiveness going forward.

Any regulatory and supervisory process ought to start with a need, problem or opportunity that needs to be addressed or attended to. Traditionally this should be discussed with relevant stakeholders that are involved. As shown in the following figure, research of a relevant issue at hand kicks off at a desk study level and where possible thereafter stakeholders are interviewed or approached to provide additional details that could not be obtained at the desk study level.

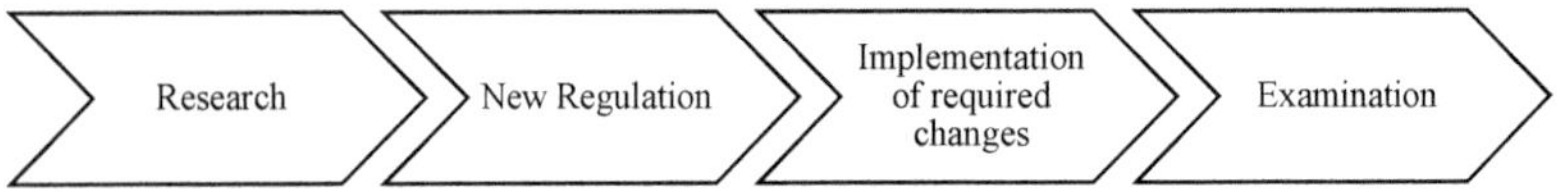

Figure 18.1. Regulatory and Supervisory Process

The process to start developing a new regulation using research output as a springboard commences. Consultations are critical prior to issuing a new regulation to make sure that the final regulation is understandable to impacted stakeholders and institutions. Once a new regulation has been issued or gazetted, what follows is the monitoring of the implementation of the regulatory instrument. This stage of the process is what is sometimes called examination or oversight.

Examination or oversight can be broken down into two important parts. There is off-site analysis and on-site examination. Off-site analysis is done at premises of the regulator with its aim being to browse through reports and conduct detailed analysis to uncover the level of compliance. Questions that arise during off-site analysis are used when carrying out on-site inspection, which is done by a regulatory authority at the premises of regulatory institutions. Visits at the premises of regulated entities can be scheduled or impromptu. Failure by any institution to accord a regulator the opportunity to inspect affairs of a regulated entity can result in a fine being issued.

Costs and Benefits of Regulation

What are the benefits and costs that are associated with regulations? Do you still remember what we stated above? Imagine a market with regulations that have been put in place and another market where there are no regulations at all for a certain portion of the market. Suppose users of a mobile services operator complain now and again of calls being dropped during a transaction process.

Some regulations are useful especially if they are well thought through. A regulation that compels a mobile services operator to make necessary changes to limit calls being dropped during a transaction process is a good regulation because it aims to reduce complaints, encourages quick check-out at the point-of-sale, and leads to an increase in sales, productivity and eventually economic growth. It is clear in this case that the society benefits as a whole.

Does a mobile services operator feel the same way? There can be a level of discomfort on the side of a service operator on this. Investment outlay is involved and it can be expensive to implement such a change especially in the shortest time possible. Besides, implementing such a change can lead to service disruption and this is not a good situation for any operator to be in.

What is the net effect in view of the discomfort that might be there for such a change to be implemented? The net effect is that the whole society benefits. There is minimal reputational damage on the side of the service operator. Users of financial services are delighted to be associated with stable service from the mobile services operator. Merchants on their side experience smooth check-out and an increase in sales. The above also imply general productivity and higher economic growth in society fuelled by the adoption of electronic payments and improved aggregate demand in general.

How can the cost of regulation be minimised then? Firstly, there is a need to ensure that there is adequate consultation in the process of issuing a regulation. Consultation assists in reducing ambiguity and rework. Second, a piece of regulation needs to be clear on a specific change that is required to support compliance. Enough time needs to be given to implement that change. Is there such a thing as adequate time? This is debatable, but with the right consultation approach all issues at hand can be addressed to the satisfaction of all stakeholders that are involved.

Regulated Entities and Inherent Risks

There are multiple regulated entities that are involved in any sector of an economy. In the payments, clearing and settlement sub-sector for example regulated entities include banks and non-bank financial institutions. These entities are at different levels in terms of their economic activities. Some of these are new entrants while others have accumulated a vast amount of experience in their areas of operation.

The approach to regulation and supervision of all entities that are authorised to operate in a given sector or sub-sector should therefore be similar, subject to certain nuances that need to be accommodated, given the fact that entities are at different levels of development. However, certain things are true. Each entity, whether small or big, has the ability to introduce risks into payments, clearing and settlement systems. Besides, each entity has the opportunity to grow from being an indirect participant to being a direct participant. It is also the fact that each entity expects a certain level of expertise and competence from others in carrying out certain aspects related to these systems. It is therefore important that the playing field be levelled so that inherent risks are properly addressed to the betterment of all stakeholders that are involved.

Regulatory Bodies in Namibia

This saying is true: On the one hand, if you want to go far in life, do what you need to do alone; on the other hand, if you want to go a step further than that, do it with others. The foregoing is factual because life in itself places a limit on the kinds of things we do, but if we seek for a helping hand, the chance increases for breaking that limit placed on us.

The field of payment, clearing and settlement systems requires co-operation with others in order to cover all applicable areas that fall within a sphere of influence and this is done through instruments such as a memorandum of understanding or agreement. This sphere of influence includes areas over which a regulatory authority has both direct and indirect control. Each regulator therefore can only regulate a certain area or sector based on enabling legislation. Co-operating with other regulatory bodies becomes critical, especially when there is a need by a specific regulator to cover a certain area it has an interest in but which falls within a jurisdiction of a fellow regulator, while at the same time affecting its own territory.

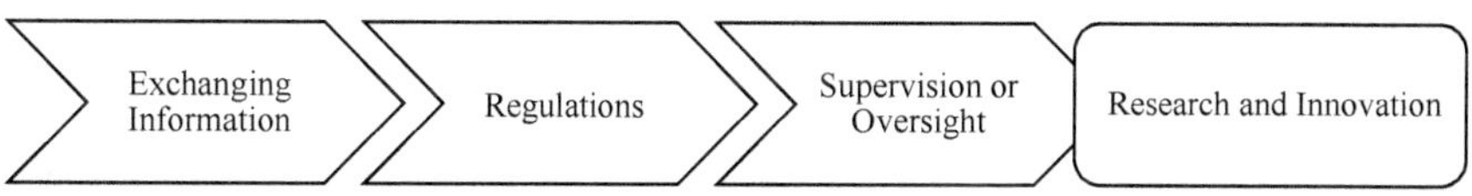

Figure 18.2. Regulatory and Supervisory Process

There are a number of areas fellow regulators and supervisors can co-operate in with the view to making sure that all aspects are covered as per the above-mentioned chart. These include exchanging of information, crafting of regulatory instruments, supervision or oversight, and research and innovation. Consider the case of multi-national companies that operate in various jurisdictions. These entities face different regulations and it becomes important for regulators to co-operate by sharing information and limiting the regulatory burden.

What springs to mind when it comes to defining communication in general? It is the exchange of messages between the sender and the receiver via a communication medium or technology. Messages need to be kept original, through encryption and other interventions, so that the receiver receives a message as expected. Communication is like a two-way street in that it should be bi-directional with a response expected after a message has been delivered. Consequently, there is a need for a regulatory authority in the area of communication to protect the needs of all stakeholders.

Communications Regulatory Authority of Namibia (CRAN) was established on 18 May 2011 in terms of the Communications Act, 2009 (Act No. 8 of 2009) to regulate telecommunication, broadcasting and postal sectors. Entities such as MTC Namibia, Telecom Namibia Limited, Namibian Broadcasting Corporation (NBC) and NamPost are some of the organisations that are regulated by CRAN.

Bank of Namibia is the principal regulator of the national payment system supported by the Payment Association of Namibia. Participants in the national payment system include both banks and non-bank financial institutions. Consequently, the *Namibia Financial Institutions Supervisory Authority (NAMFISA)* authorises certain non-bank financial institutions to conduct business in Namibia and some of the entities are active participants in the national payment system through established industry structures.

NAMFISA was established in terms of the Namibia Financial Institutions Supervisory Authority Act, 2001 (Act No.3 of 2001) to supervise the business of financial institutions and financial services. Some of the entities supervised by the non-bank regulator include insurance companies, pension funds, medical aid funds, friendly societies and capital markets.

Competition, price, quantity supply and quantity demand are key discussion points in our daily lives from a microeconomics standpoint. It all starts by authorities encouraging the spirit of competition, leading to downstream impact. An increase in the number of suppliers of goods and services through an intervention in a specific sector leads to an increase in the supply of a product or service in question, resulting in a fall in the price, making a service or product affordable to the end users.

Namibian Competition Commission (NaCC) was established on 9 December 2009 in terms of the Competition Act, 2003 (Act No. 2 of 2003) to promote and safeguard fair competition across sectors in Namibia. This implies that all sectors and business entities in Namibia have to observe the competition law. Anti-competitive practices in the payments sector are not allowed.

Co-operation extends to the central banking fraternity as well. *Central banks* co-operate through various regional and international arrangements, committees and associations. In Africa there is the Association of African Central Bank Governors (AACB), and the Committee of Central Bank Governors (CCBG) at African and Southern Africa Development Committee (SADC) levels respectively. Governors also meet at the level of the Common Monetary Area (CMA). Internationally, the Bank for International Settlement, through its structures, normally issues international principles in various sectors or areas that member countries can domesticate in their own environments.

Consequently, central banks do co-operate to make sure that cross border issues are addressed and to learn from each other on how to best regulate and supervise such activities. Sound co-operation in supervision leads to efficient markets and elimination of cross-border risks and is a springboard for investor confidence.

BOX 17

The Bank of Tanzania is the central bank of the United Republic of Tanzania and was established in terms of the Bank of Tanzania Act of 1965. One of the functions of the apex bank is the regulation, monitoring and supervision of payment, clearing and settlement systems.

Consumer protection is one of the regulatory areas of the Bank of Tanzania. Section 47 (1) of its National Payment Systems Act, 2015 (Act No. 4 of 2015) states that a payment system provider shall protect the privacy of a participant and customer information; and not disclose information of a participant or customer unless the disclosure is made in compliance with the law of a court or with the express consent of the system participant or customer concerned (The United Republic of Tanzania, 2015).

Chapter Summary

This chapter discussed regulation of payments, clearing and settlement systems. The chapter covered a number of key sections that include regulation and supervision, the regulatory and supervisory process, and benefits and costs of regulations. An attempt was made to differentiate between regulation and supervision. It was noted that regulation stops when a regulation has been issued while supervision kicks in by using a published regulation to demand observance of a regulatory instrument. The chapter indicated that the net effect of regulation is that the whole society benefits if a regulation has been well thought through.

Review Questions

1. Illustrate in the form of a diagram the regulatory and supervisory process that you have learned.
2. Define the following terms related to regulation of payment, clearing and settlement systems:
    a. Regulation
    b. Supervision
    c. Off-site analysis
    d. On-site examination
3. Outline and write short notes on regulatory bodies related to payment, clearing and settlement systems.

Selected References

Cooper, B., Hougaard, C., Perez, L.M., Loots, C., Peter, R.T., Ferreira, M., & Dunn, M. (2018). *Payment system in Sub-Saharan Africa – Note 1 – themes and imperatives for national and regional payment systems that enable remittances.* Bellville, South Africa: Cenfri. Retrieved from https://cenfri.org/

Government of the United Republic of Tanzania, (2015). *The National Payment System Act.* Dar es Salaam, The United Republic of Tanzania: Government of the United Republic of Tanzania. Retrieved from https://www.bot.go.tz/

CHAPTER 19

Self-Regulation

Self-regulation is an important concept in payment, clearing and settlement systems. It reminds one of the old saying: attempt to do your best even if no one is watching. We can apply this to payment, clearing and settlement systems, where the one who is watched can be referred to as a participant and the one who is or could be watching is a regulator. Is it better to do something all the time without necessarily being told when to do it or is it better to wait and be told to do something? It is good to ponder this question as you go on reading this chapter.

Learning Objectives

By the end of this chapter, you should be able to

- know what self-regulation is all about;
- understand how self-regulation is organised in Namibia; and
- take note of challenges that are associated with self-regulation.

Description of Self-Regulation

Let us use an illustration of a traffic light to make the concept of self-regulation clear. Traffic light signals consist of three primary colours: red for stop, yellow for wait and green for go. They are unassisted although controlled remotely by a computer system. Traffic lights are normally found at busy intersections or T-junctions in urban centres. It would not be practical to install traffic lights in a rural setting or at points where there is limited traffic.

What if traffic lights malfunction? The result is a normal three-way or four-way stop. In a situation like this, drivers are expected to control themselves, giving each other the right of way. This is sometimes not possible though, especially during rush hour when parents, guardians and service providers need to go to work or drop kids to school. Traffic officers are then required to be present to handle the movement of cars smoothly.

The above illustration implies that drivers can control themselves by giving each other right of way in normal situations. In other situations when the system does not work as expected, traffic officers need to be at the scene to make sure that motor vehicles proceed unhindered. The first situation, when a system works as expected, means there is self-regulation, while if there is a disruption such that drivers cannot give themselves the right of way or there is a need to smooth traffic flow, it follows that control is required in the form of a traffic officer being present at the scene.

Self-regulation in payment, clearing and settlement system happens along the lines as described above. In this set-up, participants are expected to regulate and monitor their affairs according to the expectations of a primary regulatory authority. It starts with the creation of an association not for gain which fulfils the regulatory and supervisory part on behalf of a primary or principal authority. Such an association is owned by the members and recognised by a principal authority – in most cases a central bank. Members, who are the participants, need to make sure that there is an appropriate and well-resourced organisational structure to perform secretarial functions on behalf of a board or group of boards and committees.

Finance for the operational affairs of the secretariat comes from contributions made by members or participants as well as the central authority. Outside sourcing of funds from say philanthropists is also possible. Philanthropists are committed, wealthy individuals and entities with surplus financial means to contribute to causes that can uplift the living standard of a community through initiatives or projects requiring funding.

The assumptions around self-regulation are many. Some of these include the fact that the central authority can be relieved of certain activities, but the ultimate responsibility, in terms of ensuring that the market remains intact, still rests with it. There is a widely held belief that a particular market is awash with skills, knowledge and know-how and if entities or participants are put to work together through forums, committees and boards such skills, knowledge and know-how can be put to good use. Another assumption is that national interests are put first on the list ahead of interests of the respective institutions. This stems from the fact that decisions that are made through forums, committees and boards are reflective of a need to come up with initiatives of national importance and not those that are aimed at promoting the interest of members or participants.

What a self-regulatory body and its members need to do is to report to the central authority over time, as per agreed reporting frequency, informed by mutual agreement that is in black and white, so that expectations from each side are clear. The secretariat mandated by its board needs to highlight achievements, ongoing matters and aspects where attention may be required. Reporting needs to focus on strategic matters as enshrined in a strategic plan or vision as well as operational matters.

Things do not always work according to plan. You might have heard of the concept of market failure. It follows that laissez-faire and moral suasion principles sometimes do not work. The result of these principles not working as expected is a need for direct regulation and supervision. There is no absolute self-control just as there is no true free market economic system. Some form of control from authorities will always be required proportionate to the situation on the ground. Market failure should not be viewed as negative, to say the market has completely failed, but rather to reason that guidance from the central authority is sometimes required with the view to directing a particular market accordingly.

Practices in Namibia

The system of managing and overseeing the national payment system in Namibia is called self-regulation. This involves the Bank of Namibia being the principal regulator and the Payment Association of Namibia (PAN), a payment system management body, as a self-regulatory authority or delegated regulator in line with the payment system management act, 2023 (Act No. 14 of 2023). Some of the responsibilities of PAN include assisting the central bank in managing the national system, creating forums so that participants can discuss issues of mutual concern in a co-operative space, and putting in place standards that can be used to effect required changes or that are necessary to manage the participation of members in the national payment system (Government of the Republic of Namibia, 2023). There is a defined working relationship between the payment system management body and the central bank via instruments such as the legislation, memorandum of agreement, and oversight policy. It is the duty of PAN to report to Bank of Namibia periodically on aspects related to operational affairs and strategic matters such as those that are covered in the Namibia National Payment System Vision and Strategy document. This document expires in 2025 and it is expected that another one will be crafted by the industry, covering the next five years.

PAN has an organisational structure that enables it to carry out its day-to-day responsibilities. At the apex of the structure is the PAN management council (PMC), which is the highest decision-making organ, and it is supported by the chief executive officer who in turn is supported by a group of senior managers and operational staff. The new payment system management act allows for changes to be made on the governance structure of PAN. On a day-to-day basis, PAN discharges its responsibilities through forums, committees and working groups across relevant streams. Streams in this case include card, electronic funds transfer and immediate settlement. While the first two streams handle low-value payments, the third covers high-value transactions. Governance documents such as constitutions or terms of reference and agreements assist in the smooth running of the respective forums, committees and working groups. All the forums, committees and working groups need to provide periodic reports to PAN on their activities. Participants, system operators, service providers, Bank of Namibia and PAN are represented in these structures.

How are the activities of PAN funded? Funding comes chiefly from members. It all starts with a budget. A budget is a financial plan that lists expected income and expenditure. The bottom line can be a deficit or surplus. Surplus or balanced budget is good, but with a deficit there is a need to look for additional resources to fund the shortfall. This funding can be done through various ways, including external sources or drawing on savings or investments.

Once the budget has been drawn up it goes through an approval process within the payment system management body and consequently requesting members to settle their respective obligations. It is a regulatory obligation to settle the amount due as failure to do so results in a member not being in good standing. This is not a situation an entity needs to be in as that has various implications. Any member of the association has the opportunity to participate in industry forums, committees and working groups. Participation in industry structures enables all entities to shape the modernisation of the national payment system so that it is comparable to payment industries in other parts of the world. Consequently, there is every reason for any member of the association to be in good standing in order to continue enjoying the benefits associated with being a participant at industry level.

There is no doubt that PAN has performed well in terms of discharging its responsibilities since establishment in 2006. Performance indicators that can be used include but are not limited to the creation of relevant forums, collaboration at industry level, putting in place an organisational structure that responds to current needs, reporting on industry affairs, commitment to implement the vision and strategy document, and managing industry projects. One expects the industry to pull all resources together to ensure full implementation of the said vision and strategy blueprint. The following box article provides information about the Payment Association of South Africa (PASA):

BOX 18

PASA was established in 1999 and is recognised as a payment system management body by the South African Reserve Bank. PASA exists to manage payment systems in the interest of economic and social development of South Africa; it aspires to be acknowledged as world-class in assisting in the evolution and oversight of the payments industry; and its mission is to manage and develop the national payment system and facilitate integration with international payment standards (Payment Association of South Africa, 2022).

PASA has a constitution that governs its business and is headed by a chief executive officer (CEO) who is accountable to PASA council. The CEO is assisted by executive committee members to run the day-to-day activities of the institution. There are a number of structures that assist PASA in carrying out its mandate. These include payment clearing house participant groups; strategy, legal and risk committees; stakeholder forums; and project steering committees.

Challenges of Self-Regulation

There are challenges that are related to self-regulation in general and these should not be associated with any entity. These challenges viewed at an aggregate level include but are not limited to funding, relevance, conflict of interest, and capacity. Each challenge is discussed separately by looking at a problem statement and possible solution for each challenge. Special reference is made to the payment, clearing and settlement systems environment when discussing each challenge.

The first challenge relates to funding that is required to defray operational, capital and other expenses. Limited funding can force an entity to focus on operational activities and neglect investing in long term assets, key to its survival down the line. Funding in general is hard to come by in view of global challenges that are affecting many nations at present. It is important therefore to prioritise diversifying revenue sources to complement traditional ones. With a good proposal on what additional funding is for and outlining core initiatives that need to be done, the likelihood is there that financial services providers, donors and philanthropists are able to provide the requisite resources.

Are associations relevant? The simple answer to this question is yes. These are entities that are delegated by their principals to do certain activities on their behalf so that the one that delegates can focus more on strategic issues. Payment associations have proved to be useful in Africa and on other continents as they tend to bring industry stakeholders together to share skills, knowledge and experience with the view to take modernisation forward. There is value in collaboration to make sure that all initiatives that ought to be done are actually done within a defined period of time.

Conflict of interest is another issue that can affect associations, including payment associations. This is inherent as long as there are different entities that are involved. The issue is not if conflict of interest is likely, but rather what needs to be done to manage it when it is detected. Excusing oneself from a decision if conflicted, disclosure principles and a more independent board can assist in limiting chances of conflict of interest.

There is an issue around capacity whenever there is a general discussion on associations in general and payment associations in particular. Associations are expected to deliver in terms of output as per the mandate given to then. There is a risk of a mandate being taken away from associations if performance is not as expected. No one envisages that to happen as there are always structures in place to control performance to the desired level. Training and development as well as additional manpower are key interventions in addressing capacity challenges.

Chapter Summary

This chapter handled self-regulation in payment, clearing and settlement systems. The chapter shows that in self-regulation participants are expected to regulate and monitor their affairs to the expectation of a primary regulatory authority and it starts with the creation of an association not for gain, which fulfils the regulatory and supervisory part on behalf of a primary or principal authority. Despite varied challenges, payment associations can contribute to the betterment of a national payment system by bringing stakeholders with key skills, knowledge and experience together to address issues of mutual concern.

Review Questions

1. Write short notes on how the Payment Association of Namibia is organised including highlighting the relationship with Bank of Namibia.
2. Explain the following terms that are associated with self-regulation:
   a. Self-regulation
   b. Payment Association of South Africa
   c. PAN management council
3. Discuss challenges that payment associations face today.

Selected References

Government of the Republic of Namibia, (2023). *Payment System Management Act*. Windhoek, Namibia: Government of the Republic of Namibia. Retrieved from https://www.bon.com.na/

Payment Association of South Africa, (2022). *PASA Integrated Report 2022*. Johannesburg, South Africa: Government of the Republic of Namibia. Retrieved from https://www.bon.com.na/

CHAPTER 20

Regional Payments

What comes to mind when a discussion on regional payments comes into the picture? The word region can have a double meaning. It can mean a section within a country, consisting of villages, settlements, towns and cities. For example, Namibia has 14 regions. These regions can be referred to as provinces in South Africa and states in the United States of America. That same word can refer to a group of countries that have formed an alliance or an economic bloc. There is the Economic Community of West African States (ECOWAS) in West Africa, consisting of fifteen-member countries. This chapter moves the focus from domestic payments to regional payments, focusing on payments made between countries within a given bloc or region of countries.

Learning Objectives

By the end of this chapter, you should be able to

- reflect on regional economic communities;
- understand regional payments and regional systems; and
- outline regulatory and governance bodies and challenges in implementing regional systems.

Regional Economic Communities

Integration either at a regional or continental level is key for driving economic prosperity and other aspirations. Economic integration takes many forms including free trade area, customs union, common market, monetary union and, ultimately, political union. Free trade area relates to free movement of goods and services between countries; customs union is similar to free trade area, but includes common external tariffs; common market includes free movement of labour; monetary union is about the use of one common currency with another variation to this being other currencies pegged to one currency; and political union refers to the adoption of one system of governance for all member states. The following table shows the Africa Union and various regional economic communities.

Table 20.1
African Union and Regional Economic Communities

Community	Year Established	Members
African Union	1976	All 55-member states: Central Africa, Eastern Africa, Northern Africa, Southern Africa and Western Africa.
Arab Maghreb Union (UMA)	1989	Algeria, Libya, Mauritania, Morocco and Tunisia.
Common Market for Eastern and Southern Africa (COMESA)	1993	Burundi, Comoros, Democratic Republic of Congo, Djibouti, Egypt, Eritrea, Eswatini, Ethiopia, Kenya, Libya, Madagascar, Malawi, Mauritius, Rwanda, Seychelles, Somalia, Sudan, Tunisia, Uganda, Zambia and Zimbabwe.

Common Monetary Area (CMA)	1986	Eswatini, Lesotho, Namibia and South Africa.
Community of Sahel – Saharan States (CEN-SAD)	1998	Benin, Burkina Faso, Cabo Verde, Central African Republic, Chad, Comoros, Cote D'Ivoire, Djibouti, Egypt, Eritrea, Gambia, Ghana, Guinea, Guinea Bissau, Kenya, Liberia, Libya, Mali, Mauritania, Morocco, Niger, Nigeria, Sao Tome and Principe, Senegal, Sierra Leone, Somalia, Togo and Tunisia.
East African Community (EAC)	1999	Democratic Republic of Congo, Burundi, Kenya, Rwanda, South Sudan, Uganda and United Republic of Tanzania.
Economic Community of Central African States (ECCAS)	1983	Angola, Burundi, Cameroon, Central African Republic, Chad, Congo, Democratic Republic of Congo, Equatorial Guinea, Gabon, Sao Tome and Principe.
Economic Community of West African States (ECOWAS)	1975	Benin, Burkina Faso, Cabo Verde, Cote D'Ivoire, The Gambia, Ghana, Guinea, Guinea Bissau, Liberia, Mali, Niger, Nigeria, Senegal, Sierra Leone and Togo.
Intercontinental Authority on Development (IGAD) 2	1996	Djibouti, Eritrea, Ethiopia, Kenya, Somalia, South Sudan, Sudan and Uganda.
Southern African Customers Union (SACU)	1910	Botswana, Eswatini, Lesotho, Namibia and South Africa.

Southern African Development Community (SADC)	1992	Angola, Botswana, Comoros, Democratic Republic of Congo, Eswatini, Lesotho, Madagascar, Malawi, Mauritius, Mozambique, Namibia, Seychelles, South Africa, United Republic of Tanzania, Zambia and Zimbabwe.
West African Economic and Monetary Union (WAEMU)	1994	Benin, Burkina Faso, Cote D'Ivoire, Mali, Niger, Senegal, Togo and Guinea Bissau.
West Africa Monetary Zone (WAMZ)	2000	Gambia, Ghana, Guinea, Liberia, Nigeria and Sierra Leone.

There are eight regional economic communities that are recognised by the African Union and these are Arab Maghreb Union (UMA), Common Market for Eastern and Southern Africa (COMESA), Community of Sahel – Saharan States (CEN-SAD), East African Community (EAC), Economic Community of Central African States (ECCAS), Economic Community of West African States (ECOWAS), Intercontinental Authority on Development (IGAD) 2, and Southern African Development Community (SADC). ECOWAS includes two sub-regional blocs: West African Economic and Monetary Union (WAEMU) for French-speaking West Africa, and West Africa Monetary Zone (WAMZ) for English-speaking West Africa.

The central message around regional or continental integration efforts is the promotion of movement of goods and services. This needs to be complemented by payment or market infrastructures to support the movement of money so that obligations of different actors or players can be smoothly concluded.

Description of Regional Payments

Several terms can be associated with regional payments. Some have referred to these payments as cross-border payments while others say common monetary area (CMA) payments or international payments. Regional payments or common monetary area payments all refer to payments within a particular regional bloc. As an example, CMA payments are payments that are done and concluded within the four countries belonging to the regional community. Cross-border and international payments are payments that are processed and concluded not only within a given regional bloc but beyond as well. It is a matter of semantics and the above terms can be used interchangeably.

Regional transactions therefore are transactions that are processed, cleared and settled between two countries within a particular regional economic community. This implies that the paying and the beneficiary customers are located in different countries. The payments are made possible through regional systems, correspondent banking and card schemes.

Regional Systems

Regional systems can take many forms that include clearing and settlement systems at a regional level. They support the movement of goods and services. It is easy to have a view of the value and volume of transactions that flow through such systems compared to a situation where such systems did not exist. Besides, regional systems are implemented in order to ensure compliance to treaties and agreements that are in place.

The multilateral monetary agreement signed by the CMA countries indicates, in article 7, that the CMA may participate in the integrated cross-border payment system infrastructure to effect cross-border payments (Central Bank of Eswatini, 1992). In addition to this, state parties in the Southern African Development Community (SADC) shall ensure co-operation amongst their respective central banks in relation to payments, clearing and settlement systems (Southern African Development Community, 2006).

Payments, clearing and settlement systems therefore need to be in place as a result of agreements, treaties and protocols that have been put in place. A multilateral monetary agreement was signed by the CMA countries while the SADC protocol on finance and investment was put in place for the SADC region.

There are several regional systems one finds in the regional economic communities. Regional economic communities in this case are SADC and CMA. This implies that the clearing and settlement systems to be outlined are those that have been implemented in these two regions. The focus is not on payment methods or instruments that are used to initiate transactions via respective channels, but rather the discussion is at the level of clearing and settlement arrangements that have been put in place. These systems to be considered are the SADC real time gross settlement system (SADC RTGS) and low-value systems that are operated by the regional clearing and settlement operator (RCSO).

SADC RTGS was implemented in 2013 to facilitate the settlement of high-value payments in the SADC region, which is inclusive of CMA. The implementation was preceded by elimination of cross-border cheques at a regional or cross-border level. High-value payments are transactions that are above a certain threshold in a given country and for Namibia this is NAD5 million. Single low-value transactions can also be directly settled via this settlement system and such an arrangement is for an interim period when it is put in place. SADC RTGS is owned and operated by the South Africa Reserve Bank (SARB) on behalf of other central banks in the SADC region. Transactions are currently settled in the South African Rand (ZAR) and other currencies can be introduced as per determination by regional regulators.

There is no way a discussion around *low-value, cross-border payment clearing systems* in the SADC or CMA regional economic communities comes up without mentioning the regional clearing and settlement operator (RCSO). Low-value payments are transactions that are below a certain threshold in a given country and for Namibia this is for transactions below NAD5 million. These transactions are collected, grouped or batched in a settlement file by the RCSO for settlement in SADC RTGS.

The RCSO in this case is called BankservAfrica, which is located in Johannesburg, South Africa. It can be traced to 1972 and presently clears retail transactions not only for its home market, South Africa, but also for CMA and SADC. Participants can integrate or connect to BankservAfrica in three ways: directly, via a domestic clearing and settlement operator, or through a payment hub, which is a way non-bank financial institutions can integrate or connect to BankservAfrica.

BankservAfrica has put in place clearing solutions for low-value, cross-border payments for the regional communities with the view to meet regulatory requirements and expectations. The difference between interim and long-term solutions needs to be understood. An interim solution is a solution for low-value, cross-border credit and debit payments that has been put in place to sponsor transactions from other CMA countries into the South African national payment system while a compliant and dedicated arrangement for the region was being put in place. This implies migration from an interim to a long-term clearing arrangement for the region. Transactions cleared on an immediate basis (TCIB) is one of the solutions, services, systems or rails for low-value, cross-border payments. TCIB is available 24 hours a day, 7 days a week; it is available for all customer segments; all balance of payment codes can be used; and transactions can be cleared in ZAR and other currencies.

There are some high-value transactions that are not processed and settled directly via the SADC RTGS, but rather through *correspondent banking*. This is an arrangement where the paying and beneficiary banks conclude transactions between themselves outside the SADC RTGS system through a vostro and nostro account relationship. Vostro account is a facility that bank A in country A holds for bank B in country B. Similarly, nostro account is a facility that bank B in country B holds for bank A in country A. Kenton (2023) notes that correspondent banking is applicable when sending and receiving banks do not have agreements in place for wire transfers and when it is not feasible for a domestic bank to open branches in another location or country.

Regulatory and Governance Bodies

There are regulatory and governance bodies that are crucial for driving integration efforts in the SADC and CMA regional economic communities. Some of these bodies fulfil a regulatory and supervisory role, while others assist regulators in carrying out their responsibilities. These regulatory and governance bodies include Committee of Central Bank Governors Sub-Committees, SADC Banking Association, SADC Payment Oversight Committee, CMA Cross Border Payments Oversight Committee, and SADC Payment Scheme Management Body.

Committee of Central Bank Governors in SADC (CCBG) was established in 1995 to bring about close co-operation among central banks in the region. It works through four sub-committees, which include the Banking Supervision Sub-Committee, Exchange Control Sub-Committee, Financial Markets Sub-Committee, and Payments Sub-Committee. These are specialised committees with a mandate to achieve certain milestones in their areas of specialisation. The payments Sub-Committee is critical for the realisation of integrated clearing and settlement systems in SADC. The Exchange Control Sub-Committee is critical in the harmonisation of BOP codes across the SADC region. BOP and codes are briefly described in the box article below.

BOX 19

Balance of payments (BOP) is a key focus area in macroeconomics. The field of macroeconomics deals with the study of key macroeconomic variables such as inflation, unemployment, economic growth, money supply, exchange rates and balance of payments. BOP is a record of a country's transactions with the rest of the world. This implies that each country maintains this record, traditionally with the regulatory authority or a central bank, to indicate the size of transactions with other countries covering such things as balance of trade, current account and capital account. The trade account contains transactions associated with physical goods while the current account includes the trade account and trade in services. The capital account records long-term capital movement such as long-term investment in factories in the host country.

Cross-border, regional or international payments need to be reported to regulators by participating banking or financial institutions to enable dissemination of information in statutory publications. This is where the BOP codes, description or reason for payment becomes important. BOP categories are normally specified for inward and outward payments covering such things as BOP category, code and description. As an example, a transaction with code 40100 has a description called gifts, falling under the BOP category of transfers of a current nature or current payments (First National Bank, 2019).

SADC Banking Association (SADC BA) was established in 1998 to co-ordinate projects and activities, where banks are involved, in the region. One of the important projects carried out is the SADC payments project covering clearing and settlement components. Banking associations in the region are represented on the board of SADC BA. The entity provides training activities aimed at boosting human resources capacity across member banking institutions.

SADC Payment System Oversight Committee (SADC PSOC) was established in 2013 to regulate and oversee the cross-border payment, clearing and settlement systems, activities and institutions. Since the SADC RTGS is owned by SADC, central banks in the respective member countries have an interest and responsibility to promote the safety and efficiency of the SADC RTGS system, including any payment matters pertaining to the region (SADC Payment System Oversight Committee, 2019).

CMA Cross-border Payment Oversight Committee (CMA CPOC) looks at regulatory and oversight affairs relating to cross-border payment, clearing and settlement systems, activities and institutions in the CMA region as opposed to SADC PSOC that focusses on the SADC region. Heads of national payment system departments of the central banks in the CMA region form part of CMA CPOC, while heads of national payment system departments of the central banks in the SADC region form part of SADC PSOC.

SADC Payment Scheme Management Body (SADC PSMB) is a structure within SADC BA and assists SADC PSOC in carrying out its regulatory and oversight activities. SADC PSMB registers or appoints payment service providers or system operators after endorsement by SADC PSOC. As an example, BankservAfrica was initially appointed by SADC PSMB after endorsement by SADC PSOC as the regional clearing and settlement operator for the SADC region.

Challenges in Implementing Regional Systems

Implementation of regional systems is not without challenges. Regional systems take many forms that include clearing and settlement systems to support the movement of goods and services at a regional level. These challenges include but are not limited to the following:

- Governance structures and administrative support. Institutions that provide regulatory and oversight responsibilities are important. There should be resources dedicated to rendering day to day operational support in order for regional governance structures to function effectively. The use of fulltime employees of regulators and regulated institutions creates challenges in attending to regional matters as these resources need to be accountable to their respective employers as well.
- Settlement currency to use. It is likely that one settlement currency can be adopted for the go-live of a settlement infrastructure. There might be a need to add other eligible currencies at some point once the system has matured. Adoption of multiple currencies encourages the use of a system while at the same time minimising exchange rate risk.
- Legal and regulatory framework. Putting a legal and regulatory framework at a regional level is a challenging activity. A legal and regulatory framework outlines a number of areas including but not limited to governance arrangements, how transactions need to be cleared and settled, the process of registering entities to be service providers or system operators, and harmonisation of practices and policies.
- Location of clearing and settlement systems. This is traditionally done at a policy level. A treaty, protocol or sub-ordinate legal or regulatory instrument can provide details on where these systems should be located, especially when it comes to settlement systems. An operator can decide on the location when it comes to a clearing system, at times subject to authorisation from a regulatory body.
- Multiple membership. Belonging to multiple regional economic committees cannot be avoided, but it can be a challenge. It can have an impact on resource allocation, stakeholder availability, stakeholder participation, and commitment to all regional blocs. Related issues can be avoided, minimised or managed with involvement from senior stakeholders in all activities related to regional blocs.

Chapter Summary

This chapter covered regional payments. Regional transactions are transactions that are processed, cleared and settled between two countries within a particular regional economic community. It is noted that regional systems take many forms that include clearing and settlement systems to support the movement of goods and services at a regional level. Regional economic communities, regulatory and governance bodies, as well as challenges in implementing regional systems, were also covered.

Review Questions

1. List and write short notes on regulatory and governance bodies in SADC and CMA regions.
2. Outline and describe the regional payment systems in SADC that you have learned.
3. Discuss challenges that are associated with implementing regional systems.

Selected References

Central Bank of Eswatini, (1992). *Multilateral Monetary Agreement between the Government of the Kingdom of Lesotho, the Government of the Republic of Namibia, the Government of the Republic of South Africa, and the Government of the Kingdom of Swaziland. Mbabane, Eswatini: Central Bank of Eswatini*. Retrieved from https://www.centralbank.or.sz/

First National Bank, (2019). *Global Transacting Balance of Payment – Category Codes*. Johannesburg, South Africa: First National Bank. Retrieved from https://www.mailers.fnbweb.co.za/

Kenton, (2023). *Correspondent Bank: Definition and How it Works*. New York, NY: Investopedia. Retrieved from https://www.investopedia.com/

SADC Payment System Oversight Committee, (2019). *SADC Payment System Oversight Committee Report August 2017 – March 2019.* Pretoria, South Africa: South African Reserve Bank. Retrieved from https://www.resbank.co.za/

Southern African Development Community, (2006). *SADC Protocol on Finance and Investment.* Gaborone, Botswana: Southern African Development Community. Retrieved from https://www.sadc.int/

CHAPTER 21

Continental Payments

There are seven continents of the world – Asia, Africa, Europe, North America, South America, Oceania and Antarctica – and some points can be made from this list. Asia is believed to be the largest continent followed by Africa, while Oceania is understood to be the smallest continent. Antarctica is not inhabited and Oceania is sometimes referred to as Australia. Each continent has regional economic communities, where this is possible. One finds countries in each regional economic community. Reference to continental payments in this chapter is to Africa.

Learning Objectives

By the end of this chapter, you should be able to

- understand what it means by continental payments;
- know aspirations around African Continental Free Trade Area and Agenda 1963; and
- be clear on developments in settlement and retail payment systems.

Basic Challenges of the African Continent

There are basic challenges about the African continent from a payment, clearing and settlement perspective that can be highlighted. These are: interoperability of payment systems, access to mobile connectivity or internet, and financial exclusion. The challenges are not insurmountable, but rather they can be addressed with time. Great efforts being made across the continent need to be complimented. Fixing such challenges will result in ensuring that these systems continue to work for all stakeholders thereby having a positive impact on economic growth as well as economic development.

Limited interoperability in payment, clearing and settlement systems is one of the challenges that is worth noting. This implies that there is inadequacy of interconnectedness of these systems resulting in payment instructions between regional economic communities not being sent and received effectively and efficiently. Consequently, the systems are like wallet or walled gardens whereby there is limited interoperability of systems to facilitate movement of goods and services across regional economic communities.

The following table shows real time gross settlement systems (RTGS) in selected regional economic communities:

Table 21.1
Selected Regional Economic Communities and Real Time Gross Settlement Systems

Community	Name	Notes
Common Market for Eastern and Southern Africa (COMESA)	COMESA Regional Payment and Settlement System (REPSS)	Operated by COMESA Clearing House, Central Bank of Mauritius acts as settlement bank for final settlement of net positions at end of day. Pre-funding is done through a central bank and settlement currencies are United States Dollar (USD) and Euro.
East African Community (EAC)	East African Payment System (EAPS)	Went live in 2013 and transactions are made through commercial banks in EAC regional currencies. EAPS integrates with real time gross settlement systems of member states. There is same-day settlement. East African Payment and Settlement Systems Integration Project is underway.
Economic Community of West African States (ECOWAS)	West African Monetary Zone (WAMZ) Real Time Gross Settlement System; ECOWAS Regional Payment and Settlement for WAMZ; and West African Economic and Monetary Union (WAEMU) Digital Financial Services Interoperability Project	WAMZ Real Time Gross Settlement System is a multi-currency system for English speaking West Africa and went live in 2012. ECOWAS Regional Payment and Settlement for WAMZ has a project delivery date of 2024. In addition, WAEMU Digital Financial Services Interoperability Project for French speaking West Africa was scheduled for 2023.

Southern African Development Community (SADC)	SADC Real Time Gross Settlement System (SADC RTGS)	Went live in 2013. South African Rand (ZAR) is the settlement currency. The system is operated by the South African Reserve Bank (SARB).

Source: African Development Bank Group (2023), Bank of Zambia (2016), Central Bank of Kenya (2013), East African Community Secretariat (2023), West African Monetary Institute (2021), Central Bank of West African States (2023)

These systems are not interconnected. As an example, SADC Real Time Gross Settlement System (SADC RTGS) and East African Payment System (EAPS) are not interconnected – in other words there is no interoperability. This is because these systems are meant for their respective regional economic communities. However, interoperability is key for encouraging trade across these communities and serves as a springboard for continental integration.

Mobile connectivity in particular or internet in general is still low in Africa. There are signs of progress being made. The Covid-19 pandemic has shown how important connecting to the internet is, as during that time many people and stakeholders worked from home and some employers are still encouraging this new form of working, albeit in a hybrid format. Queues in banking halls were limited, customers transacted via their cellphones and this pushed for a perennial need for a move towards electronic means of payment.

The prediction for sub-Saharan Africa is that by 2025 there will be about 40 million 5G connections, while 4G adoption is expected to reach a third of total connections, and there will be 50 percent mobile subscriber penetration (GSMA, 2022). There are several aspects to consider as far as this prediction is concerned. Data needs to be affordable, and affordability therefore needs to be in tune with the global strategy that the move is towards electronic payments and not paper-based payments. Handsets also need to be affordable. Although feature phones are relatively cheaper than smart phones, the former are limited in terms of capacity to handle multiple applications.

Financial inclusion is another challenge for continental integration in Africa. This relates to access or usage of financial services by underbanked and unbanked stakeholders across the continent. Payment channels, availability and affordability of smartphones, data affordability and internet connectivity are all important to realising financial inclusion or serving as springboards for adequate consumption of banking and payment services across various regional economic communities.

Description of Continental Payments

There is a difference between domestic, regional and continental payments. Domestic payments are transactions that are routed through clearing and settlement systems domestically while regional payments are transactions that are transmitted through clearing and settlement systems at a regional level. Besides, continental payments are those that are processed via continental clearing and settlement systems. Regional systems within regional economic communities can be enabled to interoperate with continental systems thereby facilitating transactions at a continental level. These regional economic communities that are recognised by the African Union were noted: Arab Maghreb Union (UMA), Common Market for Eastern and Southern Africa (COMESA), Community of Sahel – Saharan States (CEN-SAD), East African Community (EAC), Economic Community of Central African States (ECCAS), Economic Community of West African States (ECOWAS), Intercontinental Authority on Development (IGAD) 2, and Southern African Development Community (SADC). Ideally, each regional economic community should have clearing and settlement systems to facilitate transactions within the bloc.

Suppose a banking institution in Namibia wants to send a transaction to another in Tanzania. The banking institution in Namibia is a participant in SADC RTGS in this example, while the other in Tanzania participates in the East African Community RTGS system. There are three options or process flows that are involved. One option is direct access to continental clearing and settlement systems by banking institutions and the second is ensuring that RTGS systems in regional economic communities are interlinked to continental clearing and settlement systems for transactions to happen end to end. The last option is the use of the traditional correspondent banking arrangement if the options mentioned above are not practical.

African Continental Free Trade Area

A free trade area is the basic form of economic integration from the perspective of international economics. Different forms of economic integration were noted earlier: free trade area, customs union, common market, monetary union and ultimately political union. The term "free trade area" relates to free movement of goods and services between countries; customs union is similar to free trade area, but includes common external tariffs; common market includes free movement of labour; monetary union is about the use of one common currency with another variation to this being other currencies pegged to one currency; and political union refers to the adoption of one system of governance for all member states.

The African Union saw a need to create a free trade area for all the countries of the continent of Africa. This form of integration has several implications to consider. Free movement of goods and services is traditionally accompanied by removal of trade restrictions (or in certain situations reduction of trade barriers) between and among member states. Free movement of goods and services is not going to be fully realised if other regions in Africa still maintain customs union arrangements. Free trade area implies that the manufacturing sector in each member state needs to scale up to realise benefits associated with this economic integration arrangement. There is a common belief that there is more trade taking place with other countries outside Africa than with countries in Africa. This theory can be tested with the free trade area in Africa by promoting intra-Africa trade in goods and services.

African continental free trade area (AfCFTA) is one of the key projects of the African Union. It aims to accelerate intra-Africa trade as an engine of growth and sustainable development by doubling intra-Africa trade and strengthening Africa's common voice and policy space in global trade negotiations and is to be realised through the AfCFTA agreement (African Union Development Agency, 2022). Doubling intra-Africa trade will require collaboration of all stakeholders in order to realise aspirations around this initiative or project.

Agenda 2063

The word agenda means different things to different people. It can entail a list of items or topics to be discussed during a meeting. This word can also imply actions, tasks, deliverables or milestone to be executed with the view of realising a certain aspiration. As an example, if a vision is to realise a prosperous Africa compared to the current state, it follows that a list of initiatives or projects need to be implemented to realise the end state. The list of projects is then referred to as an agenda.

Agenda 2063 is Africa's development blueprint for achieving inclusive and sustainable socio-economic development over a 50-year period and it is divided into aspirations and goals with tracking of performance done via continental-level reports (African Union Development Agency, 2022). These aspirations and goals are listed in the following table:

Table 21.2
Agenda 2063 Goals and Aspirations

Aspirations	Goals
1. A prosperous Africa based on inclusive growth and sustainable development	Goal 1. A high standard of living, quality of life and wellbeing. Goal 2. Well educated citizens and skills revolution underpinned by science, technology and innovation. Goal 3. Healthy and well-nourished citizens. Goal 4. Transformed economies and job creation. Goal 5. Modern agriculture for increased productivity and production. Goal 6. Blue / ocean economy for accelerated economic growth. Goal 7. Environmentally sustainable climate resilient economies and communities.
2. An integrated continent, politically united and based on the ideals of Pan-Africanism and a vision of the African renaissance	Goal 8. United Africa (federal or confederate). Goal 9. Key continental financial and monetary institutions established and functional. Goal 10. World class infrastructure criss-crosses Africa.

3. An Africa of good governance, democracy, respect for human rights and the rule of law	Goal 11. Democratic values, practices, universal principles of human rights, justice and the rule of law entrenched. Goal 12. Capable institutions and transformed leadership in place at all levels.
4. A peaceful and secure Africa	Goal 13. Peace, security and stability are preserved. Goal 14. A stable and peaceful Africa. Goal 15. A fully functional and operational African peace and security architecture.
5. Africa with a strong cultural identity, common heritage, value and beliefs	Goal 16. African cultural renaissance is pre-eminent.
6. An Africa whose development is people driven, relying on the potential of the African people	Goal 17. Full gender equality in all spheres of life. Goal 18. Engaged and empowered youth and children.
7. Africa as a strong and influential global partner	Goal 19. Africa as a major partner in global Affairs and peaceful co-existence. Goal 20. Africa takes full responsibility for financing her development.

Source: African Union Development Agency (2022)

Payment, clearing and settlement systems are important for the realisation of AfCFTA as well as aspirations and goals as enshrined in Agenda 2063. These systems support the movement of goods and services at cross border level. Such systems can be addressed under goals 9 and 10 under aspiration 2 of Agenda 2023 with a view of attaining an integrated or interconnected continent of Africa.

Continental Clearing and Settlement Systems

Clearing and settlement systems at continental level are equally as important as clearing and settlement systems at national and regional levels. These systems support the movement of goods and services at all levels of society. While the systems are well established at domestic and regional levels, work is still required with the view to build on the current status at continental level thereby contributing towards the achievement of AfCFTA and Agenda 2063 aspirations.

The Pan African payment and settlement system (PAPSS) was implemented out of the need to have a settlement system for the African continent. PAPSS is the brainchild of the African Union and the first continent-wide digital payment system, and seeks to: facilitate intra-African payments; offer alternatives to correspondent banking; and facilitate low-cost, low risk clearing and settlement of transactions (Monye & Monye, 2022). There are distinguishing features of PAPSS that are worth noting (Pan African Payment and Settlement System, 2023):

- Payments (instant or real time) are sent and received in local currency within 120 seconds subject to compliance, legal and sanctions validations.
- Payments are pre-funded via in-country central bank crediting participant's prefunded account. PAPSS is notified and then credits the direct participant's clearing account.
- Settlement in local currency is done within 24 hours and net settlement happens at 11:00 coordinated universal time (UTC) each day.

- Each central bank has a hard currency settlement account in Afreximbank. This is debited / credited depending on net position or payment instruction from PAPSS.
- Payments are based on an ISO 20022 messaging system, allowing for interoperability and rich data in payment instructions.
- Transaction types include wholesale payments, retail payments, request to pay and remittances.
- System enjoys the support of the African Union and central banks in Africa.
- The governance architecture for PAPSS includes byelaws, governing council, management board, and management team.
- Implementation in West African Monetary Zone (WAMZ) serves as springboard for wider connectivity across Africa and beyond.

BOX 20

African Export-Import Bank, commonly known as Afreximbank, has a crucial role to play in Africa payments. It is understood that the bank was established in 1993 by African governments, African private and institutional investors, and non-African financial institutions and private investors with the purpose of financing, promoting and expanding of intra-African and extra-African trade (World Economic Forum, 2023). Afreximbank is headquartered in Cairo, Egypt.

Intra-African trade refers to trade within the borders of Africa, while extra-African trade implies trade with counterparts that are located outside Africa. Counterparts outside Africa include those in the diaspora, while counterparts in Africa are those in Southern Africa, Central Africa, Western Africa, Eastern Africa and Northern Africa. Consequently, Afreximbank has a drive to ensure continent-wide connectivity as far as the implementation of Pan African payment and settlement system (PAPSS) is concerned. This will require the support of multiple stakeholders going forward.

The outlook around clearing and settlement systems at a continental level is positive in view of the above box article as well. It is expected that PAPSS will be implemented in other regional economic communities beyond WAMZ and by extension ECOWAS. A regulatory framework on how to join this system from the perspective of regulators is likely to be introduced and communicated. There is an expectation that central banks will be involved in matters around clearing and settlement systems for Africa going forward. This in line with one of the purposes of the Association of African Central Bank Governors, which is to promote co-operation in the monetary, banking and financial spheres in the African region (Association of African Central Bank Governors, 2021).

Development in Retail Payments

Retail payments have been defined as low-value transactions below a specific threshold viewed from the perspective of each regulatory authority in a given country. This is the opposite of wholesale or high-value payments, which have been described as those transactions above a specific threshold viewed from the perspective of each regulatory authority in a given country. Low-value transaction types therefore include card, electronic funds transfer and electronic money related transactions.

There is an expectation as well on how retail payments will be initiated, processed, cleared and settled via recognised or approved clearing systems at a continental level. Clearing models are well entrenched at country and regional levels and these practices can be replicated at a continental level. More collaboration by all stakeholders including service providers, system operators, banking associations, payment associations, regulators and other stakeholders is expected on retail payments at an Africa level going forward.

Chapter Summary

The focus of this chapter was on continental payments. Domestic payments are transactions that are routed through clearing and settlement systems domestically while regional payments are transactions that are transmitted through clearing and settlement systems at a regional level. This chapter noted that continental payments are those that are processed via continental clearing and settlement systems. Regional systems within regional economic communities can be enabled to interoperate with continental systems thereby facilitating transactions at a continental level. There is an expectation that central banks will be involved in matters around clearing and settlement systems for Africa going forward.

Review Questions

1. Why was PAN African Payment and Settlement System (PAPSS) implemented? List five of the distinguishing features of this African system.
2. Outline seven aspirations of Agenda 2063.
3. Discuss three basic challenges of the African continent with regard to payment, clearing and settlement systems.
4. African Continental Free Trade Area (AfCFTA) and Agenda 2063 are closely related. Explain this statement.
5. Write short on the following systems:
    a. COMESA regional payment and settlement system
    b. East African payment system
    c. SADC real time gross settlement system

Selected References

African Development Bank Group, (2016). *Harmonisation of the Existing Payment System Infrastructure across ECOWAS.* Abidjan, Cote D'Ivoire: African Development Bank Group. Retrieved from https://www.adfi.org/

African Union Development Agency, (2022). *Second Continental Report – On the Implementation of Agenda 2063.* Johannesburg, South Africa: African Union Development Agency. Retrieved from https://www.au.int/

Association of African Central Bank Governors, (2021). *Statutes of the Association of African Central Bank Governors.* Dakar, Senegal: Association of African Central Bank Governors. Retrieved from https://www.aacb.org/

Bank of Zambia, (2016). *Overview of Payment System in Zambia.* Lusaka, Zambia: Bank of Zambia. Retrieved from https://www.boz.zm/

Central Bank of Kenya, (2013). *Commencement of the East African Payment System (EAPS)* Press Release. Nairobi, Kenya: Central Bank of Kenya. Retrieved from https://www.centralbank.gov.ke/

Central Bank of West African States, (2023). *Annual Report 2022.* Dakar, Senegal: Central Bank of West African States. Retrieved from https://www.bceao.int/

East African Community Secretariat, (2023). *East African Community Secretariat General Procurement Notice.* Arusha, Tanzania: East African Community Secretariat. Retrieved from https://www.afdb.org/

GSMA, (2022). *The Mobile Economy Sub-Saharan Africa 2022.* London, United Kingdom: GSMA. Retrieved from https://www.gsma.com/

Monye, O., & Monye, B. (2022). Regional Integration in Africa: Proposals for an Africa-wide Payment System. *Law Democracy & Development,* 22, 190-218. https://doi.org/10.17159/2077-4907/2021/ldd.v26.8

West African Monetary Institute, (2021). *WAMZ Payment System Development Project – Consultancy Service for the Recruitment of a Procurement Specialist for the UBI and DI Project.* Accra, Ghana: West African Monetary Institute. Retrieved from https://www.wami-imao.org/

World Economic Forum, (2023). *African Export-Import Bank.* Geneva, Switzerland: GSMA. Retrieved from https://www.weforum.org/

CHAPTER 22

Foreign Exchange Payments

There are several market types, including but not limited to foreign exchange, money, capital, financial, product and labour markets. Buying and selling of foreign exchange takes place on the foreign exchange market. The money market is a market place for short-term securities or financial instruments while the capital market is a market for long-term securities or financial instruments. The financial market is a collection of markets and includes the money market, capital market and foreign exchange market. The product market is a market for goods and services. While goods are tangible, services are intangible. The labour market is a market for the supply of and demand for labour. Individuals who are looking for a job participate in the labour market, along with entities with job openings.

Learning Objectives

By the end of this chapter, you should be able to

- understand key concepts related to the foreign exchange market;
- know continuous linked settlement and how settlement happens; and
- appreciate the size of foreign exchange deals and related benefits of CLS to banks and corporates.

Foreign Exchange Market

The foreign exchange market, commonly abbreviated as the FX market, is a place where foreign exchange is bought and sold. Foreign exchange is another name for foreign money or foreign currency. Foreign exchange transactions occur in currencies such as United States Dollar (USD), Euro (EUR), Japanese Yen (JPY), British Pound (GBP), Swiss Franc (CHF), Canadian Dollar (CAD), Australian Dollar (AUD), and the South African Rand (ZAR). Countries in the common monetary area (CMA) accept the ZAR as a legal tender. End-users are aware that trading in foreign exchange happens via over-the-counter or electronic trading systems. The exchange rate is the price at which foreign currency is bought and sold.

There are seven key points to remember about the FX market (Chaboud, Rime and Sushko, 2023). First, it is a place where relative prices of the world's major currencies are determined for international transactions in goods, services and financial assets. Second, participants in the FX market are many and include but are not limited to end-users and market intermediaries. Third, the FX market is the largest financial market in the world compared to markets such as the global equity market. Fourth, currency trading takes place around the world and around the clock, with a weekly cycle beginning early Monday morning in the Asia / Pacific region and ending Friday afternoon in the Americas. Fifth, the top three traded currencies are the USD, the EUR and JPY with the USD accounting for 90 percent of all global FX transactions. Sixth, the FX market shows a high degree of concentration, and liquidity provision is concentrated among a relatively small number of global banks and non-bank liquidity providers. Seventh, the FX market is an over-the-counter (OTC) market in which electronic trading has grown rapidly over the years.

Sound management of risks in the FX market is important in view of the abovementioned points. This market is the largest of the financial markets and any form of disturbance can have a ripple effect not only in the financial market but in the rest of the global economy as well. Risk containment measures have been put in place to manage risks resulting from activities in the FX market. One such risk that requires active management in the FX market is settlement risk.

Foreign Exchange Settlement Risk

Settlement risk is inherent in any market where counterparties are involved for a trade or transaction to be concluded. This risk has been described as a possibility of insufficient funds in a paying bank's settlement account at the point of settlement in a real time gross settlement system (RTGS). Some terms that are associated with settlement risk include liquidity risk and funding risk. The above definition can relate to a domestic or regional RTGS environment with limited foreign currency exposure and where settlement currency is common to participants in the system.

Settlement risk in the context of foreign exchange is an extension of the foregoing. In the FX market, settlement risk is sometimes referred to as Herstatt risk after the collapse of Bankhaus Herstatt in German in 1974. It is a risk of loss incurred by a counterparty when it pays out the currency it sold but does not receive the currency it bought, and in the case of Bankhaus Herstatt it had already received Deutsche marks from its counterparts, but it had not yet made the corresponding USD payments in New York, a situation that led to other banks stopping outgoing payments until their own payments due had been received (Chaboud, Rime and Sushko, 2023).

There are two legs to any transaction, consisting of a paying portion and a receiving portion, and the challenge in the FX market is to ensure that the two sides do happen close to real time thereby avoiding any form of settlement risk and the resultant impact to the entire financial system. Bankhaus Herstatt received Deutsche marks from its counterparts in Germany and the entity did not make corresponding USD payments in New York in this asynchronous situation, resulting in an imbalance and its eventual closure by German authorities.

Payment versus Payment

The term "payment versus payment" in the literature on payment, clearing and settlement systems is aimed at the need to eliminate FX settlement risk. Funds that move in the FX market are large and it makes perfect sense that the values in the two separate currencies are delivered, or paid and received, at the same time. Let us go back to the previous example of Bankhaus Herstatt. The bank received Deutsche marks from its counterparts and yet it did not make corresponding USD payments at the same time. If it had, there would not have been any form of imbalance, settlement risk or even systemic risk in this wholesale market.

Sissens (2023) notes that payment-versus-payment (PvP) eliminates FX settlement risk because it creates simultaneous exchange of the currency ownership, which can only take place once both sets of funds have moved, providing the assurance that one party continues to own their funds until their counterparty has met their transfer obligations. The key words to note from this description are "simultaneous", which means "at the same time" and "funds", referring to the situation where two currencies are involved in a transaction, while "ownership" implies that full ownership can happen once transfers on the two sides of a transaction have taken place.

CLS Governance

Continuous Linked Settlement (CLS) was created out of the need to minimise FX settlement risk in the FX market. Spinney (2009) notes that the only way to eliminate settlement exposure of this nature entirely is to settle both transactions, payment-versus-payment, using a real-time settlement system and it was for this purpose that the hybrid CLS system was designed by the world's 20 largest foreign exchange banks, to eliminate Herstatt risk in the foreign exchange market. Minimising or reducing settlement risk therefore means moving towards a PvP state, a condition where the receipt of value in one currency and the payment of value in another currency all happen at the same time. The overall benefit is the realisation of efficiency as well as avoidance of systemic risk in the global FX market.

CLS is international payment system which was launched in September 2002 for the settlement of foreign exchange transactions and is overseen by all central banks involved, with the Federal Reserve Bank of New York acting as a lead overseer, and consists of three related companies that are worth describing (Magerle and Maurer, 2009). First is the *CLS Bank International* that is based in New York and is responsible for the management of the system and across whose accounts transactions are settled, falling under the oversight regime of the Federal Reserve Bank of New York. Second is the *CLS Services* that is situated in the United Kingdom and provides operational and technical back office and information technology services for CLS. The above-mentioned companies are subsidiaries of *CLS UK Holdings Limited*, which is wholly owned by CLS Group Holdings AG based in Switzerland.

Mechanics of Settlement

All FX transactions are settled in the CLS system on a net basis, as opposed to gross basis, resulting in reduced funding and settlement obligation on the part of the settlement participant. It all starts with ensuring that each currency account of a settlement participant is adequately funded and consequently making sure that instructions are validated and matched for actual settlement to take place. There is no need for collateral as all settlement obligations are prefunded. The following points show how settlement works in the CLS system for FX transactions (Spinney, 2009):

- Settlement is on a real-time net basis, within a five-hour window, when all the relevant real-time gross settlement (RTGS) systems are open and able to make and receive payments. Settlement cycle starts at 07:00 and ends at 12:00 Central European Time (CET).

- Operations are conducted from London, which gives the maximum window of opportunity for processing of foreign exchange transactions between the different international currency centres.
- Major participants in CLS include shareholders, settlement members, user members, third parties, liquidity providers, nostro agents, third-party service providers, central banks, and vendors.

BOX 21

South Africa joined the CLS system in 2004 and the South African Rand (ZAR) is one of the settlement currencies in the settlement system. The South African Reserve Bank (SARB) took a position that the ZAR should be included as a CLS currency (Mitchell, 2007) for three important reasons. First, CLS is an important development in terms of forex settlement risk. Second, other emerging economies have joined CLS. Third, if the ZAR is not included, and if the South African banking industry does not participate directly in CLS, domestic banks could incur additional transactions costs (to manifest through a two-tier pricing structure in terms of correspondent banking arrangement for non-CLS transactions), and there could be limited forex market acceptance.

The above provides motivation to would-be members and users of the CLS system going forward. There are about 18 settlement currencies in the CLS system and more than 70 settlement members, while over 35000 financial institutions make use of CLS services (Continuous Linked Settlement, 2023). FX settlement risk is reduced if more participants join the settlement system.

- CLS bank holds RTGS settlement accounts with each of the participating central banks and each of its settlement members has multicurrency accounts with CLS bank.
- Each settlement member pays in the required currency amounts, from a funding perspective, either directly via an approved payment system and in this case an RTGS system if they are participants, or by using nostro agents.
- CLS bank only settles instructions that have been validated and matched against settlement criteria and those that fail this check are queued for the next cycle.
- CLS does not require the deposit of collateral, as most RTGS systems do, to cover daylight overdrafts at each central bank.
- CLS bank, settlement members, national RTGS systems and third parties communicate via SwiftNet, thus allowing CLS to settle transactions simultaneously in real time. SwiftNet is an infrastructure provided by Society for Worldwide Interbank Financial Telecommunication (Swift).

Foreign Exchange Deals

FX market is the largest financial market in the world in terms of transactions settled. It is the size of this market that makes it necessary to have these transactions processed via a secure and widely regulated and supervised settlement mechanism, the CLS. There are non-CLS transactions though, that are processed and settled through correspondent banking. Going forward, there is therefore an expectation of a further decline in correspondent banking transactions and a general increase in transactions that are processed and settled via CLS.

Spinney (2009) points out that CLS settles on average over USD5 trillion a day, which accounts for 95 percent of the daily traded value in the 17 currencies traded and that the Bank for International Settlements estimates that CLS eliminates over USD4 trillion of FX settlement risk per day. Approximately USD6.6 trillion in FX payments, on an average day, is subject to settlement risk (Sissens, 2023). Continuous Linked Settlement (2023) indicates that each day it settles over USD6.5 trillion of payments in 18 of the most actively traded currencies globally, protecting members and clients from the most significant risk in the FX market, settlement risk, and these currencies and respective issuers appear in the following table:

Table 22.1
Currencies and respective issuers

Issuer	Currency
Banco de Mexico	Mexican peso
Bank of Canada	Canadian dollar
Bank of England	Pound sterling
Bank of Israel	Israel shekel
Bank of Japan	Japanese yen
Bank of Korea	Korean won
Danmarks Nationalbank	Danish krone
European Central Bank	Euro
Federal Reserve Bank of New York	US dollar
Hong Kong Monetary Authority	Hong Kong dollar
Magyar Nemzeti Bank	Hungarian forint
Monetary Authority of Singapore	Singapore dollar

Norges Bank	Norwegian krone
Reserve Bank of Australia	Australian dollar
Reserve Bank of New Zealand	New Zealand dollar
South African Reserve Bank	South African rand
Sveriges Riksbank	Swedish krona
Swiss National Bank	Swiss franc

Source: Continuous Linked Settlement (2023)

Chaboud, Rime and Sushko (2023) show that the establishment of CLS and other actions led to a substantial reduction in FX settlement risk. The above trend provides useful insight. Value that CLS settles is more than USD6 trillion and CLS will continue to play a significant role in eliminating settlement risk. Continuous decrease in the use of correspondent banking and the increase in transactions settled through CLS is a good sign that settlement risk has fallen. Consequently, CLS provides a number of benefits to a wide range of stakeholders such as banks and corporates. As an example, banks are not required to post collateral for settlement and there is associated reduction in liquidity requirements given that CLS is a netting based system (a netting arrangement is a situation where obligations and receipts of a paying financial institution are set off against each other before final obligation is determined in the settlement system, thus reducing funding requirement). Corporates then do not need to deal with different banks and systems and there is an opportunity to realise straight-through processing. The detailed benefits for banks and corporates are displayed in the following table:

Table 22.2
Benefits of CLS for banks and corporates

Benefits for banks	Benefits for corporates
• It reduces the risks associated with settling high-value FX transactions using international fund transfers. • It reduces the cost involved with such transactions as a netting system. • It operates throughout the transaction window, providing for faster settlement of transactions. • It does not require the deposit of collateral to cover daylight overdrafts at each central bank. • It gives banks the opportunity to re-engineer their liquidity management to take advantage of the fact that less money is tied up in the system either as collateral in the form of money market instruments or as central bank balances.	• It offers treasurers greater certainty in terms of trade execution and hence allows them to improve their cash management. • It eliminates the risks associated with different banks and different settlement systems. • It offers advantages in terms of straight-through processing and reporting opportunities for each of the participating currency zones. • It allows multinational companies to rationalise their correspondent banking arrangements and further improve their global cash management.

Source: Spinney (2009)

Financial institutions and monetary authorities that are interested in joining CLS can do a cost benefit analysis or feasibility study in view of the benefits that are outlined above. There are different options on how to join the system depending on whether the aspiring stakeholder is a participant in the domestic real time gross settlement system (RTGS) or not. Traditionally, in-country monetary authorities do take a lead in ascertaining whether a country or financial sector needs the services that CLS brings. More participants in the settlement infrastructure lead to reduction in settlement risk in the FX market.

Chapter Summary

This chapter focussed on foreign exchange payments with special emphasis on continuous linked settlement system (CLS). CLS was created out of the need to minimise FX settlement or Herstatt risk through settling transactions on a payment-versus-payment basis. South Africa joined the CLS system in 2004 and the South African Rand (ZAR) is one of the settlement currencies in the settlement system. This provides motivation to would-be members and users of the CLS system going forward. FX settlement risk is reduced if more participants join the settlement system.

Review Questions

1. Name and write short notes on the three companies that form part of the CLS international payment system.
2. Outline how settlement for FX payment instructions takes place within the CLS payment system.
3. State four benefits of the CLS settlement system for banks and corporates respectively.
4. Name three reasons why South Africa joined the CLS settlement system.
5. Explain the following terms related to the FX market:
    a. Foreign exchange market
    b. FX settlement risk
    c. Payment versus payment

Selected References

Chaboud, A., Rime, D., & Sushko, V. (2023). The Foreign Exchange Market. *BIS Working Papers*, 1094, 1-28. Retrieved from https://www.bis.org/

Continuous Linked Settlement, (2023). *CLS Settlement.* Pretoria, South Africa: South African Reserve Bank. Retrieved from https://www.cls-group.com/

Magerle, J., & Maurer, D. (2009). *The Continuous Linked Settlement Foreign Exchange Settlement System (CLS).* Berne, Switzerland: Swiss National Bank. Retrieved from https://www.snb.ch/

Mitchell, D.C. (2007). *Information Paper – South Africa's Participation in the Continuous Linked Settlement System.* Pretoria, South Africa: South African Reserve Bank. Retrieved from https://www.resbank.co.za/

Sissens, D. (2023). *Why the increased Adoption of PvP Settlement will enhance Cross-border Payments.* London, United Kingdom: FinTech Futures. Retrieved from https://www.fintechfutures.com/

Spinney, W. (2009). The Great FX Fix. *The Treasurer*, 6-9. Retrieved from https://www.treasurers.org/

CHAPTER 23

Securities Settlement Systems

The overriding objective of settlement systems in payments is final settlement of transactions under the principles of finality and irrevocability. This basically means that there is no need to reverse a transaction as a settlement process has been completed. Securities settlement systems are an integral part of the settlement process, ensuring that the above stated principle continues to be realised through ensuring that payment instruments are processed from end to end without any friction.

Learning Objectives

By the end of this chapter, you should be able to

- understand securities for settlement of payments;
- comprehend the *delivery versus payments* principle; and
- know security settlement systems and how they are linked to payment systems.

Description of Security

Security has applications not only in commercial bank lending, but in central bank lending as well. Synonyms associated with security include collateral or collateral security. Imagine a working individual who applies for a home loan and a small and medium enterprise (SME) owner seeking financial assistance to expand his business. The primary security or collateral for a home loan is a salary in case of an individual, while for an SME security can include such assets as revenue, movable assets or fixed assets, depending on the amount of money that is borrowed.

Commercial banks or financial institutions also borrow money to meet their funding or payment needs. Sources of borrowing include other commercial banks or financial institutions and the central bank. Simplifying assumptions can be made. First, a commercial bank borrows from a central bank. Second, borrowing is necessary to meet funding requirements in the domestic real time gross settlement system (RTGS). Third, this form of borrowing kicks in only if there are insufficient funds in a commercial bank's settlement account with a central bank. Fourth and last, borrowing is during the day and assets pledged as security exchange hands or are returned by the end of the day.

Security is therefore an asset belonging to the borrower that is pledged, committed or encumbered for liquidation when payment obligation in favour of a creditor is not honoured. Liquidation or converting assets into cash is a last resort as the understanding is that monthly premiums, for the case of an individual or SME, will be made as agreed or, in the case of a commercial bank, that there will always be sufficient funds in its settlement account in the RTGS system to meet funding and payment obligation.

Securities for Settlement of Payments

It is stated above that securities have application in central banking especially when it comes to settlement of payment instructions. Real time gross settlement systems are traditionally prefunded, implying that there should be funds in a participant's settlement account to honour incoming settlement obligations. There is an exception that sometimes funds are not sufficient hence the need to make sure that transactions are settled at all times.

There are different forms of securities that can be used for settlement from a perspective of payment and settlement systems. These securities include those that a settlement operator (funds transfer settlement systems operator) has determined are eligible or classified as collateral for settlement. An asset can be used as security for settlement if it meets certain conditions and one of these is that such an asset should be liquid and acceptable to the settlement operator and in most cases the central bank. A liquid asset is easily converted into cash without unnecessary delay or cost and examples can include but are not limited to treasury bills, short-term loans and short-term investments. Assets eligible for collateral can be maintained in a book entry system of a central bank or housed with a central securities depository (CSD), which can be a separate entity outside a central bank. CSD is a financial market infrastructure that is critical in the transfer, ownership, immobilisation and dematerialisation of securities.

Delivery versus Payments

The concept of delivery-versus-payments (DvP) can best be understood by means of examples. The first example involves Bank A and a central bank. Bank A pledges security for settlement of payment instructions in the real time gross settlement system (RTGS) and a central bank on its part provides intra-day funding or credit for Bank A to settle in the RTGS system. Transfer of credit happens after security has been pledged with the central bank with ownership of security reversed after Bank A has paid back borrowed funds by the end of the day.

The second example involves a seller of security or securities and an investor who needs to invest in securities. In this example, a seller issues these securities to an investor, who pays for them before ownership is transferred. Issuing securities and payment for these happen at the same time. This guarantees that the seller of securities has the funds due to them and the investor has proof of ownership of securities.

Delivery-versus-payment, sometimes called receive-versus-payment, is predominantly related to the second example. It means a condition whereby ownership of security can only be realised when payment for security has taken place and the opposite is true. There should be integration between a system that is used to hold or maintain securities and a funds transfer system that is used for actual settlement of payment instructions under principles of finality and irrevocability.

Deloitte Consulting (2018) notes that a DvP transaction is one where the cash payment for a purchased security occurs prior to or upon its delivery to protect counterparties from principal risk, with the risk of the seller of a security failing to receive payment despite fulfilling delivery, or the risk of the buyer of a security failing to receive delivery despite fulfilling payment. DvP method essentially gained popularity after the global market crash of October 1987.

Security Settlement Systems

Security settlement system (SSS) is an important financial markets infrastructure in a country's financial system. There is a distinction between SSS and a real time gross settlement system (RTGS). Whereas the latter is a funds transfer settlement system traditionally in the books of the central bank, the former is rolled out to realise DvP, a situation where both the delivery leg of a security and the payment leg happen at the same time. The more specific name for SSS is central securities depository (CSD).

The settlement process and models from a securities settlement system are depicted in the following table:

Table 23.1

Settlement process and settlement models

Key Stages of the Settlement Process	
Name	Description
Pre-settlement and clearing	Matching the trade instructions supplied by each counterparty, ensuring that seller has sufficient securities, and that buyer has sufficient funds to cover purchase cost.
Settlement	The legal title of ownership of the securities is transferred from the seller to the buyer in exchange for the equivalent value in cash.
Post-settlement	Management of failed transactions and the subsequent accounting of the trades.
	Cash Settlement Models
Name	Description
Commercial bank money model	Cash leg of the settlement process uses commercial bank money with cash settlement taking place within a commercial bank.
Interfaced model	Cash leg of the settlement process utilises the central bank's real time gross settlement system (RTGS) and there is an interface between the securities settlement system (SSS) and the central bank's RTGS system.
Integrated model	Central bank outsources all the related cash settlement processing activities to the SSS, which operates the entries directly in dedicated accounts on the books of the central bank.

Source: Capital Markets Authority (2019)

The settlement process for a securities transaction includes pre-settlement and clearing, settlement and post-settlement. Cash settlement models include commercial bank money, interfaced model, and integrated model. An interfaced model is the most preferred model and has been implemented in several markets such as Kenya, Ghana and South Africa (Capital Markets Authority, 2019). This model has been implemented in Iceland as well, as per the following box article:

BOX 22

The Central Bank of Iceland (CBI) was established in 1961. It performs the same functions as any other central bank. One of the tasks that it undertakes is promoting a safe, effective financial system including domestic and cross-border payment intermediation. The CBI owns and operates the real time gross settlement system (RTGS), while Icelandic Securities Depository owns and operates the securities settlement system.

There is an agreement between the Central Bank of Iceland and Icelandic Securities Depository (ISD) on settlement of securities transactions. This agreement provides key information including fees that ISD pays to the CBI for settlement of securities transactions; sharing of information on system changes as well as turnover and number of transactions; and the roles or responsibilities of each party in terms of the agreement (Central Bank of Iceland, 2009).

The above discussion on securities settlement arrangements provides useful information. The implementation of a securities settlement system or central securities depository is private-sector-led while the operation of an RTGS system remains the responsibility of a central bank. Some countries that have not rolled out a security settlement system can learn from countries that have done so. Besides, the Central Bank of Iceland provides an example on the integration of an RTGS system and securitics settlement system and this integration is key for minimisation of principal risk.

Chapter Summary

This chapter provided information on securities settlement systems. These systems are traditionally implemented to realise delivery-versus-payment. The term delivery-versus-payment is a condition whereby ownership of security can only be realised when payment for security has taken place and the opposite is true. Integration between a system that is used to hold securities and a funds transfer system that is used for actual settlement of payment instructions, via an interfaced model, is important to minimise principal risk.

Review Questions

1. Outline and discuss the key stages of the settlement process from securities settlement standpoint.
2. Name and explain the cash settlement models that you have learned from securities settlement systems standpoint.
3. Write short notes on the following terms:
    a. Security settlement system
    b. Delivery-versus-payment
    c. Principal risk

Selected References

Capital Markets Authority, (2019). *Cash Settlement Using Central Bank Money*. Kampala, Uganda: Capital Markets Authority. Retrieved from https://www.cmauganda.co.org/

Central Bank of Iceland, (2009). *Agreement on Settlement of Securities Transactions*. Reykjavik, Iceland: Central Bank of Iceland. Retrieved from https://www.cb.is/

Corporate Finance Institute, (2023). *Delivery versus Payment (DVP)*. Vancouver, Canada: Corporate Finance Institute. Retrieved from https://www.corporatefinanceinstitute.com/

Deloitte Consulting, (2018). *Delivery versus Payment on Distributed Ledger Technologies*. New York, NY: Deloitte Consulting. Retrieved from https://www2.deloitte.com/

CHAPTER 24

Open Banking

Consider this scenario. A non-bank financial institution (NBFI) wants to introduce a product in a certain market, but it does not have profiles of potential customers in the market in question. It was informed about the possibility of data sharing and, based on this understanding, it decides to approach a fellow financial institution for an engagement leading to data sharing. However, the NBFI then realises that data sharing is a highly regulated environment!

Open banking is not only a recent discussion topic, but it is an important one from a payment systems standpoint. Does open banking relate to the sharing of data between or among financial institutions? What is the point in sharing data? Is there a relationship between open banking and competition in the provision of financial services? This chapter clarifies these and other related matters as far as open banking is concerned.

Learning Objectives

By the end of this chapter, you should be able to

- understand what open banking is all about;
- be aware of the operating model for open banking;

- know various technologies that are associated with open banking; and
- appreciate some public policy instruments for open banking.

Description of Open Banking

Open banking is a recent discussion point in payment systems. This area has enjoyed interest from professionals and policy makers due to a number of reasons and changes. These include the entry of NBFIs in the banking sector, the need for competition in this sector, regulatory requirements, technological changes especially in terms of rules of engagement that should apply, and tastes and preferences from the perspective of consumers.

Several definitions of open banking have surfaced from a number of angles. One is that it is the removal of entry barriers for persons to establish a banking or payment business, while another is that it is the introduction of services to the unbanked and underbanked members of the public from a financial inclusion standpoint. In addition, open banking allows for sharing of data, after a banked customer has given consent, for the beneficiary service provider to introduce financial services to a target market. Industry professionals agree that open banking relates more to the sharing of data between service providers, that is banks and financial technology (FinTech) companies.

Briones De Araluze and Cassinello (2022) note that open banking started in the United Kingdom in 2015 and the concept has spread to continental Europe, America and Asia and covers four applications or drivers: business model, financial technology, data sharing and regulation. Robin and Smith (2022) point out that open banking refers to the opening up or sharing of a customer's or a business' data, held by one party, to the other parties via secure digital channels for the customer's own benefit and with their consent. There are key words that need to be unpacked in this definition. The titles *customer* and *business* all refer to a client of one party. A party in this case is a financial institution such as a bank or FinTech with the digital channel being the medium through which client data is shared between service providers. Data cannot be shared if a customer has not given consent or authority beforehand. This consent can be given at account opening or at some time thereafter during a party's relationship with a client.

Operating Model

An operating model refers to how open banking ought to work and the building blocks that need to be present to realise successful implementation. The building blocks are the key elements or components that serve as a springboard for successful implementation of open banking in a way that meets the expectations of a multitude of stakeholders. Open banking can be viewed as a success if data is shared in a secure environment, unbanked and underbanked stakeholders continue to access financial services, and there is competition in the provision of financial services.

Table 24.1
Operating model for open banking

Model	Description
Legal and regulatory	Laws, regulations and oversight bodies. Legal and regulatory frameworks need to include aspects related to protection of personal information.

Governance	Stakeholders, decision making, rules, and ownership and operation. Open banking needs to embrace environment, social and governance (ESG) principles.
Participation	Participation and incentives, roles and rights, registration process, investment and return on investment.
Infrastructure	Information technology infrastructure, technical standards and cybersecurity.

Source: Robin and Smith (2022)

The above table outlines four elements that form part of the operating model for open banking: legal and regulatory framework, governance, participation and infrastructure (Robin and Smith, 2022). Protection of personal information and cybersecurity are important aspects that need to be addressed during the operation of open banking. This is because an environment characterised by customer information being compromised is a breeding ground for reputational, operational and systemic risks.

Technologies

It is noted above that open banking relates to the sharing of customer data between financial institutions. The issue at hand is how to realise that grand objective. This can only be achieved through employing certain technologies that are typically mentioned in the banking and payments literature. These technologies are: application programming interface (API), cloud computing, artificial intelligence (AI) and machine learning (ML), as well as blockchain, as depicted in the following table:

Table 24.2
Technologies

Technology	Description
Application Programming Interface	An API is a set of programming codes and protocols that works as an intermediary to allow two applications to talk to each other. A third-party service provider or Fintech in need of customer data can submit a request to the bank via an API call.
Cloud Computing	This resilient and scalable platform makes it possible to collect, store, analyse and distribute huge data volumes negating the need for on-premises legacy systems that lack required agility.
Artificial Intelligence and Machine Learning	AI involves simulation to allow machines to perform tasks performed by humans while ML is a type of AI that helps increase the accuracy of software applications in predicting outcomes without explicit programming. Both AI and ML assist financial institutions in analysing huge volume of data in areas such as processes, products and services.
Blockchain	This technology is compatible with privacy regulations or policies in that financial institutions do not store customer data in a blockchain model, with the burden of responsibility being on the customers and not financial institutions.

Source: Kshetri (2023)

There is a lot of discussions at a global level around the above technologies, especially in relation to the impact on the labour market. It is noted in the above table that AI and ML are key in areas such as processes, products and services and that these technologies can perform tasks that humans are able to perform. Technology experts are of the view that AI and ML can bring efficiencies in performing certain tasks while opponents are of the view that these technologies are likely to result in layoffs. This calls for a thorough impact analysis to understand exactly what these technologies need to do compared to what humans are supposed to do in the workplace.

Public Policy

Open banking has received support from policy makers across the world. Policy makers and implementers have a focus in ensuring access to financial services by the underbanked and unbanked members of society. Access to these services becomes possible if financial institutions across the divide do all they can to share customer data through appropriate technologies for the benefit of those to whom these services are due.

There is a multitude of regulations or pieces of legislation that have been issued in a number of countries and regional blocs to promote open banking. The objectives for issuing these instruments include promoting competition in the delivery of financial services, ensuring consumer protection and bringing about a sound environment in which data of consumer profiles can be shared. Selected instruments are briefly outlined below:

- *Payment services directive for the European payments area.* The payment services directive number 2 (PSD 2) was introduced in Europe in 2015 to strengthen consumer protection through secure customer authentication (SCA) and the creation of account information service providers (AISP) and payment initiation service providers (PISP). The new framework, payment services directive number 3 (PSD 3), aims to strengthen consumer protection, define parameters within which open banking should operate and level the playing field through allowing non-banks to participate directly in the Single European Payments Area (SEPA) scheme (KPMG, 2023). The payment services directive is one of the notable payment regulations that have been issued and it is serving as a springboard for defining open banking legal instruments around the world.

BOX 23

Single Euro Payments Area (SEPA) is a payments scheme in the euro areas that allows customers to do non-cash transactions to the European Union and non-European Union countries. The scheme can be traced to 2008 and became fully implemented in 2016. Payment streams that are covered include credit and debit transfers.

The payment integration triggered by SEPA has contributed to the efficiency and competitiveness of the European economy as a whole by eliminating differences between national and cross-border payments by harmonising standards in all the participating countries (European Central Bank, 2024).

- *Position paper on the feasibility of open banking within the Namibian financial sector.* The Bank of Namibia plans to mandate open banking after a period of 18 months from the issuance date of the position paper and a legal framework is expected to include components of consumer protection, data protection and cybersecurity requirements, and conditions for participants within the open banking initiative (Bank of Namibia, 2022).
- *Privacy regulations.* These include General Data Protection Regulation (GDPR) and California Consumer Privacy Act and have enabled financial institutions and other companies to adopt personal data minimisation policies to help protect themselves from liabilities arising from a negligent act related to data handling (Kshetri, 2023).

Chapter Summary

Open banking is a recent discussion topic in payment systems and has enjoyed interest from professionals and policy makers due to a number of reasons and changes. These include the entry of NBFIs in the banking sector, need for competition in this sector, regulatory requirements, technological changes especially in terms of rules of engagement that should apply, and tastes and preferences from the perspective of consumers. It started in the United Kingdom in 2015 and the concept has spread to continental Europe, America and Asia and covers four applications or drivers, namely a business model, financial technology, data sharing and regulation. Open banking refers to the opening up or sharing of a customer's or a business' data held by one party to the other parties via secure digital channels for the customer's own benefit and with their consent.

Review Questions

1. Outline three public policy instruments related to open banking that you have learned.
2. Name and briefly discuss open banking technologies in payment systems.
3. Elaborate on the key elements of the operating model for open banking.
4. Write short notes on the following terms:
    a. Open banking
    b. Application programming interface
    c. Cloud computing

Selected References

Bank of Namibia, (2022). *Position Paper on the Feasibility of Open Banking within the Namibian Financial Sector.* Windhoek, Namibia: Bank of Namibia. Retrieved from https://www.bon.com.na/

Briones De Araluze, G.K., & Cassinello, N.P. (2022). Open Banking: A Bibliometric Analysis-Driven Definition. *Plos One*, 17(10), 1-19. https://doi.org/10.10.1371/journal.pone.0275496

European Central Bank, (2024). *Single Euro Payments Area (SEPA).* Frankfurt, German: European Central Bank. Retrieved from https://www.ecb.eu/

KPMG, (2023). *PSD3 / PSR and SEPA Instant Legislation.* London, England: KPMG. Retrieved from https://assets.kpmg.com/

Robin, R., & Smith, D. (2022). Open Banking and Regulation: Please advise the Government. *Journal of Information Technology Teaching Cases*, 12(2), 108-114. https://doi.org/10.1177/20438869221082316

CHAPTER 25

Sanctions Screening

Screening has wide application in several fields of study including medicine, human resources management and payment systems. Think about someone who complains that they are unwell and decides to visit a physician. Upon arrival at a medical facility this person is examined to detect a problem and treatment is given to make him or her feel better. Or consider the recruitment process followed before someone is hired to fill a vacant position. This entails perusing each candidate's documentation and if need be performing police clearance. The end result ensures that the best individual performs according to expectation when hired at the end of the recruitment process. This chapter provides fundamental information on how screening is done from the perspective of payment, clearing and settlement systems.

Learning Objectives

By the end of this chapter, you should be able to

- define sanctions screening and understand its levels;
- appreciate that there are sanctioning controls and sanctions lists;
- comprehend the sanctions screening process; and
- know principles for effective sanctions screening program.

Description of Sanctions Screening

Sanctions screening or screening for sanctions is one of the most important areas that payments and compliance professionals need to be familiar with. It is a compliance requirement for accountable institutions to have systems in place to screen persons and transactions with the view to identify sanctioned targets; failure to do so can attract sanctions, penalties or associated risks.

Sanctions are directed at states, individuals or legal entities involved or suspected of being involved in illegal activities, and are issued by governments and institutions such as the United Nations (UN), Office of Foreign Assets Control (OFAC)) and the European Union (EU) with financial institutions expected to implement them as required by international and domestic regulatory organisations (Deloitte AG, 2000). Sanctions screening means processing up-to-date and accurate data, as well as conducting thorough queries across pertinent sanctions lists; and its purpose is to prevent legal, reputational, and financial damage caused by non-compliance and involvement in illegal trade operations, money laundering, terrorist financing and similar activities (Stankeviciute, 2023). LexisNexis (2024) says that sanctions screening involves screening individuals, groups or companies against designated sanctions lists according to the territories in which an organisation trades, the currencies they trade in, and their partnerships and alliances. This is in line with the work of`Financial Crime Academy (2023), which shows that the primary component of anti-money laundering (AML) compliance is AML screening.

BOX 24

Money that has been obtained or possessed legally can fulfil all its functions, such as being a medium of exchange for purchases of goods and services. However, when money is "laundered", we are referring to money whose origin has been concealed – it's as if it has been "washed clean", like laundering clothes. The money then appears as if it was obtained legally, and it is introduced and integrated into the financial system and subsequently into other sectors of the economy. Activities that are involved in money laundering include placement (depositing in an account), layering (spreading to other accounts and do transactions), and integration (money can now be withdrawn for other uses).

Authorities across the world have put in place measures, procedures and laws aimed at combating money laundering or financing of terrorism. Ogbeide, Thomson, Gonul, Pollock, Bhowmick, and Bello (2023) note that these measures, procedures and laws are based on Financial Action Task Force (FAFT) recommendations, to meet intricate compliance requirements, verify the identity of customers, check sources of funding and do transactions monitoring.

There are associated benefits and challenges related to sanctions screening. Benefits of sanctions screening include avoiding costly fines, reputational damage and legal issues, fraud detection, financial insurance, and regulatory compliance, while challenges include lengthy processes, human errors and false positives (Tamkivi, 2023). These benefits and challenges are described in the following table:

Table 25.1
Benefits and Challenges

Benefits	
Name	**Description**
Costly fines	Sanctions screening helps organisations avoid costly fines that may arise.
Reputational damage	Sanctions screening assists organisations in minimising reputational risk associated with negative publicity.
Legal issues	Sanctions screening helps organisations avoid legal issues that are related to dealing with sanctions targets.
Fraud detection	Sanctions screening can help detect fraudulent transactions by cross-referencing sanctions lists.
Financial insurance	Sanctions can lead companies to financial risks, especially when their business partners or customers are unexpectedly sanctioned.
Regulatory compliance	To maintain compliance, some regulated entities and financial institutions must conduct sanctions screening.

Challenges	
Name	**Description**
Lengthy processes	Screening large volumes of data manually makes it hard to keep up with the amount of data that needs to be screened or entered manually.
Human errors	Flaws in screening can occur due to typos, especially for foreign entities.

False positives	Businesses often face false positive results or duplicates when they don't have an effective sanctions screening system in place.

Source: Tamkivi (2023)

Fraud detection is therefore key to sanctions screening and this can only be achieved through a robust fraud detection or screening programme being in place. Financial institutions therefore have a duty, as accountable institutions, to comply with applicable regulatory requirements through putting in place controls aimed at detecting sanctioned targets. The above table shows that businesses often face false positives and this can be minimised with effective sanctioning screening tools (a false positive is an outcome of a screening process that comes out positive when in the true sense it should be negative).

Screening Controls

There are primary levels, controls, approaches or types of screening that are performed from a sanctions screening standpoint. These are: name or customer, payment or transaction, real time and batch screening (Financial Crime Academy, 2023). While name screening is typically done at the point of onboarding or at some point later when it is required, payment screening is carried out when a customer is transacting using their preferred payment instruments. The bottom line is that name and payment screening are carried out by comparing or matching internal records against a sanctions list. These levels of screening are outlined and described in the following table:

Table 25.2
Screening

Level	Description
Name screening	This is the process of matching an internal record against a sanctioned list either manually or through an automated screening tool. The two functions of name screening are to create a risk assessment and to assist organisations in detecting and reporting suspicious activity. Customer Due Diligence (CDD), Enhanced Due Diligence (EDD) and Know Your Customer (KYC) are additional compliance programs that assist businesses in developing risk assessments.
Payment screening	It focuses on screening payment messages and takes place with current customers and is performed before a payment or message is processed. This is related to reference screening, which allows a financial service provider to look for potential matches in banking or payment reference texts.
Real time screening	This form of screening can be associated with name screening and can take place prior to accepting or onboarding a new customer. Payment screening takes place in real time or ex-ante before payments are processed and its main benefit is that it ensures that institutions stop payments on a sanction target before the fact.
Batch screening	The form of screening that takes place ex-post or after the transaction has been processed and its main drawback is that it fails to ensure that institutions stop payments on a sanction target.

Source: Financial Crime Academy (2023), Tamkivi (2023)

Name and payment screening are all important from an operational and regulatory standpoint. The world is trending towards real time screening as opposed to batch screening. Real time screening is the *now form* of screening as it focuses on screening a customer before a relationship is established with a financial service provider and before a payment is concluded. This minimises regulatory or compliance and reputational risks, especially when a financial services provider processes a transaction related to a sanctioned target and only finds out after the fact.

Sanctions screening can be further categorised into domestic screening and cross-border screening. Domestic screening relates to screening customers and payments at a domestic level while cross-border screening has to do with screening customers and payments at a cross-border level. Domestic screening appears to be easier to implement compared to cross-border screening, especially when it comes to sharing information between the paying financial service providers and the beneficiary service providers.

Sanctions Lists

Sanctions lists provide a basis for sanctions screening. Internal records or client databases need to be compared with sanctions lists to detect fraud or sanctioned targets. Consequently, it is a challenge to perform sanctions screening if there are no sanctions lists in place. Sanctions lists are instructions for regulated institutions that have a legal obligation to comply with sanctions screening requirements and these do not always align across sanctioning bodies (Stankeviciute, 2023). The list of primary sanctions lists appears below:

- The Office of Foreign Assets Control (OFAC) sanctions list. It applies to all US citizens and corporate entities incorporated in the US, and any entity that trades in US dollars, US goods and components, or has a US parent or affiliate.

- The EU consolidated list of sanctions. This applies to all citizens and corporate entities that are established in a member state and overseen by the EU Council.
- His Majesty's Treasury (HM Treasury) sanctions list. It is enforced by the Office for Financial Sanctions Implementation (OFSI) and applies to all individuals and legal entities that operate or conduct business activities within the United Kingdom, including UK nationals and legal entities established under UK law.
- The UN sanctions list. This is overseen by the UN Council and applies to all countries that are members of the United Nations.

Technology

Financial service providers (and other providers) are believed to have a huge number of customers and transactions. It is also important that customers are onboarded as soon as possible so that a relationship can begin, for the benefit of both the service provider and the end user. Transactions need to be sieved through to uncover fraudulent transactions before these are introduced in payment, clearing and settlement systems. The foregoing implies that automated screening, as opposed to manual screening, is critical to assist service providers in locating sanctions targets and related fraudulent transactions.

LexisNexis (2024) notes that sanctions screening can take the form of manually inputting a name into an online search tool, checking a customer database for any sanctions alerts en masse, or automatically screening customer and stakeholder databases. A service provider has an option to implement either a manual solution or an automated solution. There are advantages and disadvantages associated with any solution. Notwithstanding this, a manual solution, although cheaper, is prone to errors compared to an automated solution, which can be costly in the short-term but more effective in the long-term.

Sanctioning screening is a process that leads to a determination of whether fraud is likely to be committed or has been committed. The use of an appropriate technology assists greatly in arriving at an outcome. Deloitte AD (2000) outlines a process that is involved in sanctioning screening, depicted in the following figure:

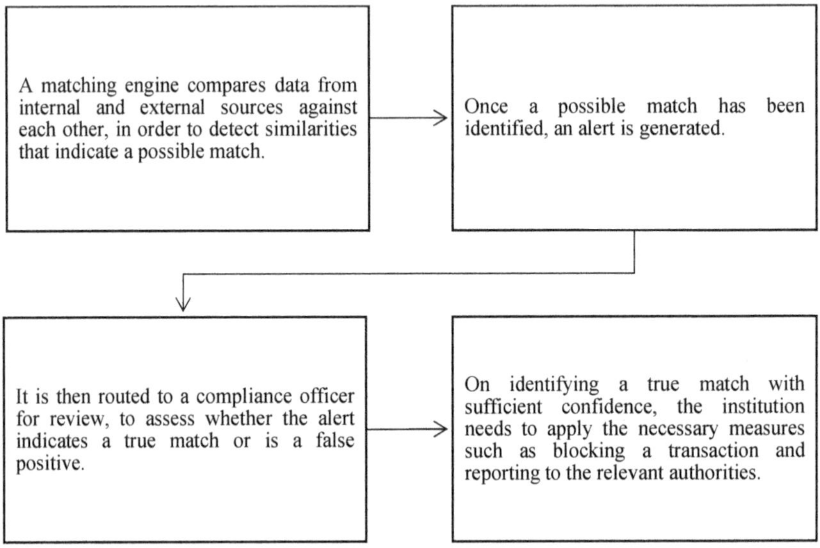

Figure 25.1. The Sanctions Screening Process

The above shows four key steps in sanctions screening: the sanctions list, matching, alerts and reporting. The sanctions list is therefore the basic first step in any sanctions screening activity, with reporting to respective authorities being the last one. All fraudulent activities are expected to be reported to the regulators from a sanctions screening perspective so that a financial system is kept clean at all times with the view to promoting the required confidence. A sound confidence in a given financial sector engenders investment and economic growth.

Principles for Effective Sanctions Screening Programme

The goal of any sanctions screening programme is to assist in detecting fraudulent activities and have these reported to the relevant authorities for actioning. However, this goal cannot be realised if such a programme is not as effective as intended. Implementing best practices can go a long way in making sure that a sanctions screening programme remains as effective as possible.

In view of the foregoing, LexisNexis (2024) provides tips for effective sanctions screening, as outlined and described below:

- Prepare customer data well. Customer data needs to be up to date, as incomplete and inaccurate data will result in false positives given the millions of customers that companies screen daily.
- Use proven and reliable technology to support screening. The screening software should be fit for purpose and some considerations in this regard include capacity to handle high volumes, being user-friendly with customisable settings, and using proven technology with the ability to automate.
- Screen against high quality and comprehensive sanctions data. The data against which customers are screened should be up-to-date, comprehensive and consolidated with other watchlist databases such as politically exposed persons lists.

Accurate customer data, appropriate technology and comprehensive sanctions data are all key to an effective sanctions screening programme. This requires availing resources to ensure that all these ingredients are in place with a view to detecting fraudulent activities and minimising false positives.

Chapter Summary

This chapter covered sanctions screening. Sanctions and sanctions screening are closely related. Sanctions are directed at states, individuals or legal entities involved or suspected of being involved in illegal activities on one hand. On the other hand, sanctions screening involves screening individuals, groups or companies against designated sanctions lists according to the territories in which an organisation trades, the currencies they trade in, and their partnerships and alliances. Consequently, persons and payments that these persons engage in need to be screened, as doing so engenders confidence in a given financial system, which is key for attracting investment to support economic growth.

Review Questions

1. Outline and explain four basic levels or forms of sanctions screening that you have learned.
2. What is the difference between domestic and cross-border screening?
3. List and explain the benefits and challenges for sanctions screening.
4. Write short notes on the following terms:
    a. Sanctions list
    b. Sanctions screening
    c. Name screening
5. Rearrange the following items to make a complete end-to-end sanctions screening process:

Process	Student Response
Sanctions list	
Reporting	
Alerts	
Matching	

Selected References

Deloitte AD, (2000). *Data Management: Why it matters for Effective Sanctions Screening*. Zurich, Switzerland. Retrieved from https://www2.deloitte.com/

Financial Crime Academy, (2023). *Name Screening and Payment Screening: Comprehensive Comparison between Name and Payment Screening*. Dublin, Ireland: Financial Crime Academy. Retrieved from https://www.financialcrimeacademy.com.org/

LexisNexis Risk Solutions, (2024). *A Guide to Sanctions Screening and Sanctions Lists*. London, United Kingdom. Retrieved from https://www.idenfy.com/

Ogbeide, H., Thompson, M.E., Gonul, M.S., Pollock, A.C., Bhowmick, S., & Bello, A.U. (2023). The Anti-Money Laundering Risk Assessment: A Probabilistic Approach. *Journal of Business Research*, 162, 1-15. https://doi.org/doi:10.1016/j.jbusres.2023.113820

Stankeviciute, G. (2024). *The Complete Sanctions Screening Guide*. Kaunas, Lithuania. Retrieved from https://www.idenfy.com/

Tamkivi, T. (2023). *The Complete Guide to Sanctions Screening*. Tallinn, Estonia. Retrieved from https://www.salv.com/

CHAPTER 26

Interchange in Payments

Interchange is one of the topical issues in recent times not only from a policy maker's standpoint but also from participants that are involved in the clearing and settlement of payment instructions. This subject matter forms part of discussions around fees and charges that are levied to end users. Policy makers are interested in consumer protection through regularisation of fees and charges while participants or financial institutions require compensation on varied investments they deploy in the market.

Learning Objectives

By the end of this chapter, you should be able to

- know the description of interchange and its importance;
- understand the basic interchange model; and
- comprehend how interchange is determined.

Description of Interchange

Interchange is a cost and benefit at the same time. It is a fee collected by one party on behalf of another party in a transaction. Parties to a transaction include paying and beneficiary participants. The transaction can be via a card, an electronic funds transfer, or a transaction concluded via an alternative payment channel. Much of the discussion in this chapter focusses on the card payment stream.

Calvano (2011) notes that interchange fees serve to determine how costs are shared between acquirers and merchants on the one hand and issuers and consumers on the other; knowing only the costs provides no information on how they should be shared. On their part, Weiner and Wright (2005) indicate that interchange is an instrument that card associations can use to achieve a desired balance of cardholder usage versus merchant acceptance across the two sides of the market. Interchange encourages the development and introduction of interoperable payment systems that ultimately provide end-users with access to a wide range of payment services (Bank of Namibia, 2022).

The above discussion mentions two-sided markets or two sides of the market. There is an issuer and card holder on one side and acquirer and merchant on the other side. The issuer issues a payment card to the customer and the acquirer installs a speed point terminal at the premises of a merchant or supermarket. Interchange is therefore important for the development of interoperable payment systems and traditionally flows from an acquirer to the issuer especially in case of transactions conducted at speed point terminals.

Interchange Determination Process

The determination of an interchange fee structure or model is a process with an expected start and finish. There are steps that are involved in this process (as per the following figure): identification of a need, hiring of a consultant, engagement with key stakeholders, and publication of a policy instrument by a regulatory authority.

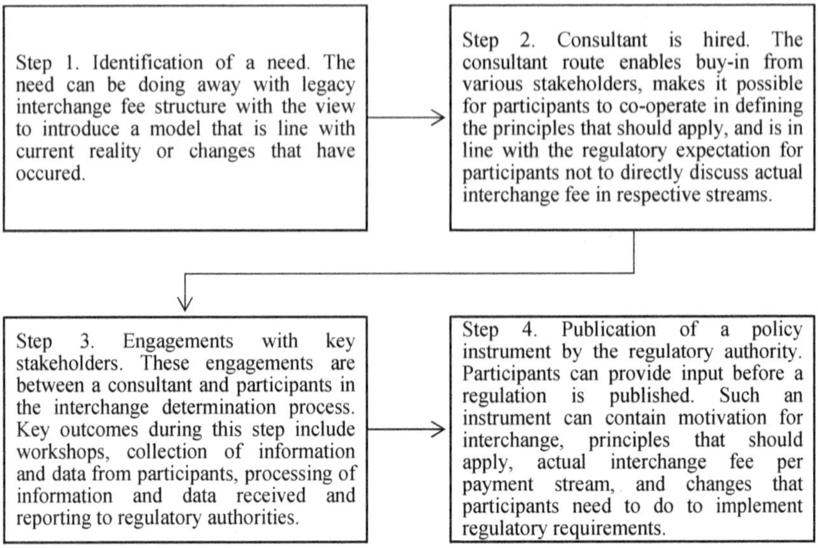

Figure 26.1. Interchange Determination Process

What is the key outcome of the above defined interchange determination process? It is a regulation that is issued to the market by a regulatory body. Such a regulation has an implementation date and the respective interchange fees that should apply. It is at this point that participants or stakeholders are expected to make changes to their systems so that the interchange structure that is outlined in a given regulation is implemented. The actual implementation ensures that the issuer, as an example, receives the required interchange revenue whenever goods and services are bought via speed point terminals.

Interchange Types and Rates

There are different forms of interchange in the card market. The card market is made up of cardholders, merchants, issuers, acquirers and a switch, just to mention but a few of the stakeholders. The variety of interchange types and rates is due to the presence of various channels where cardholders can conduct their transactions. The participants involved include issuers and acquirers. Additionally, there are several transaction types one finds in the card market.

In Namibia, the Bank of Namibia introduced the Determination on Card Interchange and ATM Surcharging (PSD-11), effective from 1 October 2024, which determination provides the card interchange rates and ATM surcharging fees for interbank transactions in the national payment system (Bank of Namibia, 2022). The following table covers interchange rates as published by the regulator, Bank of Namibia:

Table 26.1
Interchange types and rates

Types	Rates
A. Card Interchange for Retail Transactions	
Debit card	0.50%
Hybrid card	0.90%
Credit card	1.60%
B. Card Interchange for Fuel Transactions	
Debit card	0.50%
Hybrid card	0.80%
Credit card	0.80%
C. Interchange for Cash Back Transactions	
Debit card	NAD0.90
Hybrid card	NAD0.90
Credit card	NAD0.90
D. Reserve Interchange for ATM Financial Transactions	

Successful ATM Withdrawal	NAD3.00 plus NAD0.60 per NAD100
Unsuccessful ATM Withdrawal	NAD3.60
E. Reserve Interchange for ATM Non-Financial Transactions	
E.1 Non-Financial ATM Transactions	
Balance enquiry	NAD0.50
Invalid PIN	NAD0.50
Excess PIN tries	NAD0.50
Negative card	NAD0.50
Access restricted	NAD0.50
Expired card	NAD0.50
Invalid transactions	NAD0.50
Insufficient funds	NAD0.50
Withdrawal balance	NAD0.50
Daily limit exceeded	NAD0.50
Excess daily limit withdrawal	NAD0.50
Transaction cancelled	NAD0.50
Foreign card	NAD0.50
E.2 Own Financial Institution (Issuer) Errors	
Host unavailable	NAD0.50
Invalid PAN	NAD0.50
Unable to process	NAD0.50
Denied	NAD0.50
Invalid PIN block	NAD0.50
Balance unavailable	NAD0.50
Slow authorisation	NAD0.50

Invalid data	NAD0.50
No reply	NAD0.50
E.3 Other Financial Institution (Acquirer) Errors	
Invalid PIN block service provider	NAD0.50
Invalid data	NAD0.50
Partial dispense	NAD0.50
ATM fault	NAD0.50
Slow ATM mode	NAD0.50
Unable to capture	NAD0.50
No request	NAD0.50

Source: Bank of Namibia (2022)

Several points can be made from the abovementioned table. There is *normal* and *reserve interchange* in card transactions. The issuer is compensated for normal interchange while it is the acquirer that is compensated for reserve interchange. Normal interchange is realised as a result of retail, fuel and cash back transactions at a speed point terminal. Reserve interchange is generated for transactions done at ATMs and these can be financial and non-financial transactions.

Credit card interchange for retail transactions is higher at 1.60% compared to those for hybrid and debit cards. Retail transactions are the normal purchases done at the merchant, be it buying milk, bread, fruits or vegetables. A credit card allows a cardholder to have access to an unsecured line of credit hence a need for this card type to be associated with a relatively higher interchange rate. An unsecured credit is a form of loan whereby the lender does not require collateral, but ability to pay or creditworthiness for such a facility to be extended to the borrower. The interchange rate for credit and hybrid cards is the same at 0.80% compared to that of debit cards for fuel purchases.

BOX 25

Several countries have adopted a regulatory process for determining interchange rates especially in the card payments environment. Interchange balances the two sides of the market, that is, the issuer side and the acquirer side. The issuer side has a relationship with the cardholder while the acquirer side has a relationship with the merchant. This balance is key as the two sides have each made investment in the market. Cardholders need the means to transact and merchants have a desire to provide goods and services to their varied customer base.

The South African Reserve Bank (2021) through its National Payment System Department determined interchange rates for its national payment system environment covering automated teller machines, debit card, credit card and cash-back at point-of-sale terminal. Some rates are in percentages while others appear in Rand terms. Rand is the South African currency. There is an effective implementation date associated with each interchange rate.

There are interchange rates associated with cash back transactions. Card transactions can be split into two parts: normal retail and cash back transactions. The last transaction type allows the cardholder to get physical cash at a till, as part of the total purchase. Interchange is the same at NAD0.90 for all cash back transactions as per the above table.

Determinants of Interchange Fees

A determinant is a factor that explains a change in the other factor. This means that if there is a change in one factor there is likely to be a change in the other factor, be it negative or positive. Holding other factors the same, an increase in card usage at a particular shop leads to an increase in the number of goods and services sold. Said differently, a decline in card usage at certain shop leads to a decrease in the number of products sold. This is a positive change as the two factors increased at the same time.

Table 26.2
Determinants of interchange fees

Determinant	Description
Demand consideration	The choice of interchange fee will not be optimal if there is very high demand from cardholders but few merchants are willing to accept cards, and the opposite to this is true.
Costs	Higher issuing costs or demand by merchants results in higher interchange fees, and higher acquiring costs or demand by cardholders results in lower interchange fees.
Price-cost margin	The interchange fee increases in the price-cost margin of issuers and decreases in the price-cost margin of acquirers. This implies that higher issuer margins lead to an increase in card fees and requires higher interchange fees to optimally balance the two sides of the market.
Shifting revenue to issuers	If issuer get to retain some of the higher interchange revenue obtained from any increase in interchange fees, the result is setting interchange fees higher that is optimal from a balancing perspective.
Merchant competition	The result of competition between merchants is an increase in interchange fee.
Inter-system competition	This refers to competition with alternative payment schemes such as between credit cards and debit cards or between MasterCard and Visa, and implies that greater inter-system competition leads to a reduction or increase of interchange fees, depending whether a customer carries a single type of card or holds multiple cards.

Source: Weiner and Wright (2005)

The above table outlines key determinants of interchange fees, which include demand consideration, costs, price-cost margin, shifting revenue to issuers, merchant competition and inter-system competition (Weiner and Wright, 2005). Consider one of the determinants such as price-cost margin. A high profit margin from an issuer perspective means a need for high interchange fee.

Chapter Summary

This chapter focussed on interchange in payments. The chapter showed that interchange is an instrument that card associations can use to achieve a desired balance of cardholder usage versus merchant acceptance across the two sides of the market. It was indicated that in other markets, interchange determination is a regulatory process. As an example, the Bank of Namibia introduced the Determination on Card Interchange and ATM Surcharging, which provides the card interchange rates and ATM surcharging fees for interbank transactions in national payment system.

Review Questions

1. How much is due to the issuer if interchange rate is 1.60% for a credit card purchase worth NAD1000 at your favourite local merchant?
2. Outline and comment on key determinants for interchange rates.
3. Discuss the interchange determination process that you have learned.
4. Write short notes on the following terms:
    a. Interchange
    b. Reserve interchange
    c. Two-sided market in card payments

Selected References

Bank of Namibia, (2022). *Determination on Card Interchange and ATM Surcharging (PSD-11)*. Windhoek, Namibia: Bank of Namibia. Retrieved from https://www.bon.com.na/

Calvano, E. (2011). *Note on the Economic Theory of Interchange.* Washington, DC. Retrieved from https://www.federalreserve.gov/

South African Reserve Bank, (2021). *Implementing Interchange Rates: Automated Teller Machines, Card and Cashback at Point of Sale.* Pretoria, South Africa: South African Reserve Bank. Retrieved from https://www.resbank.co.za/

Weiner, S.E., & Wright, J. (2005). Interchange Fees in Various Countries: Developments and Determinants. *Review of Network Economics,* 4 (4), 290-323. Retrieved from https://www.newyorkfed.org/

CHAPTER 27

Contactless Payments

The speed of checkout at the point-of-sale is one of the challenges that continues to challenge practitioners, service providers, merchants and policy makers in payment and clearing systems. This becomes an issue especially if a comparison is made between cash and non-cash payments. Cash transactions are instantaneous while non-cash ones are not and, given the migration from paper to electronic, instantaneous or near instantaneous payments become a need and not a want.

Learning Objectives

By the end of this chapter, you should be able to

- know the description of contactless payments;
- outline advantages and disadvantages of contactless payments; and
- comprehend the basic model of contactless payments.

Description of Contactless Payments

The word *contact* in our everyday conversation means to touch, like touching a payment card and using it for payment of goods and services. Traditionally, a payment card needs to get in touch with delivery channels such as automated teller machines and speed points for in-person transactions to be concluded. Recent developments such as policy, technological and other environmental changes, including the Covid-19 pandemic, have led to the increasing adoption of contactless payments in many markets across the world. Contactless payments are more associated with the card stream than other payment streams such as paper, electronic funds transfer and immediate settlement streams.

Discussions about contactless payments revolve around the extent to which a payment card touches a payment terminal and the associated limits that apply. Contactless payments are also called tap-and-go payments whereby the cardholder initiates a transaction by tapping the card at the payment terminal with a transaction immediately verified if its value is below a recognised limit or threshold and additional verification required, like entering a personal identification number, if the value of such a transaction is above a recognised limit (Brown, Felber, & Meyer, 2003). Okunbor, Adekunle and Adebayo (2020) note that contactless payments is the use of mobile phones, electronic cards and other devices with near field communication (NFC) technology to conduct transactions that do not require a physical connection between the point-of-sale (POS) terminal and the device of the consumer and that NFC refers to wireless technology that is used to transfer card payment data from the device to the payment terminal via radio waves.

BOX 26

Consider this scenario: the cardholder quickly calls a pharmacy to deliver medicine at home for a sick child who just developed fever. The transaction is concluded over the phone and a delivery driver later knocks at the door with the order. It is a payment-on-delivery order, meaning that the transaction needs to be settled when the goods arrive at the purchaser's home.

What follows is that the merchant representative requests the cardholder to tap the card at the handheld mobile speed point. The transaction is authorised online and a slip is handed over to the cardholder without a need to enter a PIN for this payment instruction that is worth NAD150 and falls within the threshold communicated by the financial services provider.

A discussion takes place as the cardholder seems curious as to why she did not enter a PIN to authorise the transactions. The motorcycle driver is willing to shed more light on this innovative technology that is less common in the market, to the satisfaction of the cardholder, and they part ways. The cardholder subsequently becomes a little bit concerned about security around such a transaction, but at the same time understands the big picture that includes the need for speed at the point-of-sale and the relatively small transactions involved for *tap and go* technology.

In view of the above and the related box article, transactions below the value limit are tap and go transactions, with no additional verification required when the card is tapped at the payment terminal. Transactions above the value limit are chip-based transactions, with additional verification like a personal identification number needed and the card is inserted into the terminal if this is the preferred option. Additionally, NFC is the key technology that connects a customer's device and the POS device.

Advantages and Disadvantages of Contactless Payments

There are advantages and disadvantages that are associated with contactless payments. Advantages of contactless payments, according to Zakonnik, Czerwonka, and Zajdel (2018), are outlined below:

- Time saving. There is no need to provide additional validation such as entering a PIN code.
- Convenience. This is related to time saving in that there is no need to insert a card in the point-of-sale terminal nor is there a need to enter a PIN code when a cardholder is prompted to do so.
- Increased level of security. This relates to the fact that for contactless payments, there is no need to provide the card to the merchant for a transaction to be concluded.

Zakonnik, Czerwonka, and Zajdel (2018) also provide details on disadvantages associated with contactless payments and these are listed below:

- Associated security vulnerabilities as a result of no validation for transactions below an agreed threshold. Determining the number of consecutive operations that can be done without entering a PIN is one of the measures that can be employed to minimise impact on cardholders.
- Multiple payments for the same product. There is a possibility of multiple payments for the same product especially if the cardholder is too close to the payment terminal.
- Possibility of card information being collected by surveillance systems. For example, special scanners could be installed at the entrances and exits of premises. Special covers can prevent unwanted communication with such scanners.

Basic Model

The figure below shows a cardholder who has an enabled contactless card and walks over to the speed point. Making transactions below a specific limit allow a cardholder to check out quickly as there is no additional verification required. "Card limit" in this case refers to a limit as communicated to the client by the financial services provider or as agreed at an industry level. Additional verification is associated with transactions above the agreed threshold. Verification kicks in when the cardholder is prompted to enter a PIN or asked to sign a slip before a transaction is concluded.

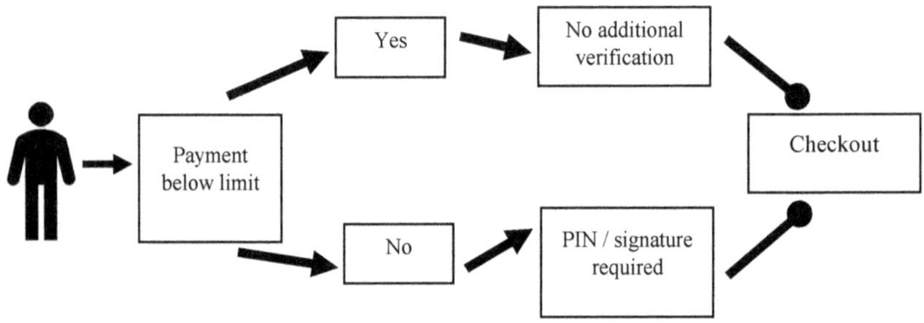

Figure 27.1. Contactless Payments

The last point in the above illustrated model is the checkout. This refers to the point at which the customer walks away from the point-of-sale-with the goods or services bought after the card verification process has been completed. Verification in this case entails checking if the amount is below or above an agreed threshold as well as providing a PIN or signature if the amount in question is above this threshold.

Chapter Summary

This chapter touched on contactless payments. The chapter noted that contactless payments is about the use of mobile phones, electronic cards and other devices with NFC technology to conduct transactions that do not require a physical connection between the POS terminal and the device of the consumer, and that NFC refers to wireless technology that is used to transfer card payment data from the device to the payment terminal via radio waves. These payments have reduced checkout delays at the point-of-sale, to the delight of clients, especially for small payments falling below agreed threshold.

Review Questions

1. Illustrate and describe the basic model that shows transaction flow of contactless payments.
2. Mention advantages and disadvantages of contactless payments that you have learned.
3. Write short notes on the following terms:
    a. Contactless payments
    b. Near field communication
    c. Additional verification in contactless payments

Selected References

Brown, M., Felber, L., & Meyer, C. (2003). *Consumer Adoption and use of Financial Technology "Tap and Go" Payments.* SNB Working Papers, 8. Zurich, Switzerland: Swiss National Bank. Retrieved from https://www.snb.ch/

Okunbor, C.O., Adekunle, Y.A., & Adebayo, A.O. (2020). The Challenges of Contactless Payment Models using Near Field Communication Enabled Devices. *International Journal of Computer Applications Technology and Research*, 9(4), 133-138. Retrieved from https://www.ijcat.com/

Zakonnik, L., Czerwonka, P., Zajdel, R. (2018). Contactless Payments in Poland - Advantages and Disadvantages based on Surveys of a Selected Group of Users over the Years 2011-2028, *SHS Web of Conferences*, 57(01033), 1-7. Retrieved from https://doi.org/10.1051/shsconf/20185701033

CHAPTER 28

Virtual Assets

Virtual assets as a field of study in payments, clearing and settlement systems is relatively new and important for the general public and practitioners alike to understand. When people hear of these assets, what quickly comes to mind are terms such as digital assets, cryptocurrencies, Bitcoin, private sector digital currencies, and blockchain. These assets should be understood with a bigger picture in mind; that is, they are associated with the end goal of realising cash lite. The latter entails the migration from paper-based payment methods to an electronic way of paying for goods and services.

Learning Objectives

By the end of this chapter, you should be able to

- describe what virtual assets are all about;
- list different types of virtual assets;
- comprehend the risks related to virtual assets; and
- appreciate regulatory and supervisory aspects for virtual assets including the travel rule.

Description of Virtual Assets

The term "virtual assets" is made up of two key words. "Virtual" implies something that exists or is represented in a non-physical form. On the other hand, "assets" are things that we own. Virtual assets, based on the above understanding, are assets that exist or are represented in a non-physical form. The implication is that there is a conversion process that happens to turn an asset from one state, that is physical, to another state, that is virtual or non-physical. There are several use cases for an asset that has been made virtual and these include for payment and investment.

Virtual assets should not be confused with real money or electronic money. These payment instruments were discussed in the previous chapters. This is in line with the work of Rysin and Rysin (2021) that says that virtual currencies are considered different from traditional currencies and electronic money. Virtual assets are distinct from fiat currency, that is real currency, real money or national currency, which is the money of a country that is designated as its legal tender. "Virtual asset" refers to a digital representation of value that can be digitally traded or transferred and can be used for payment or investment purposes, including digital representation of value that functions as a medium of change, a unit of account and/or store of value (LexisNexis Risk Solutions, 2019). Hrytsai (2022) implies that virtual assets are also referred to as cryptocurrencies, virtual currencies or digital assets and notes that cryptocurrency is a decentralised convertible currency based on mathematical principles that are protected using cryptographic methods, that is, using cryptography to create a distributed, decentralised and secure information economy, and using public and private keys to transfer currency from one person to another. Government of the Republic of Namibia (2023) notes that a virtual asset is a digital representation of value that can be digitally transferred, stored or traded; uses a distributed ledger technology or similar technology; and can be used for payment or investment purposes.

Crypto assets and related technologies are part and parcel of the crypto asset industry. The sector can be broken down into different components with each part being essential for proper functioning of the industry.

Hacibedel and Perez-Saiz (2023) provide six categories in the crypto asset ecosystem:

- Issuers design or issue crypto assets.
- Miners or validators verify and validate transactions, sometimes by solving complex cryptographic problems, and getting a reward for it.
- Crypto exchanges or platforms provide custodian services and facilitate transactions between players.
- Wallet providers promise the secure storage of crypto assets in exchange for a fee.
- Investors as a category includes individuals and institutions.
- Payment providers enable clients to use crypto assets to pay merchants or transfer funds abroad using crypto assets, in addition to other payment services.

The above description shows that there is an agreement on what virtual assets are all about, that is, digital representation of value available for trading, payment and investment in the virtual asset ecosystem. These assets are powered by a specific technology and traded via an organised arrangement or platform. Technology in this case is the distributed ledger technology such as blockchain. Trading arrangement can be an organised exchange or over the counter method depending on the extent of development of a given cryptocurrency market.

Different Types of Virtual Assets

Virtual assets manifest in a variety of forms. Some of these are commonly known to many people while others are less known. These assets are bitcoin, altcoin, stablecoin and token as per the following table. The assets can be broken down in subcategories as well. As an example, Ethereum is one of the use cases within the altcoin range of assets.

Table 28.1
Types of Virtual Assets

Type	Description
Bitcoin	It was launched in 2009 as a decentralised cryptocurrency powered by blockchain technology, which can be sent, received and stored. Bitcoin was developed to solve the possibility of fraud and it is pseudo-anonymous; that is, an individual involved in the transaction is not known, but the chain of transactions can be traced end to end.
Altcoin	This cryptocurrency was launched in 2011, as an alternative to Bitcoin. Types of altcoins include but are not limited to: Ethereum, Ripple, Bitcoin Cash, Litecoin, EOS.IO, Dogecoin, Zerocoin and Anoncoin.
Stablecoin	A cryptocurrency that is stable or low in volatility with value tied to physical assets or currency reserves. Types of stablecoins include Tether, Dai and Paxos.
Token	Tokens can be used as a means of payment and are a unit of account and are classified into capital tokens, service tokens and tokens secured by assets.

Source: Hrytsai (2022)

Bitcoin is known to be the first virtual asset that came into the cryptocurrency market in 2009. A few years later, further developments led to the creation of other assets including altcoin, which is the alternative to bitcoin. This is in line with Hrytsai (2022) who indicated that altcoin was created as an alternative to bitcoin and coined during Bitcointalk, one of the specialised forums in the cryptocurrency market, and popularised by Wall Street Journal.

Risks in Virtual Assets

Financial products and services are associated with inherent risks, and virtual assets are no exception. It has been well known for a while that virtual currencies have been used in online criminal payments and particularly in large-scale cybercrime and on the dark web (LexisNexis Risk Solutions, 2019). This does not mean that if a certain product or service has risks attached to it then such a product or service should be discarded. There is a close and positive relationship between risk and reward such that, holding other things the same, reward tends to be higher if the associated risk is high and vice-versa. Risk management is important to ensure that risks are minimised to the required level for the benefit of all stakeholders.

BOX 27

The market for cryptocurrencies is growing. More interest is seen in the private sector (privately issued digital currencies and not necessarily central bank digital currencies) in terms of offering and acquiring these assets. Emanuel-Burns (2024) noted that central bank digital currencies (CBDCs) fall into two categories, that is retail and wholesale, and that 93 percent of central banks are actively involved in CBDC development in recent years with the Bahamas, Jamaica and Nigeria being live on the retail side. Interest in cryptocurrencies has served as a basis for the regulatory fraternity to be prepared for what is ahead. While some countries have embraced digital assets within the existing legal and regulatory frameworks, others have opted to issue new legal and regulatory instruments.

Devitt (2024) shared that it is not in the Swiss National Bank's best interest to hold Bitcoin (BTC) as a reserve currency as there are downsides to holding the top crypto asset and this is despite campaigns from the crypto stakeholders pushing for a portion of the reserves to be in BTC. South Africa, under the auspices of Financial Sector Conduct Authority (FSCA), was expecting cryptocurrency platforms or digital asset exchanges to seek permits or approvals to operate before 30 November 2024 (Daily Investor, 2024).

Virtual assets literature is awash with risks that are specific to the virtual assets or crypto assets industry. These risks are not only felt at micro-environment level but also extend into the macro environment, that is the real sector. Hacibedel and Perez-Saiz (2023) categorise risks that are associated with virtual assets into micro risks (credit risk, market and liquidity risks, concentration and propagation risks, cyber risk, and legal and regulatory risks) and macro risks (risks on households and corporates, risk to the fiscal sector, risk to the external sector, and less effective monetary policy), as outlined in the following table:

Table 28.2
Risks in Virtual Assets

Type	Description
Credit risk	This risk refers to the inability to fulfil a financial claim by the counterparty in a financial exchange. It is not substantial in some crypto assets, like Bitcoin, that do not have a claim on the issuer and are considered nonfinancial assets. Stablecoins are prone to credit risk as they have a claim on the issuer, and there are concerns about the quality of the assets or effectiveness of the algorithms used to back their value.
Market and liquidity risks	These risks are present in crypto assets with market risk being a risk of price volatility or adverse information that can affect the quality of the issuer's assets. Runs on the issuer not only induce price pressures, they also lead to fluctuations in an asset as well as worsening liquidity risk.
Concentration and propagation risks	Despite the decentralised design of crypto assets, concentration has increased in this sector over the years due to the dominance of Bitcoin and Ethereum or the emergence of large exchange platforms and wallets.
Cyber risk	Emerging financial technologies, like those in the crypto asset industry, are exposed to cyber-attacks, given their reliance on technology as well as poor governance and fewer controls and risk management procedures on the part of specialised crypto firms.

Legal / regulatory risks	These risks can manifest if regulatory or legal instruments are not in line with prudent best practices being recommended by standard-setting bodies.
Risks on households and corporates	Market ambiguities and price fluctuations have a wealth effect on households especially if accompanied by excessive risk taking and leveraged exposure. The integration of crypto assets into payment systems makes corporates more vulnerable in terms of profitability, asset versus liability mismatches and cash flows.
Risk to the fiscal sector	Fluctuations in crypto assets especially in case of downturns negatively impact economic growth and budget deficit, notably in countries where these assets are legal tender or where governments depend on financing from crypto platforms.
Risk to the external sector	Lower transaction costs could trigger highly volatile capital flows in the external sector.
Less effective monetary policy	Cryptos could accelerate bank disintermediation, currency substitution, reduce the effectiveness of capital controls, and undermine traditional credit transmission channels, thus limiting the effectiveness of monetary policy.
Money laundering and terrorist financing (ML/TF) risks	The speed of transactions, global reach and potential for increased anonymity and obfuscation of transaction flows and counterparties make crypto assets particularly suitable for criminal uses especially if regulated financial institutions do not apply preventative measures such as customer due diligence, record keeping and suspicious transaction reporting.

Source: Hacibedel and Perez-Saiz (2023), Coelho, Fishman and Ocampo (2021)

There is a total of ten risk categories in the above table, of which the first five relate to the micro environment and the last five are associated with the macro environment. While the micro environment includes the impact on the virtual assets and service providers, the macro environment focuses on the real sector that cover such entities like households, corporates and government. As an example, market risk arising from adverse media coverage or price fluctuation can have a negative impact on asset value as well as the ability of a service provider to honour a claim. An expected and sustained boom in the crypto sector can lead to fiat currency substitution and consequently less effective monetary policy.

Regulation and Supervision

Regulation and supervision of virtual asset service providers (VASPs) is important to make sure that inherent and money laundering and terrorist financing risks (ML/TF) are minimised or mitigated. Bank of Namibia (2022) states that a virtual asset service provider is a natural or legal person that conducts one or more of the following activities or operations for or on behalf of another natural or legal person:

- Exchange between virtual assets and fiat money.
- Exchange between one or more forms of virtual assets.
- Transfer of virtual assets.
- Safe keeping and / or administration of virtual assets or instruments enabling control over virtual assets.
- Participation in and provision of financial services related to the issuer's offer and / or sale of virtual asset.

Pavlidis (2020) provides a framework, based on the work of Financial Action Task Force (FATF), an international standards setting body, that is key for regulation and supervision of virtual asset service providers and this framework, as per the diagram below, has components such as the nature of virtual assets, risk-based approach to virtual assets, registration of virtual asset service providers, regulation and supervision of virtual asset service providers, preventative measures, and international cooperation.

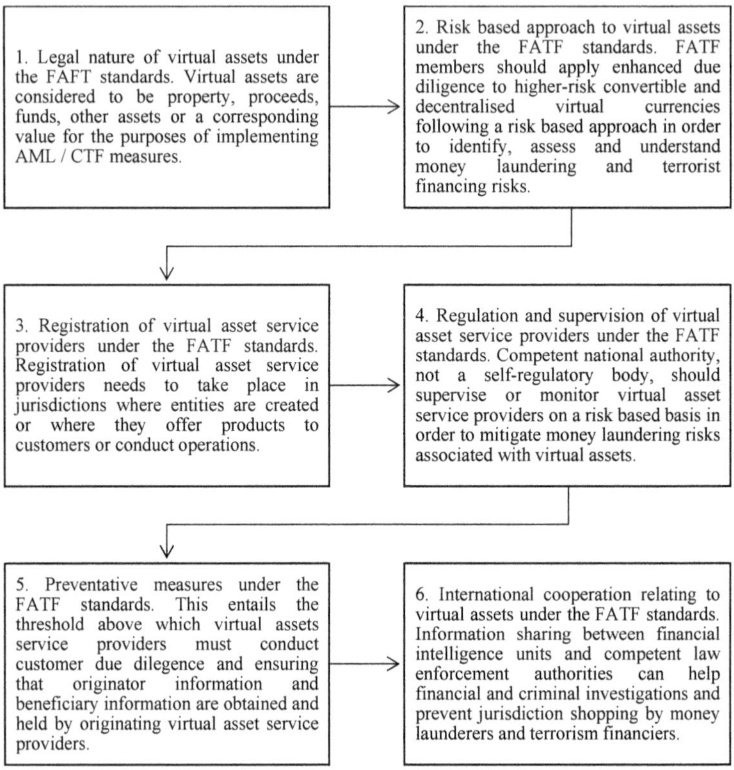

Figure 28.1. Regulation and Supervision of Virtual Assets

FATF standards are being domesticated in member jurisdictions around the world in the form of principal legal instruments such as a payments law or subordinate regulations such as a directive. Domesticating these standards leads to effective regulation and supervision, based on a risk-based approach, and prevents jurisdiction shopping. A risk-based approach to regulation and supervision focusses on key risk areas and not all risk issues to prevent overstretching of resources. Jurisdiction shopping is a situation where entities or service providers look for doing business in jurisdictions with weak legal and regulatory frameworks.

Recommendation 15 and Travel Rule

Contact and financial details of originator and beneficiary are crucial in payment, clearing and settlement systems. This is not only to ensure that a transaction is completed from end to end to realise straight-through processing but also to make sure that necessary information is available when requested by third parties or regulatory bodies as part of the effort to contain money laundering and terrorist financing risks. Recommendation 15 of the Financial Action Task Force highlights that financial institutions have to identify and evaluate the money laundering or terrorist financial risks and those risks may emerge due to the evolution of financial products and business practices, in particular those that provide the newest methods of distribution, and the application of new technologies for both existing and promising products and services (Rysin and Rysin, 2021). Virtual assets are one of the newest financial technologies, products or services and they are not immune from the risks related to money laundering and terrorist financing.

The travel rule entails a need by governments to require cryptocurrency firms to collect accurate originator information and required beneficiary information on transactions and share those details with other firms involved in the payment chain (LexisNexis Risk Solutions, 2019). The application of the FATF's wire transfer requirements in the virtual asset context is called the travel rule and mandatory information for the originator includes the name of the originator, account number and originator's address while for the beneficiary the required information is the name of the beneficiary and the account number (Financial Action Task Force, 2021). While the travel rule has been an obligation in the United States since 1996 for payments of USD3000 and above, other jurisdictions remain uncertain on how to apply the travel rule, in light of the fact that the robust infrastructure available to support compliance for banks is lacking for crypto asset providers, making compliance for them technically feasible but much less efficient than for banks (Coelho, Fishman and Ocampo, 2021). The above shows that the travel rule is one of the key preventative measures that can be applied by all stakeholders in reducing money laundering and related risks if supported and implemented by all institutions not only for wire transfers but also virtual assets related payments.

Chapter Summary

This chapter covered one of the important and emerging topics in payment, clearing and settlement systems: that of virtual assets. The chapter noted that a virtual asset is a digital representation of value that: can be digitally transferred, stored or traded; uses a distribution ledger technology or similar technology; and can be used for payment or investment purposes. It has been well known for a while that virtual currencies have been used in online criminal payments and particularly in large-scale cybercrime and on the dark web. The aforementioned reality has motivated the Financial Action Task Force to put in place regulatory and supervisory best practices that can assist countries in containing money laundering and terrorist financing risks.

Review Questions

1. Discuss key risks in virtual assets that you have learned.
2. List and explain the types of virtual assets.
3. Illustrate the framework for the regulation and supervision of virtual assets.
4. Write short notes on the following terms:

a. Jurisdiction shopping
b. Virtual assets
c. Virtual asset service providers
d. Bitcoin
e. Travel rule
f. Stablecoin

5. Match the stakeholders (wallet providers, issuers, miners and exchanges) to the statements or functions by giving feedback under the space that is provided:

Statements or functions	Student Response
Issues cryptos	
Validates transactions	
Facilitates transactions	
Provides storage of cryptos	

Selected References

Bank of Namibia, (2022). *Revised Position on Virtual Assets and Virtual Asset Service Providers*. Windhoek, Namibia: Bank of Namibia. Retrieved from https://www.bon.com.na/

Coelho, R., Fishman, J., & Ocampo, D.G. (2021). Supervising Crypto Assets for Anti-Money Laundering. *FSI Insights on Policy Implementation, No. 31*. Basel, Switzerland: Bank for International Settlements. Retrieved from https://www.bis.org/

Daily Investor. (2024). FSCA set to License 60 Crypto Exchanges in South Africa. Pretoria, South Africa: *Daily Investor*. Retrieved from https://www.dailyinvestor.com/

Devitt, C. (2024). Swiss Central Bank's Chairman says He's Dubious about Holding Bitcoin. Los Angeles, California: *The Daily Hodl*. Retrieved from https://www.dailyhodl.com/

Emanuel-Burns, C. (2024). The Asian CBDC is Ready to Bloom. London, United Kingdom: *FinTech Futures*. Retrieved from https://www.fintechfutures.com/

Financial Action Task Force, (2021). *Updated Guidance for a Risk-Based Approach to Virtual Assets and Virtual Asset Service Providers*. Paris, France: Financial Action Task Force. Retrieved from https://www.fatf-gafi.org/

Government of the Republic of Namibia, (2023). *Payment System Management Act*. Windhoek, Namibia: Bank of Namibia. Retrieved from https://www.bon.com.na/

Hacibedel, B., & Perez-Saiz, H. (2023). Assessing Macrofinancial Risks from Crypto Assets. *IMF Working Paper, WP/23/214*. Washington, D.C: International Monetary Fund. Retrieved from https://www.imf.com/

Hrytsai, S. (2022). The Place of Virtual Assets in the Structure of Digital Financial Technology. *International Science Journal of Management, Economics & Finance*, 1(3), 34-48. Retrieved from https://doi.org/10.46299/j.isjmef.20220103.3

LexisNexis Risk Solutions, (2019). A Risk-Based Approach to Virtual Assets and Virtual Asset Service Providers – White Paper. Chandler, Arizona: *LexisNexis Risk Solutions*. Retrieved from https://www.risk.lexisnexis.com/

Pavlidis, G. (2020). International Regulation of Virtual Assets under FATF's new Standard. *Journal of Investment Compliance*, 21(1), 1-8. Retrieved from https://doi.org/10.1108/JOIC-08-2019-0051

Rysin, V., & Rysin, M. (2021). Vulnerability of Virtual Assets to Illicit Financial Flows. *Journal of Economics, Entrepreneurship and Management*, 8(1), 35-42. Retrieved from https://doi.org/10.23939/eem2021.01.035

CHAPTER 29

Social Media Payments

Social media platforms are ubiquitous. The platforms come in different forms and people subscribe to them for diverse uses. Presently, uses of these applications include but are not limited to: advertising products and services; searching for employment and training opportunities; connecting with family, friends and other stakeholders; and raising funds for certain needs. An emerging trend is the integration of these platforms to the world of payment, clearing and settlement systems.

Learning Objectives

By the end of this chapter, you should be able to

- describe what social media is all about;
- understand different social media platforms;
- know social media payments and related technologies; and
- comprehend challenges associated with social media payments and adoption of these payments in future.

Description of Social Media

There is a need to differentiate between media and social media. The word media refers to ways that information and entertainment are transmitted or communicated to as many people as possible and includes newspapers, magazines, radio, television and internet. Consequently, media can be print such as newspaper, broadcast like radio and online via the internet. Social media then refers specifically to the main ways that people or communities send, receive or share information, entertainment or data via the internet.

Koukaras, Tjortjis and Rousidis (2020) show that people use social media to communicate, connect and interact with users through virtual communities and networks, and share and propagate information at a greater rate; and such data includes posts, photos, videos and so on. Social media networks have also connected people and communities that are at a distance from one another. The volume of data being shared is massive and has increased over the years, an increase made possible by more and more people and communities that are being connected, availability of smartphones, affordability of data and proximity of communication networks.

Types of Social Media Platforms

Social media can be divided into several types. Koukaras, Tjortjis and Rousidis (2020) propose three types: social, entertainment and profiling networks, typically capturing emerging social media platform services.

Table 29.1
Types of Social Media

Type	Description
Social networks	The primary utility covers connecting, multimedia, professional broadcasters / recruiters and sharing. Examples include Facebook, You Tube, Instagram, Twitter, and LinkedIn.
Entertainment networks	This refers to social media with primary utility being entertainment such as games, sports, cinema and travel. Examples include Facebook.
Profiling networks	Comprise social media that offer functions for promoting skills, goals and personal journals with primary utility being profiling. Examples include Facebook and LinkedIn.

Source: Koukaras, Tjortjis and Rousidis (2020)

The table shows types of social media in the left-hand column and the description of each network in the right-hand column. Major social media examples include Facebook, You Tube, Instagram, Twitter and LinkedIn. Several conclusions can be made from the abovementioned table, as shown in the additional table below:

Table 29.2
Examples of Social Media

Examples	Social Networks	Entertainment Networks	Profiling Networks
Facebook (Meta)	1	1	1
You Tube	1		
Instagram	1		
Twitter	1		
LinkedIn	1		1
Total Count	5	1	2

Looking at the above table, social networks are the most common types (total count is 5) followed by profile networks (total count is 2) ending with entertainment networks (total count is 1). With respect to examples of social networks, Facebook is the most common as it used for social, entertainment and profiling purposes. LinkedIn has proved to be useful across these forms of networks as it is utilised for both social and profiling. The other three, that is, YouTube, Instagram and Twitter are mainly social network examples. There are several ways social media networks are being used today and the following box article provides an example:

BOX 28

Social media can be classified into social, entertainment and profiling networks. They provide a number of benefits to subscribers including for connecting and sharing information or data, entertainment and promoting skills.

Social media platforms are being used to a great extent today. Consider an example of an individual who would like to organise a function. The event in this case is a matriculation farewell party that is scheduled to happen the day after the formal gathering has been concluded. A committee is established with the sole purpose of raising money totalling NAD10,000 to cover associated expenses. About 100 individuals are expected to attend. As a result, it is agreed that each person contributes NAD100 to make up the required amount. Mobile phone number of the finance person, who should receive all contributions, is shared on the group's chat or social media platform, WhatsApp. Consequently, all goes according to plan and the party is held to the satisfaction of everybody.

One example of social media that is not shown in the above tables is called WhatsApp. This can be classified as a social network example and not necessarily falling into the categories of networks like entertainment and profiling. WhatsApp as a social network provides for uses such as connecting, multimedia and sharing as well.

Social Media Payments and Technologies

There is a positive correlation between the growth of social media and social media payments. Social media payments are transactions that are done through the app, either within the app or outside the app in collaboration with payment service providers. Growth in social media platforms creates a need to integrate with payment systems. As social media continues to evolve, more and more platforms are exploring the world of payments and in 2012, Snapchat introduced *Snapcash* to allow users to send money to each other through the app; in 2015 Pinterest introduced *Buyable Pins,* allowing users to purchase products directly from the platform; and in 2020, TikTok launched its own payment feature making it possible for users in certain countries to link their credit or debit cards and make purchases within the app (Tomych, 2023).

Social media transactions can be divided in several forms or use cases. Tomych (2023) outlines three types of social media payments and these are outlined below:

- Peer-to-peer payments. This use case allows users to send money directly to other users within the same social media platform and examples are Snapchat's Snapcash and Facebook's Messenger Payments.
- In-app purchases. Users are able to buy goods and services within the app or game with purchases charged to the user's connected credit card or payment account.
- Social commerce. The use case allows users to buy products directly through a social media platform without leaving the platform and Instagram and Facebook have integrated shopping features that allow users to buy products from brands they follow without having to navigate to a separate website.

The above list shows that there are transaction types that are related to social media payments, person-to-person being one of them. In-app purchases allow users to conclude a transaction without leaving the app in question, made possible through close collaboration with other service providers in the national payment system.

Challenges related to Social Media Payments

Social media payments provide a number of benefits although there are some challenges. Baird (2023) lists different areas where personal finances and social media intersect and these include person-to-person payments (sending money to another party), crowdfunding (collecting a large pool of money for charity and other causes), social commerce (purchasing and selling products within a social media platform), and financial education (financial advice) and goes further to say that despite associated benefits, social media platforms also come with fraud related risks for consumers. The emergence of embedded finance and its ability to connect to banking services within all types of media is renewing the ambitions of certain czars in social media, person-to-person payments and blockchain technology, but obstacles that still remain include fraud and scams infecting online shopping portals, competition from established payment providers, and a growing number of fake websites masquerading as legitimate e-commerce portals (Fitzgerald, 2024). Additionally, Koenigsberg (2024) notes that embedded finance is now getting more sophisticated, and the acceleration is taking financial products and putting them into non-financial platforms, which banks should like because it gives them another touchpoint with their customers.

The foregoing confirms that there are benefits of social media payments, albeit with some associated risks. Risks such as fraud need to be managed and not left untouched as doing so can lead to propagation of additional risks like reputational and systemic risks. Institutional and industry risk frameworks can go a long way in managing risks related to social media payments.

Adoption of Social Media Payments

Full adoption of social media payments is a matter of when this can happen, rather than if it can happen. Consumer demand, availability of infrastructure, regulatory buy-in and media campaigns are some of the factors that can fuel the acceptance of these payments going forward. It all starts with the penetration of smart phones in the market and availability of social media networks on such phones. These phones are now widely available and the usage of social media is equally widespread. The uptake of social media automatically serves as a springboard for social media payments.

There should be regulatory buy-in in order for social media payments to be well received. Regulators are traditionally interested in the achievement of public policy objectives for any payment-related innovation that comes into the market. Public policy objectives include financial inclusion, affordability, competition, safety and effectiveness. As an example, the Bank of Namibia (2024) issued a position modernisation paper that covers a number of topics in the national payment system and noted that the integration of payments into social media and messaging apps is an evolving field, with social networking sites and payment service providers constantly innovating and collaborating to offer improved solutions and user experiences.

Trust from a customer's perspective is important for acceptance of social media payments. A customer can trust an innovation if there are security features, they are able to do their payments, the service is affordable and there is awareness around a given payment mechanism. This is line with Fitzgerald (2024) who advises that building consumer trust, staging awareness campaigns and improving security of these services through faster payments will be key to their adoption on social media platforms. Although social media payments are beneficial, there are also inherent risks that need to be managed.

Chapter Summary

This chapter focussed on social media payments. Social media can be broken down into social, entertainment and profiling networks which people use to communicate, connect and interact with other users through virtual communities and networks. Social media payments are transactions that are done through the app, either within the app or outside the app in collaboration with payment service providers. Institutional and industry risk frameworks can go a long way in managing risks related to social media payments.

Review Questions

1. List and briefly explain the three major types of social media that you have learned.
2. Name some of the challenges that are associated with social media payments.
3. Indicate whether the following statements are true or false:
    a. LinkedIn is a profiling as well as social network.
    b. You Tube is a social network only.
    c. Facebook is a social, entertainment and profiling network.

d. Embedded finance relates to the integration of financial products with non-financial or banking platforms.

4. Match the following broad types of social media networks (social network, entertainment network and profiling network) to the examples of social media networks by providing feedback in the space that is provided (hint: some examples might be associated with more than one broad category):

Example of Social Media Networks	Student Response
You Tube	________________
Facebook	________________
Instagram	________________

LinkedIn ____________________

____

Selected References

Baird, S. (2023). Social Media for Personal Finances: A New Trend for Millennials and Gen Z. *Payments System Research Briefing*. Retrieved from https://www.kansascityfed.org/

Bank of Namibia, (2024). *National Payment System Modernisation Position*. Windhoek, Namibia: Bank of Namibia. Retrieved from https://www.bon.com.na/

Fitzgerald, K. (2024). *What does the Future hold for Social Media-Powered Payments*. New York, NY: American Banker. Retrieved from https://www.americanbanker.com/

Koenigsberg, A. (2024). Visa's Koenigsberg sees five Emerging B2B Payment Trends in Defining 2024. *The 2024 Business Payments Outlook*. Retrieved from https://www.bottomline.com/

Koukaras, P., Tjortjis., C., & Rousidis, D. (2020). *Social Media Types: Introducing a Data Driven Taxonomy*. Thessaloniki, Greece: International Hellenic University. Retrieved from https://www.researchgate.net/

Tomych, I. (2023). *Social Media Payments: A Game-Changer for the Financial World*. Wilmington, DE: DashDevs. Retrieved from https://www.dashdevs.com/

CHAPTER 30

Quick Response Payments

Checkout at the point-of-sale without unnecessary delay remains one of the goals being pursued by regulatory and industry stakeholders. This is in line with the need to maintain or exceed customer experience in terms of meeting their tastes and preferences, creating confidence in the impacted payment stream, and aligning to international standards and developments. Quick response code is one of the ways of realising timely check out at the point-of-sale within a national payment system.

Learning Objectives

By the end of this chapter, you should be able to

- describe quick response payments;
- outline both the benefits and drawbacks for quick response payments; and
- illustrate the interbank payment and settlement process for quick response payments.

Description of Quick Response Payments

The payment for goods and services can be initiated using several methods that include traditional and non-traditional ones. Traditional payment instruments are paper based such as cash, while on the non-traditional side there are electronic types that cover cards and electronic fund transfers. It is within the electronic portion where mobile payment (m-payment) is located. Mobile payment is essentially the use of a phone such as a smartphone to conclude a transaction at the point-of-sale. The payment method is important given the global drive towards cash-lite and the need to respond to environmental challenges that favour electronic payments.

Li-Ya, Wei-Han, Xiu-Ming, Jun-Jie and Keng-Boon (2021) point out that m-payment has the potential to be a significant disruptor in many sectors and that this payment instrument uses various technologies such as a quick response (QR) code and near field communication (NFC). This aligns with the understanding that mobile payment is a very significant and critical resolution for mobile commerce with the QR code mechanism being key for enhancing user experience (Pujar, 2015).

There is a need to understand QR codes before focussing on related payments, benefits and drawbacks, and the settlement process of the payments that are initiated with QR technology. QR codes are 2-dimensional codes comprising black squares and bars on a white background; a scanner decodes the information in the code, which can be used for payments in industries such as utility companies, restaurants, street vendors and e-ticketing services (Dziuba, 2021). Peratello (2023) states that QR codes contain encoded data much like a barcode that is attached on items in the store but with the option to hold far more information.

QR payments should be understood within the field of contactless digital payments on both the issuing and acquiring sides of a payment market. Issuing here does not only mean a payment card that is presented at a contactless-enabled speed point, but also means a QR-enabled smartphone that is presented at a merchant terminal capable of handling such payments. The QR technology has its roots in the manufacturing sector, but life has moved on as the need for this now exists in other sectors as well.

Karniawati, Darma, Mahyuni and Sanica (2021) note that the QR code was first developed by Denso Wave, a division of Japanese company Denso Corporation, in 1994, with initial use being to identify vehicle parts in the manufacturing companies. Currently, the technology is used in commercial applications and payment channels aimed at mobile phone users. The scale of usage of this payment technology has increased. This is in line with the work of Marsudi and Masudin (2021), which shows that using QR codes for conducting financial transactions is now standard in the banking sector in places such as Indonesia and China. Namibia is not an exception, as specified in the following box:

BOX 29

The Bank of Namibia, through its *Guidelines on the Standardisation of Quick Response Codes*, is of the view that absence of standardised QR codes means that each payment service provider is at liberty to introduce any code that is based on proprietary standards and thus limiting innovations in the national payment system (Bank of Namibia, 2023). There are several points that stakeholders can learn from the guidelines issued by the Bank of Namibia and these points are outlined below.

Firstly, there are merchant-presented and customer-presented QR code payments. Secondly, there are static and dynamic QR codes with the former containing fixed information that is not expected to change over time and the latter providing the capability to store information that can be updated afterwards. Thirdly, there are principles for QR code standardisation in the national payment system and these include approach, technical specification, level of interoperability, security and privacy considerations, accessibility and usability, adoption and promotion strategy, and cost effectiveness.

Benefits and Drawbacks of Quick Response Payments

Non-cash payment instruments, although beneficial, are not problem free and QR payments are not an exception. These payments are a close substitute to traditional payment methods such as paper and other non-cash instruments. Additionally, such payments are not fraud free, hence a need for constant customer education on financial products and services.

There are several benefits of the QR payment method that are mentioned in the literature (Hewawasam, Jaharadak, Khatibi, and Azam, 2023):

- QR code-based payment solutions offer an alternative channel for initiating and accepting payments.
- The use of QR codes for payments eliminates the need for consumers to carry cash or credit cards and for retailers to purchase pricey point-of-sale equipment to process transactions.

Drawbacks of the QR payment method to note are outlined below (Hewawasam, Jaharadak, Khatibi, and Azam, 2023):

- Lack of knowledge about the utility and usage of the QR payment method.
- Consumers worry about their personal information being obtained by unauthorised parties thus making them reluctant to provide such information when doing digital transactions.

Payment and Settlement Process

The process to complete a transaction within a QR payment space is similar to any other interbank transaction where two banks are involved, with the difference being the payment method that is used. Location of the QR code should be clear as well, whether it is the customer who displays it or the merchant. Six steps are outlined in the diagram below with the assumption that the QR payment is based on merchant-presented mode (Dziuba, 2021):

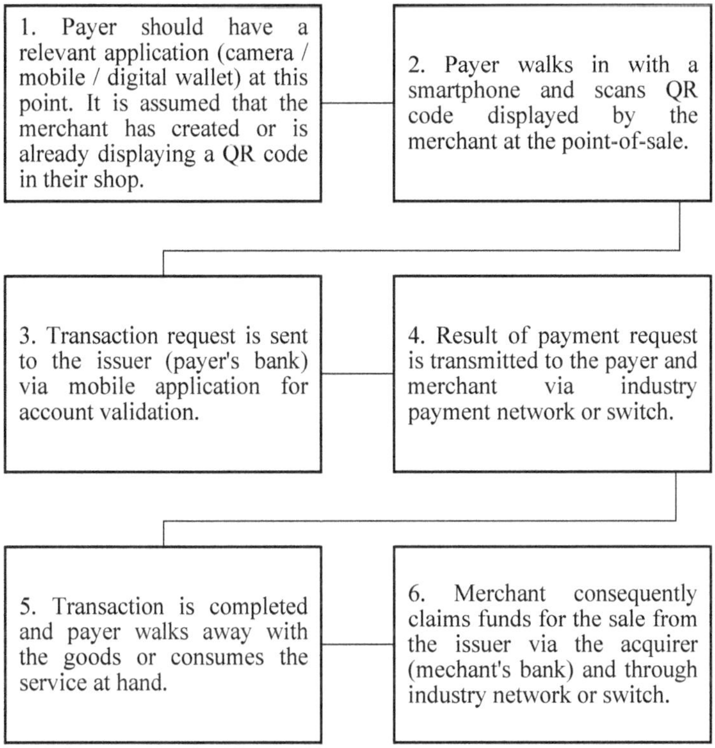

Figure 30.1. Payment Process

In the above diagram, the payer, with a relevant app-enabled smartphone, scans the QR code at a merchant outlet. What follows is the confirmation with the issuer regarding availability of funds, before goods are released or the service is fully consumed, after which the merchant initiated interbank settlement process kicks in.

Chapter Summary

The purpose of this chapter was to discuss quick response (QR) code payments. QR codes are 2-dimensional codes comprising black squares and bars on a white background and when a code is scanned a scanner decodes the information in it, which can be used for payments in various industries. One of the benefits of these payments is that they offer an alternative channel for initiating and accepting payments. There are drawbacks associated with QR code payments and one of these is the lack of knowledge about the utility and usage of the QR payment method. Despite the negatives associated with QR code payments, the future is bright for these payments given that they provide convenience to customers and are in line with strategic imperatives such as migration of customers to online and digital payments.

Review Questions

1. List the benefits and drawbacks of QR payments that you have learned.
2. Illustrate the payment process for a QR code transaction.
3. Define the following terms that are associated with QR payments:
    a. QR code
    b. QR code payment
    c. Mobile payment
    d. Merchant mode for QR transaction
    e. Payer mode for QR transaction

Selected References

Bank of Namibia, (2023). *Guidelines on the Standardisation of Quick Response Codes in the National Payment System.* Windhoek, Namibia: Bank of Namibia. Retrieved from https://www.bon.com.na/

Dziuba, A. (2021). *QR Code Payments Explained – Will 2024 be the Year of QR?* Lviv, Ukraine: Relevant Software. Retrieved from https://www.relevant.softwares.com/

Hewawasam, P. C., Jaharadak, A. A. B., Khatibi, A., & Azam, S. M. F. (2023). QR Code Enabled Payment Solutions in Creating a Cashless

Society among Sri Lankan Consumers - A Literature Review. *Journal of Service Science and Management,* 16, 110-132. Retrieved from https://doi.org/10.4236/jssm.2023.162008

Karniawati, N. P. A., Darma, G. S., Mahyuni, L. P., & Sanica, I. G. (2021). Community Perception of Using QR Code Payment in Era New Normal. *PalArch's Journal of Archaeology of Egypt / Egyptology,* 18(1), 3986-3999. Retrieved from https://www.sciencedirect.com/

Li-Ya, Y., Wei-Han, G.T., Xiu-Ming, L., Jun-Jie, H., & Keng-Boon, O. (2021). QR Code and Mobile Payment: The Disruptive Forces in Retail. *Journal of Retail and Consumer Services,* 58, 1-9. Retrieved from https://doi.org/10.1016/j.jretconser.2020.102300

Marsudi, W.W., & Masudin, I. (2021). QR Code Based Payment. Does the Consumer Intend to Adopt a Retail Buying Transaction? *Business Perspective,* 18(3), 1-14. Retrieved from https://dx.doi.org/10.21511/bbs.18(3).2023.01

Peratello, G. (2023). *Everything you need to Know about QR Code Payments.* London, United Kingdom: Wise Payments Limited. Retrieved from https://www.wise.com/

Pujar, J.S. (2015). Mobile Payment System using QR Code. *International Journal of Research and Analytical Reviews,* 2(2), 36-42. Retrieved from https://www.ijrar.org/

CHAPTER 31

Standard-Setting and International Bodies

Standards and principles are ubiquitous. They are available in every aspect of our lives and we practice them day to day. Standards are also associated with the quality of something produced. This implies that a product is considered of low quality if it falls below a certain bar or level of expectation and is of good quality if it is on par or above the level of quality in question. Standard-setting bodies continue to play a key role in devising principles or best practices that can be applied in many countries around the world. Domesticating or adopting international best practices brings about required modernisation and confidence in payment, clearing and settlement systems.

Learning Objectives

By the end of this chapter, you should be able to

- provide a description of standards in payments; and
- outline common standard-setting bodies.

Description of Standards in Payments

There are several standards and international best practices in payments. One description of a payment standard or principle is that of a rule on how a payment instruction is initiated, structured, routed and processed from the debtor's account to the creditor's account in a secure and efficient manner. Another description relates to the method of how products and services are produced for the market that consists of a wide range of stakeholders. Additionally, a standard or principle implies how risks are identified, assessed or controlled so as not to introduce unnecessary risks in a given national payment system. There is a lot that is involved in these descriptions. Consider an example that relates to the security of transactions in the payment process. This relates to operational or fraud risk that needs to be mitigated. One of the ways to mitigate this form of risk is by requiring a personal identification number (PIN) or signature before check-out at the point-of-sale. Such a rule becomes important especially in case of any dispute that arises after a transaction has been completed. Where a transaction has been fraudulent, any party in the transaction process can raise a dispute that needs to be settled in a timely fashion.

The security settlement system environment can be used as another example. Think about the international best practice called delivery-versus-payment (DvP). This denotes that payment for security and delivery of the asset need to happen at the same time to avoid credit risk. Standards setting and international bodies therefore put in place standards or principles that member countries can adopt in their local environments; some of the key bodies are listed and described in the following section.

Common Standard-Setting and International Bodies

Bank for International Settlements was established in 1930 and is presently located in Basel, Switzerland. Its mission is to support central banks in their pursuit of monetary and financial stability and to act as a bank for central banks. It carries out its work through a number of committees such Basel Committee on Banking Supervision, Committee on the Global Financial System, Committee on Payments and Market Infrastructures, Market Committee, Central Bank Governance Forum, and Irving Fisher Committee. One of the important instruments that the Bank for International Settlement has issued, through the Committee on Payments and Market Infrastructures, is the Principles for Financial Market Infrastructures (PFMI). This document is assisting countries in putting in place controls aimed at minimising inherent risks in respective national payment systems.

EMVCo was formed in 1999 with its mission being to facilitate worldwide interoperability of payment transactions through Europay, MasterCard, and Visa (EMV) standard, which entails migration from magstripe technology, using a signature for card transactions, to chip technology, with the use of a PIN for card-present and remote or e-commerce transactions. Members of EMVCo are American Express, China Union Pay, Discover, JCB International, Mastercard and Visa. Kagan (2022) outlines efforts beyond the chip technology, to ensure security of transactions in the e-commerce space, such as EMV 3-D secure (EMV 3DS), EMV secure remote commerce (EMV SRC), and EMV payment tokenisation.

Financial Action Task Force (FATF) came into being in 1989 with its head office situated in Paris, France. The organisation works to tackle money laundering, terrorist financing and weapons proliferation financing. Controlling these aspects brings about a situation where the international financial system is not abused by criminals for their own gain. The end result is confidence, safety and security in the very system that FATF tries to protect against criminals. This entity works closely with Financial Intelligence Centres (FIC) in member states in making sure that screening of customers and payments takes place and that there is sufficient information carried in a payment message based on international policy instruments and principles like FAFT recommendations. The FAFT recommendations set out a comprehensive and consistent framework of measures which countries should implement in order to combat money laundering and terrorist financing, as well as the financing of proliferation of weapons of mass destruction (Financial Action Task Force, 2023).

International Monetary Fund (IMF) was created in 1944 and is preoccupied with the need to achieve sustainable growth and prosperity for its member states through economic policies that promote financial stability and monetary cooperation. This implies that the IMF works closely with central banks, Bank for International Settlements and the World Bank. Consequently, poverty reduction is at the heart of the two sister institutions, that is, the World Bank and IMF.

International Organization for Standardisation (ISO) was established in 1946 and has a vision of making lives easier, safer and better with its goals for 2030 being standards used everywhere, meeting global needs and all voices heard (International Organisation for Standardisation, 2023). ISO has developed a number of standards since inception, covering a wide range of sectors and members in association with several committees and sub-committees. It works closely with the Committee on Payments and Market Infrastructures and SWIFT.

Office of Foreign Assets Control (OFAC) was established in 1950 and is an agency in the United States Department of the Treasury with its purpose being to administer and enforce economic sanctions programs against countries and groups of individuals. Although the entity falls within the government department, its work is felt across the world where its sanctions program is leveraged upon in the process of establishing and maintaining customer relationships from a sanctions screening standpoint.

PCI Security Standards Council (PCI SSC) was founded in 2006 and strives to strengthen global payment security with payment security standards and resources. One of the key standards that the PCI SSC drives is the Payment Card Industry Data Security Standard (PCI DSS), an instrument that is designed to protect cardholder account data. Its members are American Express, China Union Pay, Discover Financial Services, JCB International, Mastercard and Visa. Enforcement of compliance to PCI DSS is done by these payment brands. The in-country payment regulators and associations also play a role in requiring compliance to this standard.

Society for Worldwide Interbank Financial Telecommunication (SWIFT), which can be traced from 1973, is an infrastructure provider and as a result assists financial institutions to move value around the world. It has been helping the international financial community to migrate from the legacy message type (MT) to the ISO 20022 standard, which covers domestic, international, electronic funds transfer, high-value and card payments. ISO is the agreed methodology used by the financial industry to create consistent message standards across all the business processes of the industry (SWIFT, 2010)). Full migration is planned for 2025 (see example in the box below) for correspondent banking-related transactions, while operators of settlement systems around the world have their respective migration dates. Benefits of ISO migration include but are not limited to interoperability, facilitation of compliance, and richer data. FinTech Futures (2024) noted that the ISO 20022 standard is going to improve data exchange between entities and make domestic and cross-border transactions faster and more convenient. The migration of ISO 8583 for cards, to ISO 20022, is centred around the need to avoid duplication as maintaining two standards is not cost effective.

BOX 30

Migration from MT to ISO 20022 is to be implemented by the international financial community as per the SWIFT roadmap especially in the high-value payment space. This migration covers payment types, systems, regions, financial institutions, service providers, system operators, central banks and business domains. These domains include payments, cards, trade, foreign exchange, securities and derivatives.

There is notable progress in the Southern African Development Community (SADC). The SADC Real Time Gross Settlement (SADC RTGS) go-live date was set at 10 June 2024 on a "big bang" approach. This settlement system is operated by the South African Reserve Bank (SARB), the central bank of the Republic of South Africa, under a co-operative oversight arrangement. SARB is the lead overseer of the regional settlement system.

Migration from the current MT to ISO 20022 is enjoying support from participants and regulators around the world. Failure to achieve full compliance by 2025 for domestic and cross-border payments will lead to a situation where a particular participant is unable to send and receive messages as there will be no translation of financial messages after that time under normal circumstances unless there is a change at a policy level.

Wolfsberg Group is an association of 12 global banks and its origin can be traced to 2000. It aims to develop frameworks and guidance for the management of financial crime risks. The global banks are Santander, Citi, HSBC, Societe Generale, Bank of America, Deutsche Bank, JPMorgan Case, Standard Chartered, Barclays, Goldman Sachs, MUFS, and UBS. Wolfsberg Group works closely with Financial Action Task Force and Committee of Payments and Market Infrastructures on payment and settlement systems matters inclusive of financial crime risks.

World Bank Group has a vision to create a world free of poverty on a liveable planet through its five institutions. International Bank for Reconstruction and Development (IBRD) was created in 1944 and provides financial products and policy advice to recipient countries while the International Development Association (IDA) came into being in 1960 and gives grants and loans to low-income countries. International Finance Corporation (IFC) came into existence in 1956 and finances investment, mobilises capital and provides advisory services for developing countries, while Multilateral Investment Guarantee Agency (MIGA) was created in 1988 and offers political risk insurance or guarantees to investors and lenders in developing countries. International Centre for Settlement of Investment Disputes (ICSID) can be traced to 1966 and provides international facilities for conciliation and arbitration of investment disputes.

United Nations (UN) was established in 1945 and its interest is in the maintenance of peace, dignity and equality across the globe as per its founding Charter. This international organisation discharges its functions through bodies that include the General Assembly, Security Council, Economic and Social Council, Trusteeship Council, International Court of Justice and Secretariat. The UN is known to be active in areas such as sanctions screening, sustainable development goals, governance matters and health issues.

Chapter Summary

This chapter focussed on standard-setting and other international bodies. The list is not exhaustive. These bodies play a significant role in their areas of expertise and influence. As an example, *Society for Worldwide Interbank Financial Telecommunication (SWIFT)* is an infrastructure provider and as a result assists financial institutions to move value around the world while *Office of Foreign Assets Control* is an agency in the United States Department of the Treasury whose purpose is to administer and enforce economic sanctions programmes against countries and groups of individuals.

Review Questions

1. List and briefly describe the five institutions that fall within the World Bank Group.
2. Name five committees through which the Bank for International Settlements carries out it work.
3. Indicate if the following statements are true or false:
   a. PCI DSS is one of the standards that PCI Security Council drives.
   b. OFAC is an agency of the Ministry of Finance in Namibia.
   c. International Organisation for Standardisation has a vision of making lives easier, safer and better.
   d. The IMF was established in 1970.
   e. EMVCo's mission is to facilitate worldwide intra-operability.

Selected References

Financial Action Task Force, (2023). *International Standards on Combating Money Laundering and the Financing of Terrorism and Proliferation – The FATF Recommendations.* Paris, France: Financial Action Task Force. Retrieved from https://www.fatf-gafi.org/

FinTech Futures, (2024). *Driving AI Transformation in Banking and Payments*. London, United Kingdom: FinTech Futures. Retrieved from https://www.fintechfutures.com/

International Organisation for Standardisation, (2023). *ISO Strategy 2030*. Geneva, Switzerland. Retrieved from https://www.iso.org/

Kagan, J. (2024). *EMV – What it Means, How it Works, Limitations*. New York, NY: Investopedia Retrieved from https://www.investopedia.com/

SWIFT, (2010). *ISO 20022 for Dummies*. England, United Kingdom: John Wiley & Sons Ltd. Retrieved from https://www.ffdn.org/

CHAPTER 32

Balance of Payments Reporting

Reference to balance of payments (BoP) makes one to think of an individual or a business current account with a financial institution. The account shows money going out and funds coming in. There is a surplus when inflows are more than outflows, a deficit when inflows are less than outflows and it is balanced if inflows are equal to outflows – a rare state. Balance of payments is relevant at a country or macro level, where results such as surplus, deficit and balanced state can be recorded at a particular point of time. Financial authorities across the world are keen to know the reason for each transaction that goes out of a country or comes into a given economy.

Learning Objectives

By the end of this chapter, you should be able to

- understand the meaning of accounts that are associated with balance of payments;
- appreciate the need for BoP reporting; and

- know what harmonisation of BoP codes is all about.

Balance of Payments

Balance of payments (BoP) is a topic that features prominently in the field of economics and related branches. These branches or sub-fields of economics include macroeconomics, international economics and monetary economics. Economists agree that BoP is a record of a country's transactions with the rest of the world. Robinson (2004) noted that BoP is a summary of all economic transactions between domestic and foreign residents for a given period, usually a year, and is compiled using the latest edition of the BoP manual, which provides standards for concepts, definitions, classification and convention, and facilitates systematic national and international collection, organisation and comparability of BoP statistics.

Mushendami, Manuel, Shifotoka and Nakusera (2017) point out that BoP has three main accounts: the current account, capital account and financial account; and this classification is consistent with that of the Bank of Namibia (2024). The current account covers trade in goods, services, primary income, and secondary income; capital account consists of capital transfers and acquisition and disposal of non-produced, non-financial assets between residents and non-residents; and the financial account consists of direct investments, portfolio investments and other forms of investment (Central Bank of Philippines, 2019). Whether or not the balance of payments should have two or three accounts varies from one country to another. What is important though is alignment with international best practices to ensure comparability of reported transactions across countries.

BoP Reporting

Financial or resident institutions are required to report cross-border transactions to their respective central banks or monetary authorities for the purpose of BoP. Each monetary authority determines the period when reporting needs to be done by accountable institutions through an applicable electronic monitoring system. It is common for data that is transmitted to the central bank to be provided in an electronic file according to the format defined in relevant documents (Central Bank of Luxembourg, 2014).

Information furnished to regulatory or monetary authorities needs to be comprehensive as per relevant published manuals. Incoming and outgoing transactions are expected to contain reason codes or purpose in relevant fields or spaces where information needs to be captured. Bank of Zambia (2016) notes that commercial banks are expected to ensure that clients conducting cross-border financial transactions provide an accurate and full description of the payment and that includes the purpose of the transaction, the sector of entity, tax identification number and destination or source country.

There are numerous codes in the market for cross-border payments. These codes are traditionally arranged into category, sub-category and description so that each transaction is as clear to regulatory authorities as possible. The table below lists some of the common codes (South African Reserve Bank, 2020):

Table 32.1
BoP Codes

Category	Description
285	Tuition fees
301	Dividends
308	Rental
401	Gifts
402	Annual contributions

Source: South African Reserve Bank (2020)

The above table shows 285 being associated with tuition fees while the code for gifts is 401. Consider a parent whose child is studying for an advanced degree at the University of Cape Town (UCT) as an example. The parent searches for a tuition related code from the list of BoP codes as published via their preferred payment channel and completes the transaction accordingly. This makes it possible for both the paying and receiving financial institution to identify the transaction in their respective systems.

BoP Harmonisation

Harmonisation of BoP codes entails a similar interpretation of the reason for a payment by participating financial institutions in the countries involved; this applies to both incoming and outgoing payments. The matter continues to receive attention within regulatory and accountable communities at regional and international levels. Despite harmonisation being a lengthy and complicated process, given that several countries are involved, there are associated benefits. These include: straight-through processing of transactions; negating manual intervention; minimisation of misaligned codes; lessening ambiguity in interpreting transactions and related codes; and alignment to international standards in the compilation and reporting of international financial transactions.

BOX 31

Harmonisation of BoP codes is an aspiration that countries around the world are pursuing, and the Southern African Development Community (SADC) is not left out in this journey. This is because one of the key strategic principles of regional economic integration is to invest for straight-through processing (SADC Banking Association, 2019). Straight-through processing (STP) is associated with quick settlement turnaround to a beneficiary customer's bank account and related regulatory reporting.

Several stakeholders are involved in the harmonised BoP codes roadmap and these stakeholders are the SADC Banking Association, SADC Exchange Control Sub-Committee, SADC Payment System Oversight Committee, CMA Payments Oversight Committee, respective central banks and accountable institutions. Joint harmonisation of BoP codes across countries or within a specific region is preferred as opposed solo harmonisation (one country leading or another lagging behind).

Eurostat (2002) mentions that the idea of one common reporting format came about in mid-2000 and harmonisation of reporting rules increases the efficiency of the reporting process and fosters the level playing field. Israel and Munoz (2007) note that it is increasingly important worldwide to adhere to a set of international statistical standards in order to ensure the comparability of statistics. Consequently, adopting a uniform format in the categorisation of international transactions leads to efficiency and easier comparability of such transactions across stakeholders, countries and entities.

Chapter Summary

This chapter considered balance of payments reporting and specific sub-topics that were covered are balance of payments, balance of payments reporting and balance of payments harmonisation. The chapter noted that financial or resident institutions are required to report cross-border transactions to their respective central banks or monetary authorities for the purpose of balance of payments. Additionally, harmonisation of BoP codes is receiving close attention within regulatory and accountable communities at regional and international levels.

Review Questions

1. Name and describe three accounts of the balance of payments.
2. What do you understand by the term "BoP codes harmonisation"? Outline associated benefits and challenges.
3. Financial or resident institutions are required to report cross-border transactions to their respective central banks or monetary authorities for the purpose of BoP. Is this statement true or false? Give a reason for your answer.

Selected References

Bank of Namibia, (2024). *Annual Report 2023*. Windhoek, Namibia: Bank of Namibia. Retrieved from https://www.bon.com.na/

Bank of Zambia, (2016). *Electronic Balance of Payments (E-BoP) Monitoring*. Lusaka, Zambia: Bank of Zambia. Retrieved from https://www.boz.zm/

Central Bank of Luxembourg, (2014). *Definitions and Concepts for the Balance of Payments Reporting of Credit Institutions and the Financial Services of the Entreprise Des Postes et Telecommunications*. Luxembourg City, Luxembourg: Central Bank of Luxembourg. Retrieved from https://www.bcl.lu/

Central Bank of Philippines, (2019). *Balance of Payments and International Investment Position*. Manila, Philippines: Central Bank of Philippines. Retrieved from https://www.bsp.gov.ph/

Eurostat, (2002). *Harmonised Balance of Payments Reporting Rules for Multinationals*. Luxembourg City, Luxembourg: Eurostat. Retrieved from https://www.imf.org/

Israel, J. M., & Munoz, C. S. (2007). *Towards Harmonised Balance of Payments and International Investment Position Statistics – The Experience of the European Compilers*. Frankfurt, German: European Central Bank. Retrieved from https://www.ecb.int/

Mushendami, P., Manuel, V., Shifotoka, H., Nakusera, F. (2017). Empirical Analysis of the Monetary Approach to the Balance of Payment in Namibia. *International Review of Research in Emerging Markets and the Global Economy*, 3(1), 1088-1104. Retrieved from https://www.globalbizresearch.org/

Robinson, F. (2004). *Balance of Payments made Simple*. Kingston, Jamaica: Bank of Jamaica. Retrieved from https://www.boj.org.jm/

SADC Banking Association, (2019). *SADC RTGS Newsletter – Issue 1*. Pretoria, South Africa: South African Reserve Bank. Retrieved from https://www.resbank.co.za/

South African Reserve Bank, (2020). *FinSur Reporting System Operations Manual*. Pretoria, South Africa: South African Reserve Bank. Retrieved from https://www.resbank.co.za/

CHAPTER 33

Transactional Banking

The goal of a customer of financial services is to transact when given the opportunity to do so. On the part of financial services, this means making appropriate payment methods available for them to be able to initiate transactions at various delivery channels, which can be online and in-person. It takes an effort for the two sides of the market to meet for a transaction to be concluded. An issuer needs to make payment methods available while an acquirer has to supply access points via its merchant customers.

Learning Objectives

By the end of this chapter, you should be able to

- describe what transactional banking is all about;
- understand the key components of transactional banking; and
- appreciate customer segments that are involved in relationship management.

Description of Transactional Banking

The banking business can be split into corporate, transactional and retail banking with the first two being highly in-person and handling fewer, high-value accounts compared to the last (CGI, 2022). WallStreetMojo (2024) notes that transactional banking, also known as transaction banking, part of corporate banking, is defined as the banking services that have a significant role to play in the functioning of a corporate or a banking institution by enabling: the safe flow of money from one country to another; trade financial deals; mitigation of risks; cash flow management services; and even offering security services for improving relationships between banking institutions, clients and partners.

Transaction banking businesses are facing unprecedented change in terms of challenges and opportunities in the competitive landscape (Boston Consulting Group, 2012). Baller, Bear, Gate, Girompini, Graham, Hergenroeder, Hopkins, Kalyanasundaram, Leonbirth, Mukherjee, Nacamuli and Zimmerman (2014) surmise that cloud computing makes it possible to deploy customer products and services rapidly at a lower cost and that transactional banking is a high-value and high-volume environment.

Some observations can be made from the above-mentioned review. Firstly, transactional banking is a branch of corporate banking in general, or corporate and investment banking in particular. Secondly, both transactional banking and corporate banking handle few accounts that are associated with high values. Clients in this space therefore include corporate and commercial entities, government institutions, quasi-government institutions, multinational institutions and financial institutions. Thirdly, transactional banking is outward- or across-the-border- with the view to facilitate the movement of funds to cover cross-border transactions. The foregoing should not be regarded as cast in stone as transactional banking can be inward-looking as well by facilitating transactions of domestic and large customers.

Components

Transactional banking has several components, of which the most common ones are payments, clearing and settlement, cash management, trade finance, and trust and securities, with payments and cash management having been the traditional focus, while more recently the scope includes other areas as well (Wakeham, Tumer, Giacomini, Hale, Chrispin and Simon, 2009). The above implies that non-traditional areas are trade finance as well as trust and securities.

"Payments" in this case relate to collection-of-payment methods and channels that are used to initiate transactions. "Clearing and settlement" includes the determination of settlement obligations before the actual movement of funds happens between the paying and receiving financial institutions, via the applicable settlement system. Funding is key to avoid associated risks at the point of settlement. "Cash management" entails the management of inflows and outflows and the associated tools or applications that can assist in enabling the management of cash possible. "Trade finance" brings to mind how exports and imports of goods and services are financed at the right point of time. "Securities" are financial assets that are traded via an organised exchange or over the counter, movement of funds and the safe keeping of these until ownership has exchanged hands.

Customer Segments

Financial institutions categorise their customers into three or two segments based on the number of transactions and values associated with those payments. These are corporate, business and retail customers for some institutions while others combine corporate and business customers, resulting in only two segments. The following table illustrates the different types of customer segments:

Table 33.1
Customer Segments

Corporate Customers	Business Customers	Retail Customers
• Large corporate and institutional customers • Lower volume, very large value	• Business customers, small and medium sized customers • Medium volume, large value	• Individual customers, high net worth customers • High volume, low value

Corporate customers, who are often large ones pushing few transactions, but accounting for very large payments in value terms, fall under corporate banking. Business or commercial customers are served by the commercial banking segment within a financial institution and customer types are big businesses as well as small and medium sized ones. These customers are responsible for medium volume, and transactions in value terms are large. Retail banking covers individual customers including high net worth customers and this segment handles high volume and low value of transactions.

Relationship Management

Relationship management is an important activity within a financial institution that is charged with the goal of not only attracting customers but also maintaining them over a long period of time. Ramaj (2015) points out that the purpose of customer relationship management is to improve the services offered by a company to its customers, enhance customer satisfaction and contribute to maintaining long-term relationships. One of the dimensions associated with relationship management is the technical dimension, which is based on what is delivered, while the functional dimension is based on social interaction between subjects in the relationship (Cvijovic, Kostic-Stankovic and Reljic, 2017). Subjects in this case refer to the financial services provider and the customer.

BOX 32

Relationship management is key for the success of any business that is involved in the sale of goods and services. Let's imagine someone being interviewed for a job in financial services. This leadership position had both a technical and a sales component to it, and the interview process was divided into two parts. The first part covered a presentation on proposed strategies and a list of services and products to be introduced if the candidate was successful for the job in question, while the second portion consisted more of questions from the interview panel, covering a wide range of issues around the vacant position.

The interviewee's understanding of the job was more from a technical standpoint and not necessarily on the relationship part. This resulted in the panel asking the candidate about developmental intervention that may be required if the interviewee landed the job. The candidate replied that development in relationship management would indeed be required as this area was not their strong point. The interview panel appreciated this positive and honest feedback.

The technical component of the job is not enough, as can be deduced from the above box article. It has to be supported by the functional part, to make the entire product complete for the customer. Some clients are not technologically savvy, implying that a good or service has to be explained to them until such time as they are comfortable in using it. This is in line with consumer protection requirements whereby a given product needs to be explained to those who are going to consume it, as part of the general terms and conditions.

Financial products can be communicated to the end users in various ways or channels. These include print, broadcast and electronic as well as in-person. Print media covers newspapers, brochures and flyers while broadcast includes television and radio. Electronic media has to do with email, social media, phone calls, SMS and mobile application. In-person communication includes site visits as well as presentations.

Chapter Summary

This chapter covered transactional banking. It was pointed out that transactional banking relates to banking services that have a significant role to play in the functioning of a banking or financial institution. Relationship management was also addressed. Relationship management is an important activity within a financial institution that is charged with the goal of not only attracting customers but also retaining them over a long period of time. The technical component of the product delivery has to be supported by the functional component to make the entire product complete for the customer.

Review Questions

1. List and explain different customer segments in banking that you have learned.
2. Name the key components of transactional banking.
3. Define relationship management and outline the different communication channels that can be used to communicate financial products to the end users.

Selected References

Baller, A., Bear, K., Gate, R., Girompini, D., Graham, A., Hergenroeder, G., Hopkins, G., Kalyanasundaram, S., Leonbirth, P., Mukherjee, S., Nacamuli, A., & Zimmerman, D. (2014). *Transaction Banking and Cloud.* Somers, NY: IBM Corporation. Retrieved from https://www.ibm.com/

Boston Consulting Group, (2012). *The Transaction Banking Advantage – The Path to Profitable Growth.* Boston, MA: Boston Consulting Group. Retrieved from https://www.bcg.com/

Cvijovic, J., Kostic-Stankovic, M. & Reljic, M. (2017). Customer Relationship Management in Banking Industry – Modern Approach. *Industrija*, 45(3), 151-165. Retrieved from https://dx.doi.org/10.5937/industrija45-15975

CGI, (2022). *Top Trends to Watch in Corporate and Transaction Banking.* Birmingham, Alabama: CGI. Retrieved from https://www.cgi.com/

Ramaj, C.A. (2015). Customer Relationship Management (CRM) in Banking Sector in Albania. *European Journal of Economics and Business Studies*, 1(2), 130-137. Retrieved from https://www.revistia.com/

Wakeham, J., Tumer, J., Giacomini, P., Hale, M., Chrispin, J & Simon, P. (2009). *Transaction Banking Takes Off – Transaction Banking Compass.* London, United Kingdom: PricewaterhouseCoopers. Retrieved from https://www.pwc.com/

WallStreetMojo, (2024). *Transaction Banking.* Mumbai, India: WallStreetMojo. Retrieved from https://www.wallstreetmojo.com/

CHAPTER 34

Careers, Skills and Training in Payments

Consider this illustration from a daily departmental meeting of the operations department in a commercial bank. Team members Mary and Maria are relatively new, having only been in their respective roles for a few years. This is a technical-payments-related meeting, covering industry and operational matters. While other team members are actively participating, the two women are silent throughout. The team leader, noticing this, asks towards the end of the meeting if there is any additional comment before she closes. Mary and Maria still have nothing to say and the meeting adjourns. The team leader reaches out to the two colleagues for an informal chat and learns that their silence relates to a lack of training and development in the area under discussion. Consequently, the team leader assures them about continued support from a skills perspective, via training and development interventions, during their career in the department.

Learning Objectives

By the end of this chapter, you should be able to

- appreciate career options that are available in the payment, clearing and settlement environment;
- list the skills that are common to the payment, clearing and settlement environment;
- consider the training and development interventions that are relevant to the payment, clearing and settlement environment; and
- illustrate the strategic payments house as it relates to payment, clearing and settlement environment.

Career Options

There are various career options to consider in the payment, clearing and settlement environment, which has a number of components connected with it. These components include, but are not limited to, legal and regulatory framework, payment systems, clearing systems, settlement systems, stakeholders, and institutions. Given that there are a number of institutions handling payment instructions, with some being direct participants in the national payment system, it follows that there are career opportunities in the field. Broad areas will therefore be outlined and discussed and not necessarily specific job titles. These areas relate to several institutions across the divide and some of these institutions include banking institutions, non-bank financial institutions, associations, regulators, financial technology companies and research institutions. Consequently, the broad areas include operations and customer support, project management, legal and compliance, product management, and regulation and supervision.

Operations and customer support entail a number of areas. Ensuring that payment instructions are captured, authorised and sufficiently funded for settlement are some of the areas that are covered under operations and customer support. There is also an information technology component that needs to be considered. Systems that are involved in transactions delivery, recording and tracking across the payment value chain within a banking institution or across banking institutions are key.

Customers can constantly inquire about the whereabout of their outgoing and incoming payments. Outgoing payments are what customers have initiated, while incoming payments are what they are expecting. Dedicated frontline teams can handle customer queries via appropriate systems for resolution and escalation where it is required. Resolution of customer queries needs to be done in reasonable time.

Project management life cycle includes business cases, coming up with a business requirement specification, analysis, development, testing, and go live. There is a wide range of stakeholders that are involved in any project to make sure that delivery of a solution or functionality is realised. Internal and external issues that can affect project delivery are important and need to be monitored and addressed as a matter of urgency.

It is always important to have an end in mind when managing a project. This entails focusing on a goal and not necessarily on issues that can emerge around a particular project. Focussing on issues and not on the end result can derail delivery of the required implementation. Addressing project issues and risks within the required timeframe, as well as ensuring that stakeholders are informed at all times, can go a long way towards putting a project on track.

The key to *legal and compliance* is to minimise legal and compliance risks. Professionals in this area peruse legal instruments and advise businesses on legal issues and uncertainties to consider. Legal professionals will also represent an institution in a court of law where there are legal issues to address. Individuals in this area are expected to come up with legal instruments for certain products and services that fall within business units.

While legal is often forward looking, compliance is in many instances backward looking. Compliance teams look at regulations that have been issued and assist business units in achieving compliance in terms of timelines and expectations as enshrined in those regulatory instruments. These teams are in constant communication with regulators, industry and business units to make sure that all issues requiring attention are addressed.

Product management entails ownership of a particular functionality or product which is used to deliver products or services to end users. Individuals in this area participate in the project management life cycle and are expected to do the required testing to make sure that delivery to the market is without defects. They also handle queries that are specific to the product in question.

Each product or functionality has a particular life cycle. Besides, each product needs to evolve to consider other changes in customer needs and expectations. Consequently, enhancements to the product may need to happen to include certain components of a product or service that were not there before. Any enhancement needs to follow a project management life cycle as predetermined.

Regulation and supervision are career options that are closely related. Regulation entails coming up with the legal and regulatory framework that needs to be complied with. Supervision involves using that framework to assess or monitor compliance with the goal of ensuring stability in the national payment systems. Professionals in this field are typically associated with a central bank or a delegated regulator. Research is critical in coming up with regulations that need to be complied with, as well as using research as an input into innovation to address certain inefficiencies or shortcomings.

Supervision also entails finding a way to connect with stakeholders that are required to comply with legal and regulatory framework. This is traditionally done through instruments such as industry forums as well. Industry forums include representatives from all required stakeholders with an interest in the national payment system to discuss issues of mutual concern as part of a long-term modernisation program.

Skills Required

There is a wide range of skills that are of paramount importance for professionals in a payment, clearing and settlement environment. The environment in this case can be a banking institution, non-bank financial institution, payment system management body, principal regulator or other institution connected to payments. Skills can be learned – they are not necessarily inherent or inborn. Key skills that are discussed in this section include systems and technical, analytical, communication, financial, strategic thinking, project management, and relationship skills.

Systems and technical skills can be coupled together. The gist here is the ability to use a particular rare skill coupled with the understanding of certain information technology programmes to deliver on a certain task. These skills are associated with those who have studied courses in the fields of science, technology, engineering and mathematics. Individuals in other disciplines can also work with systems to trace payment instructions, troubleshoot technical inquiries coming from customers on payments made or expected, create and capture payment instructions, and monitor these transactions from end to end.

Analytical skills relate to the ability to make sense of complex or detailed data. While in some situations data is available, it follows that this is not always the case. Analytically-minded people assist in doing research and coming up with research reports or position papers in the payment, clearing and settlement environment. People who possess these skills come from diverse backgrounds both in social and other technical related fields.

There is always a need for *communication skills* to package information for the intended audience in a clear and less confusing manner. The ability to translate technical language to the level that is understood by internal stakeholders or the general public can be done by communication specialists. These individuals can proofread a wide range of documentation for internal and external stakeholders.

Financial skills are important too. Those in the finance field are able to read payment transaction numbers and calculate required financial ratios to aid decision making. They can also assist in the reconciliation and budgeting process, that is, to determine expected income and expenditure. These skills are mostly associated with those who studied accounting, finance and related disciplines.

Strategic thinking is one of the skills that are required especially in an environment associated with uncertainty. Strategic thinking is the ability to read both the internal and external environments with the view to understand the future. Strategic thinkers come from a wide range of disciplines and are mostly found in leadership positions.

Project management skills entail the ability to manage a project with the view to achieving a certain outcome. There are a number of intermediate steps in a project, leading to full implementation. Project managers work with a number of stakeholders and play an important role in bringing these stakeholders together for the sake of achieving deliverables collectively and not individually.

Relationship management skills have to do with being able to work with others to achieve a certain outcome. The ability to build the network of stakeholders which one would need at some point is a relationship management skill. Individuals with these skills traditionally work with clients to listen and attend to their problems and ensure that these are addressed in a timely manner. "Clients" in this case can refer to colleagues in other departments or external end users of goods and services.

Training and Development

Training and development are inter-related human capital interventions. While the former prepares employees to be productive in their career now, the latter gives them the opportunity to be effective at their work at some time in the future. Jia-jun and Hua-ming (2022) note that in the knowledge economy era, knowledge workers have become an important pillar of enterprises, and their engagement is crucial to the realisation of the strategic goals. Trained and developed employees therefore can assist their organisations to respond to customer needs, earn a good reputation in the market, stay competitive in the market and be able to influence policy decisions.

The approach to self-development with the view to gaining the required skills to perform better has changed over the years. Self-development is now employee centred just like learning in school is learner centred. This situation is ascribed to the above-normal supply of labour in the job market and cost cutting measures taken by a number of potential employers. Individuals who are graduating from colleges and universities are greater in number compared to a few years ago and consequently employers have a pool of potential employees to choose from.

Self-development can be short-term, medium term and long-term. Short-term intervention includes finding a way to enhance one's productivity now. Learning by doing, seeking advice from fellow colleagues on how something needs to be done, standing in for a colleague who is on leave, being active in departmental meetings and reading on topics related to one's field can all go a long way as far as self-development is concerned.

BOX 33

It is a brisk Saturday afternoon in one of the shopping malls outside the central business district and Pat and Sandie decide to sit over coffee to catch up on payments-related topics. Pat works for a mainstream payments service provider, while Sandie is associated with a non-bank financial institution (NBFI). The latter appears not to be well versed with payments as her employer does not participate in the inner core of the national payment system. This is not the case for Pat, who has vast experience and knowledge in this area of the financial sector.

Sandie expresses her interest in knowing more about payments as her employer is expected to play an active role in payments in the medium- to long-term. Pat encourages her companion to reach out if she needs more information and also to consider doing a formal course with one of the local educational institutions. Sandie appreciates the advice given and promises to act on it accordingly. Sandie's wish is for payment systems to be offered as a course or module at one of the institutions of higher learning.

Medium term interventions include requesting your line manager to allow you to be involved in a certain project whether it is a simple or near complex one. Working in a project allows an employee to work with a variety of stakeholders and benefits include enhancing communication, presentation, analytical and human relations skills. Doing short courses can also assist in developing oneself in this regard.

Long-term interventions cover doing something one has never done before such as taking a promotion or enhancing one's leadership skills to be able to play a more significant role in the delivery of certain major deliverables. Doing a professional qualification that enhances one's development potential and is job related, such as in payments, can have a positive impact on self-development. In addition, working on a complex project that spans several months would be considered long-term intervention in this regard.

Strategic Payments House

The world of payments, clearing and settlement systems is an evolving one. There are factors at play behind this evolution and these factors include but are not limited to regulations, technological changes, tastes and preferences, population dynamics and competition. Examples can be given in this regard. Bank of Namibia (2024) crafted a modernisation position on aspects or initiatives that financial institutions or payment service providers can consider in their respective internal modernisation strategies or efforts. FinTech Futures (2024) notes that the financial services industry is changing at a rapid pace and it seems like there is an innovation around the corner all the time. Ramayanti, Rachmawati, Azhar and Azman (2024) indicate that the accelerated growth of digital banking globally is driven by the expansion of mobile phone use and the tremendous growth of the internet.

Changes in the financial services industry at a global level in general, and an increase in digital banking and shifts in other market forces in particular, signal to financial services providers to seize opportunities and confront threats and challenges that come with such changes or shifts. This can only be realised through having professionals with the requisite skills, knowledge and experience in the area of payment, clearing and settlement systems. Such professionals are not readily available, but can be sourced with the right interventions at each institution's disposal.

Having a strategic payments house within each financial services provider is essential to assist top management in driving their payments strategy into the foreseeable future, given opportunities and threats arising from the general environment. The following figure illustrates this house, with key components being chief executive director, chief payments officer and various heads of areas (HoAs):

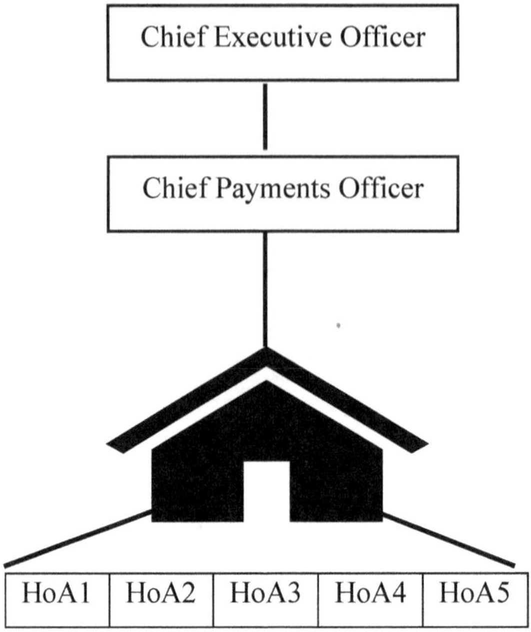

Figure 34.1. Strategic Payments House

The above figure consists of several components, including the chief executive officer (CEO) of the financial services provider and the chief payments officer (CPO), who is a C-suite executive who is accountable for and provides strategic direction to the strategic payments house. There are five key areas that follow under the CPO and they are: the card; electronic funds transfer; electronic money; research, regulatory affairs and strategic projects; and virtual assets programmes. These five areas or divisions appear in the following table:

Table 34.1
Components: Strategic Payments House

Reference Code	Area or Division	Description
HoA1	Card Programme	Issuing, acquiring, change requests, industry engagements, technical support, clearing and settlement and international standards.
HoA2	Electronic Funds Transfer Programme	Credits and debits, change requests, industry engagements, technical support, clearing and settlement and international standards.
HoA3	Electronic Money Programme	Migration to interoperability, industry engagements, technical support, change requests, clearing and settlement and international standards.
HoA4	Research, Regulatory Affairs and Strategic Projects Programme	Position papers, regulatory communiques, review of regulations, engagements with compliance team, industry engagements, regional engagements, implementing strategic projects.
HoA5	Virtual Assets Programme	Industry engagements, technical support, clearing and settlement and international standards.

The above table provides a description for each area or division. Implementing a strategic payments house like the one that is illustrated gives a payments services provider an opportunity to make sure that everything is under control from the standpoint of payments innovation and oversight.

Chapter Summary

This chapter covered careers, skills and training in payments. It was noted that trained and developed employees can assist their organisations to respond to customer needs, earn a good reputation in the market, stay competitive in the market and be able to influence policy decisions. Implementation of a strategic payments house can make this possible. Having a strategic payments house within each financial services provider is essential for top management to drive payments strategy into the foreseeable future, given opportunities and threats arising from the general environment.

Review Questions

1. Illustrate and outline key components of the strategic payments house in the national payment system.
2. Name and explain key skills required for those aspiring to be part of the strategic payments house in the national payment system.
3. List some of the career options for those looking for a career in the national payment system.

Selected References

Bank of Namibia. (2024). *National Payment System Modernisation Position.* Windhoek, Namibia: Bank of Namibia. Retrieved from https://www.bon.com.na/

FinTech Futures, (2024). *Driving AI Transformation in Banking and Payments.* London, United Kingdom: FinTech Futures. Retrieved from https://www.fintechfutures.com/

Jia-jun, Z., & Hua-ming, S. (2022). The Impact of Career Growth on Knowledge-Based Employee Engagement: The Mediating Role of Affective Commitment and the Moderating Role of Perceived Organisational Support. *Front Psychol,* 13, 1-10. Retrieved from https://dx.doi.org/10.3389/fpsyg.2022.805208

Ramayanti, R., Rachmawati, N.A., Azhar, Z., & Azman, N. H, N. (2024). Exploring Intention and Actual Use of Digital Payments: A System Review and Roadmap for Future Research. *Computers in Human Behaviour Reports,* 13, 1-17. Retrieved from https://dx.doi.org/10.1016/j.chbr.2023.100348

CHAPTER 35

Conclusion

This book is about the payment, clearing and settlement environment. Other terms that can be used are "national payment system" or just "payments". It is a banking or digital banking book in general or a payments book in particular. Payments is a sub-field of banking and not the other way around. Major topics related to payments were discussed in this guide at a greater length. There was a need to look at special topics in this sub-field of banking. These special topics related to the current developments in the environment of payments.

Payments is one of the key areas of banking. Please remember that banking is not about savings or investments, insurance and loans only. Payment methods, channels and systems are all important from a banking institution's standpoint in ensuring that funds are moved from one person, the payer, to another person, the receiver. Seamless movement of funds between and among entities, without unnecessary friction, is a springboard for supporting and expanding economic activities in a particular country. It is therefore important that all efforts are channelled towards ensuring that payment, clearing and settlement systems are available most of the time so that economic players continue to transact as efficiently and effectively as possible.

The migration from a paper to an electronic way of doing things is a long-term dream that needs to be achieved. Reference here is not about cheques. This payment method is long gone and will be remembered as such in the distant future. Manual payments in whatever nature are costly in terms of time and the actual cost in dollars. Both public and private sectors need to support the migration from a manual to an electronic way of doing things not only with payments but in other facets of life as well, as this is the future. There are good lessons from the Covid-19 pandemic!

Investments need to find a way of ensuring the reliability of networks when the general public is transacting. Efforts have already gone into this area, for which service providers need to be commended. Network calls being dropped sometimes when doing a payment is not something one needs to go through, especially when one is in front of a cashier and about to check out. The issue is most prevalent when one needs to make a transfer between accounts before swiping a card at a speed point.

Training is an important goal that can be pursued by all stakeholders with the view to learning more about banking in general and payments in particular. Short, medium and long-term goals can be pursued. Short courses and training interventions leading to diploma and degree programmes can be encouraged. There are online learning opportunities that are available around the world on payment, clearing and settlement. The time to keep on learning is now!

Financial inclusion is a public policy objective being pursued by many authorities. Milestones being pursued need to continue to promote access to financial services by the underbanked and unbanked members of our society. Financial inclusion is broad and covers several areas including payments, remittances, credit, savings and insurance. Interoperability is an important area in this environment and there is no turning back, fortunately.

There is a need by all stakeholders to invest in trying to establish what is going on around payments in other parts of the world. There are international best practices elsewhere that can be mined through research and these can be localised. Minimal investment in research for development is not a recipe for innovation. Putting in innovation programmes coupled with rewards for best innovation is a sure way to introduce new products in a market from a payments perspective.

Appendix 1 – Sample Test Paper

Logo of Post School Institution of Higher Learning
Name of Post School Institution of Higher Learning

Faculty	Name of the Faculty
Department	Name of the Department
Subject	Digital Banking
Subject Code	Code allocated for the subject (e.g. DBP 1000)
Date	Date the test is written
Duration	1 hour
Marks	40

Test Paper: Test Paper Number

Lecturer: Name of the Lecturer

This question paper consists of 2 pages including this cover page.

Instructions:

- Answer all questions.
- Write neatly and legibly.
- Observe the time limit.
- Use of a calculator is allowed.

1. Write short notes on the following terms:

   a. Payment systems (2)
   b. Debt consolidation (2)
   c. Hybrid card (2)

2. Name and explain four types of markets in which payment systems play an important role today. (12)

3. Outline three advantages and disadvantages of a debit card payment instrument. (12)

4. A credit cardholder just received a credit card statement showing the following information: opening balance NAD1,250, card limit NAD1,500, payment received NAD50, monthly management charge NAD10 (this includes value added tax of NAD5), and interest NAD25.

Required:

a. Calculate the amount to be debited to the account, closing balance and available balance (10)

Total: 40

~ The End ~

Appendix 2 – Sample Take Home Assignment Paper

Logo of Post School Institution of Higher Learning
Name of Post School Institution of Higher Learning

Faculty	Name of the Faculty
Department	Name of the Department
Subject	Digital Banking
Subject Code	Code allocated for the subject (e.g. DBP 1000)
Due Date	Date when the assignment is due
Marks	50

Group Assignment Paper: Group Number or Name

Lecturer: Name of the Lecturer

This assignment paper consists of 2 pages including this cover page.

Instructions:

- Answer all questions.
- Observe submission deadline.
- All group members are expected to contribute to the assignment.
- Assignment should be typed and presented in PowerPoint slides.
- Each group has 20 minutes to present assignment to the class and lecturer.

One licensed banking institution with automated teller machines across towns and cities in a developing country intends to offer electronic money. There is no interoperability in this payment stream. Its Chief Payments Officer who was recently recruited would like to understand this portion of the payments industry and requires your assistance.

Your group should prepare a presentation to be delivered in a classroom covering the following areas:

1. Describe interoperability in payment systems. (5)

2. Differentiate between closed-loop and open-loop payment systems. (10)

3. Present a diagrammatic illustration that shows how a payer sends electronic money to a recipient for withdrawal at an automated teller machine in a closed loop environment. (20)

4. The quality of material and delivery of presentation will attract some marks. (15)

Total: 50

~ The End ~

Appendix 3 – Sample Examination Paper

Logo of Post School Institution of Higher Learning
Name of Post School Institution of Higher Learning

Faculty	Name of the Faculty
Department	Name of the Department
Subject	Digital Banking
Subject Code	Code allocated for the subject (e.g. DBP 1000)
Date	Date the exam is written
Duration	3 hours
Marks	100

Examination Paper: Examination Paper Number

Lecturer: Name of the Lecturer

This question paper consists of 5 pages including this cover page.

Instructions:

- Answer all questions.
- Write neatly and legibly.
- Observe the time limit.
- Use of a calculator is allowed.

Question One (10)

These are multiple choice questions: write only the correct answer from the options given.

1.1 A payment card that is accompanied by a line of credit up to a certain limit and can be used to purchase goods and services at delivery channels: (1)

a. Debit card
b. Credit card
c. Gift card
d. Store card

1.2 A payment card that is issued for use at payment channels backed by available funding in a bank account: (1)

a. Debit card
b. Credit card
c. Gift card
d. Store card

1.3 The card brand that was established in 1958 and is headquartered in California in the United States: (1)

a. UnionPay
b. Visa
c. Discover
d. JCB

1.4 Domestic card scheme with its origin being India, established in 2012 to decrease cost of clearing and settlement: (1)

a. Quick Teller
b. Union Pay International
c. Ru-Pay
d. Interac

1.5 This is meant for travellers either to be encashed abroad or upon arrival from the trip: (1)

a. Stale cheque
b. Traveller's cheque
c. Self-cheque
d. Open cheque

1.6 Takes place where a debtor initiates a payment to settle indebtedness for goods or services provided: (1)

a. Direct credit payment
b. Split payment
c. Stop order payment
d. Scheduled payment

1.7 A payment channel that is associated with a USSD dial string: (1)

a. Internet banking
b. Cellphone banking
c. Automated teller machine
d. Speed point

1.8 A debit pull payment instruction initiated by a creditor: (1)

a. Creditor transfer
b. Direct debit
c. Salary transfer
d. None of the above

1.9 Participants in a given national payment system include: (1)

a. Banking institutions
b. Direct participants
c. Central banks
d. All of the above

1.10 Risk that a participant is unable to settle now but can do so later: (1)

a. Liquidity risk
b. Legal risk
c. Credit risk
d. Operational risk

Question Two (10)

Indicate if the following statements are True (T) or False (F):

1.1 Clearing refers to the exchange of payment instructions, calculation of payment obligation and the submission of an obligation of each participant for settlement. (1)

1.2 Mandatory sim card registration is aimed at facilitating the investigation of crimes committed with the aid of mobile devices and ensuring a safe digital environment (1)

1.3 Cash does not provide for instant settlement of funds within a country's national payment system. (1)

1.4 Reward or loyalty cards allow the holder to get points each time they purchase from a favourite store. (1)

1.5 Final settlement takes place when the paying account is debited and the receiving account is credited for the transaction value. (1)

1.6 Financial inclusion is a goal by governments and regulatory authorities that entails offering affordable financial services to unbanked and underbanked members of the society in urban, peri-urban and rural areas. (1)

1.7 *SADC Banking Association* was established in 1998 to co-ordinate projects and activities, where banks are involved, in the region. (1)

1.8 The payment system regulatory environment can be divided into four regulatory areas: prudential oversight, market development, consumer protection and anti-money laundering (AML) / combatting the financing of terrorism (CFT). (1)

1.9 High-value payments are transmitted to the settlement system operator for settlement or discharge of a payment obligation under principles of finality and revocability. (1)

1.10 Self-regulation involves a central bank being the delegated regulator and the payment system management body assuming the role of principal regulator. (1)

Question Three (38)

3.1 A cardholder just received a current account statement for the previous month via email and notes the following from the statement:

Transactions	NAD
Purchases at speed point	600
Withdrawal at ATM	2000
Cash purchases at till	1500
Online banking payments	200
Online banking transfers	500
Mobile App payments	300
Payments via USSD	170

Required:

a. Name the payment channels that are visible from the table. (4)

b. Which payment channel does the cardholder prefer? (1)

c. Which payment channel does the cardholder least prefer? (1)

d. Calculate all transactions that the cardholder completed electronically. (7)

e. What is the proportion of electronic transactions out of total transactions? (2)

3.2 A credit cardholder just received a credit card statement showing the following information: opening balance NAD1,250, card limit NAD1,500, payment received NAD50, monthly management charge NAD10 (this includes value added tax of NAD5), and interest NAD25:

Required:

Calculate the amount to be debited to the account, closing balance and available balance based on the above information. (10)

3.3. Consider country A with total number of automated teller machines of about 5,500 and the adult population of 400,000. Regulatory target for access points is 130 per 10,000 adults.

Required:

Calculate the number of access points per 10,000 adults (5)

3.4 The following information on processed digital transactions in the NISS settlement system and gross domestic product (GDP) is presented to you:

Year	Total value settled in NISS	Nominal GDP
2018	913	181
2019	976	181
2020	984	174
2021	1050	184
2022	1131	206

Required:

a. Calculate the optimal utilisation ratio of the NISS settlement system. (5)

b. Comment on your answer. (3)

Question Four (42)

4.1 Illustrate the framework for regulating and supervision of virtual assets. (12)

4.2 List five distinguishing features of PAN African payment and settlement system. (6)

4.3 List and briefly explain the three major types of social media that you have learned. (6)

4.4 Elaborate on the key elements of the operating model for open banking. (10)

4.5 List the benefits and drawbacks of QR payments that you have learned. (8)

Total: 100

The End

www.ingramcontent.com/pod-product-compliance
Lightning Source LLC
LaVergne TN
LVHW052029200926
848481LV00005B/1625